SELF-DETERMINATION

CANADIAN REVIEW OF STUDIES
IN NATIONALISM
(Vol. 8)

GARLAND REFERENCE LIBRARY
OF SOCIAL SCIENCE
(Vol. 394)

CANADIAN REVIEW OF STUDIES IN NATIONALISM

Series Editor: Thomas Spira

SELF-DETERMINATION
An Interdisciplinary Annotated Bibliography

David B. Knight and Maureen Davies

GARLAND PUBLISHING, INC. • NEW YORK & LONDON
1987

Library of Congress Cataloging-in-Publication Data

Knight, David B.
    Self-Determination: An Interdisciplinary Annotated Bibliography
by David B. Knight and Maureen Davies.
    p. cm.–(Canadian Review of Studies in Nationalism: v. 8)
(Garland Reference Library of Social Science: v. 394)
    Includes index.
    ISBN 0-8240-8495-0 (alk. paper): $40.00
    1. Self-Determination, National—Bibliography.   I. Davies,
Maureen.   II. Title.   III. Series.   IV. Series: Garland Reference
Library of Social Science: v. 394.

Z7164.N2K54   1987 [JX4054]   016.34126—dc19

Printed on acid-free, 250-year-life paper
Manufactured in the United States of America

To

Janet

Karen and Andrew

Gareth

Trudy and Allison

ACKNOWLEDGEMENTS

We thank Thomas Spira for encouraging us to undertake the preparation of this volume and for his continued support. We thank too the several student research assistants who helped us in our work: Stephen Blight, Melina Buckley, Marja ten Holder, Laura Hobbs, Penny Smiley and Carol Bartels. We acknowledge the various types of assistance provided us by Carleton University's Department of Georgraphy, Department of Law, and the Norman Paterson School of International Affairs. Knight's work with the International Geographical Union Study Group on the World Political Map is acknowledged. This volume represents part of our shared work on post-colonial self-determination that has been generously supported by a two-year research grant from the Social Sciences and Humanities Research Council of Canada. We most gratefully acknowledge the Council's financial support. Finally, we thank our spouses and children for everything.

Carleton University   David B. Knight and Maureen Davies

Ottawa, Canada   October, 1986

TABLE OF CONTENTS

Self-Determination

PART I

INTRODUCTION

by

David B. Knight*

Introduction

The right of a group with a distinctive identity to determine its own destiny is an ancient concept that has found special focus in the twentieth century. In contrasting ways, Lenin and Wilson defined the principle of self-determination earlier this century. The foundations they gave, or are believed to have provided, have found expression in the articulation of the desire for "self-determination" by numerous groups since then. Subsequent developments within the League of Nations and especially the United Nations (U.N.) have imbued the concept with legitimacy and currency.

The U.N. Charter and other legal instruments recognize the right of "all peoples" to self-determination, but the definition of "peoples" and territories to which it applies remains ambiguous. A major debatable issue relates to whether the "right" applies only to the total population of a state or extends to segments of the population in parts of that state. The concept of self-determination has been defined and applied variously since World War I, and further evolution can be expected. The international community tends to be conservative in prescribing limitations to the concept, although some recent human rights agreements could lead to the limits being changed if certain new dimensions are agreed upon. Current limits include giving primacy to

---

*My colleague Maureen Davies kindly read a draft of this introduction and she provided the initial draft of the section on indigenous people.

the territorial integrity of existing states versus the interests of sub-groups of people residing within those states. Despite this limitation, numerous sub-state peoples enjoy distinctive group-territorial identities, and are demanding self-determination as they define it, notwithstanding what lawyers might submit is "international law." In short, challenges to a conservative definition of the right are leading to further revisions of its content. In view of the variety of demands for self-determination, and considering the potential for disruptions within states and the international system of states, Robert Lansing's 1921 comment appraising the phrase "self-determination" as being "loaded with dynamite" remains valid.

This volume, which has assembled a wide range of literature gathered from many disciplines, explores the changing definitions, interpretations and applications of the concept of self-determination, and examines the underlying links between sub-state group identities and their territories. This investigation aims at clarifying why such group identities continue to command the attention of the world community.

The Reason for this Annotated Bibliography

There is a definite need for an interdisciplinary annotated bibliography. Scholars hailing from several fields of study, including anthropologists, economists, geographers, historians, lawyers, linguists, political scientists, psychologists and sociologists are concerned with various aspects of and wish to investigate different approaches to the concept of self-determination. However, the literature on self-determination remains largely inaccessible across disciplinary boundaries. All too frequently, scholars consult the literature from their own discipline exclusively; examples of research delving into aspects or applications of self-determination that draw upon and benefit from the perusal of interdisciplinary literature and perspectives are few in number. An annotated bibliography that is interdisciplinary in scope should spur and encourage researchers wishing to exploit the many disciplinary facets of self-determination.

The literature pertaining to self-determination is immense. Consequently, this bibliography is suggestive rather than all-embracing. The authors have selected major works and interpretations in the English language across a wide range of disciplinary approaches. This annotated bibliography also includes a selection of the important and extensive *Selbstbestimmungsrecht* literature in German, and a few pertinent French sources as well. The authors have included few reflective statements by "separatists" (or nationalists), chiefly because marΐy such declarations are likely to be transitory. The numerous articles on specific groups that appear in newspapers and newsmagazines have also been omitted. Literature on all sub-state groups could not be included in this volume, but the examples selected for inclusion should be useful for the general issues they raise.

Organization of the Annotations

The reader may elect to choose selectively from some of the nineteen thematic categories included within the collection, or decide to read the annotations from start to finish. The annotated studies have been grouped according to a conceptual framework that may assist readers to find certain themes and publication references, as well as guiding them to consider certain topics and approaches for future research. The book consists of four parts: self-determination in law and practice; identity, territory, regionalisms and power; indigenous peoples; and future perspectives. Each part is discussed in this introduction.

PART II - Practice and Interpretations

The concept of self-determination is revolutionary, because its application implies the possibility of radical change in the overthrow of a ruler or ruling class and the institution of a new form of government, or through territorial separation and the establishment of a new state. Victorious groups have generally gained the designation of "nations," because they had been able to establish the concept of popular national sovereignty to dominate over the claimed "national" territory. The French Revolution of 1789-99, the American Revolution of 1775-83 and subsequent European revolutionary experiences stimulated the diffusion of the ideal of self-determination. Between 1804 and 1830, eighteen Central and South American states, and in 1830, Belgium and Greece, gained independence, all resulting from the force generated by nationalist sentiments. Europe's abortive 1848 revolutions demonstrated the diffusion and power of nationalist ideas. In the following sixty-six years, Italy, Romania, Luxembourg, Serbia, Montenegro, Germany, Bulgaria, Norway, and Albania became virtually autonomous states, and elsewhere, Canada, Cuba, Panama, Australia, New Zealand and South Africa obtained various degrees of independence. Most peoples accepted their new international status willingly, but some, especially New Zealanders, realized only slowly that they were indeed a separate people. Simultaneously, however, some nationalist movements suffered suppression, as in Ireland and Poland, as well as in many parts of Africa, Asia and the Pacific Islands.

The idea of and various processes for attaining self-determination clearly predate World War I, yet the word "self-determination" lacked widespread usage before the end of that war. The Bolsheviks in Russia and President Woodrow Wilson in the United States formulated contrasting conceptions of what the word "self-determination" meant. Aware of the numerous centrifugal forces operating in Russia, Lenin searched for a theory that recognized the reality of nationalist sentiments, but which would not conflict with the doctrinal and organizational premises of Marxism. Tsarist "Russification" policies had heightened the nationalistic fervor of several subject groups, and Lenin hoped to capture their separatist aspirations to serve revolutionary purposes. He defined national self-determination as the political separation of nations from alien national bodies to form their own national states. At first he unqualifiedly supported a people's right to national self-determination, but he neither expected nor desired this privilege to be exercised in secession. The 15 November 1917 Declaration of the Rights of the Peoples of Russia nevertheless included the proclamation of equality and sovereignty of all national groups, and the right of each to self-determination, including the right to secede. Thereupon, many borderland groups applied these "rights" and proclaimed their independence, including Azerbaijani, Belorussians, Don Cossaks, Estonians, Finns, Georgians, Latvians, Lithuanians, Poles and Ukrainians. The Estonians, Finns, Poles, Latvians and Lithuanians resisted immediate reintegration into the Soviet state by armed force. The necessity of having to use armed might impelled the Soviet Union to reorient the concept of self-determination. In 1923, Stalin announced that the right of the working class to consolidate its power would always take precedence over the right to a people's self-determination. Stalin's reinterpretation remains in force until the present day.

Wilson considered self-determination to mean that people should be self-governed by the consent of the governed. He believed that every people had the right to choose the sovereignty under which it desired to live. What he offered as a principle, others claimed as a right. This caused tremendous pressures for the recognition of many groups to develop before and during the peace talks following World War I. Eventually, Wilson questioned the principle, because, he explained, nationalities began appearing everywhere! The key question was, to which type of community should the principle apply? Should it be limited to the successor states and the other splintered empires, or should it apply to any group that regarded itself as a nation? Czech leader Thomas Masaryk maintained that even a large minority was not necessarily a nation, and that self-determination did not imply an unconditional right to political independence.

Yet with hopes for self-determination riding high among many minorities in Europe, how could these centrifugal tendencies be arrested so that uncontrolled territorial fragmentation did not occur? Some believed language to be an adequate measure of nationality, but cited many exceptions. The application of plebiscites resulted in strange territorial alterations, some of which were difficult to intepret. In all, the Versailles and later treaties radically altered the map of Europe, as the former empires became fragmented. But the process whereby the many new states gained sovereignty did not always embody the principle of self-determination.

Over the past century, sovereignty has been applied only to territories formally constituted, accepted and recognized by other states. In its determination in the Åland Islands case, the League of Nations declared Finland's sovereignty to be a limiting factor in the Ålanders' claims for self-determination. During the later interwar years, numerous nationalist and secessionist movements became increasingly powerful in Europe and many colonially-controlled parts of the world.

In the late nineteenth century, numerous non-Western peoples were subjected to colonial rule, often within newly defined territories. The dominant European powers generally regarded this form of "national" self-determination as a unifying force, because it involved the integration of diverse peoples within "national" territories. Inherent in the colonial territorial structures, however, lurked the potential for later division. Following World War II, the quest for self-determination became an especially powerful force in the Third World. The astonishing rush to end colonialization and achieve political independence resulted in the creation of over eighty new states within a period of two decades, and generally occurred with the blessing of and prodding by the United Nations.

The United Nations Charter included the self-determination principle. The U.N. wanted to develop "friendly relations among nations based on respect for the principle of equal rights and self-determination of peoples." This principle was incorporated into other U.N. documents also, including Resolution 1514 (XV), the "Colonial Declaration," according to which "all people have the right to self-determination; by virtue of that right they freely determine their political status and freely pursue their economic, social and cultural development." The U.N. position implied, through a process referred to as external self-determination, that it was legitimate for overseas people to be released from colonial authority and to achieve self-government and sovereignty.   International law grants such self-determination only once to a territory and the people residing within it.   The territory is given primacy, as the people located within the territory are deemed to belong to it, even though the population may be complex and regionally differentiated in its plurality.

The U.N. also considers it illegitimate for a people who comprise a minority within a national territory to seek self-determination whether on its own initiative or with the help of any outside power, because such action would "dismember or impair, totally or in part," an existing state.   International law thus supports the paramountcy of the population within the total national territory over parts of the population or territory within it.   Any departure from this rule must be ratified by the majority of the total population.   The two currently accepted exceptions to the colonial limitation rule relate to people subject to a minority apartheid regime, and to the people of a sovereign state living under foreign domination.

The U.N. considers internal self-determination to be valid in the sense that a people has the right to select its own form of government. This right only applies to the total population of a state.   Agreement on how the application of this right can be measured is lacking.   Some governments claim to represent their people, although various segments of the states' total populations clearly oppose their governments.

The reader of these annotations will discover that international lawyers have been divided on whether or not self-determination is a right.   Notwithstanding the legal debate, the speedy application of the concept to most former colonial territories has been remarkable.   But such actions proved "safe," because international boundaries did not have to be altered.   In that sense, the U.N. accepted the territorial status quo.   The creation of these "new" states within the colonially-divided territorial framework provides hope for the future, because culturally diverse societies have acquired a new transtribal identity that a territorial state can provide.   If a meaningful attachment to this new national identity develops, then self-determination may be regarded as a unifying force.   Failure by some newly independent states to accommodate plural societies within their borders has ended in violence and attempted secessions.   Some of the former colonial territories became united in federal structures, but these arrangements did not last (as the defunct federations of the West Indies and Central Africa attest). Many former colonial territories have been forced to gerrymander, as they sought to accommodate the new state diversities. Nigeria is a prototype of a successful arrangement in this vein.

African leaders claim to oppose any tampering with the frontiers of colonially-derived territories, a position with which the U.N. concurs. Any attempts at border rectification or secession would undermine the territorial integrity of existing states. However, the acceptance of certain international instruments in the recent past has brought into question the hitherto clearly stipulated restrictions on the granting of self-determination. The Covenants on Civil and Political Rights and Economic, Social and Cultural Rights, as well as the nonbinding but persuasive Helsinki Final Act (of the Conference on Security and Cooperation in Europe), provide a legal basis for dissident sub-state groups to launch legitimate claims that are firmly grounded in a human rights framework. As well, there has been a worldwide upsurge of sympathy for "self-determination" that would result in a form of self-government for an aspirant people within the state, not apart from it.

Attention increasingly focuses on a different interpretation of internal self-determination, as it applies to dominant populations within portions of states. Many sub-state groups in Europe, Asia, Africa, the Americas and the Pacific are seeking self-determination of this type. At the very least, they desire increased autonomy. The form of autonomy and what it will include (cultural, educational, linguistic, economic and political facets of life) varies from group to group and from state to state, as the degree of group "self" awareness differs. However, many sub-state groups aspire to achieve full self-control, and exercise sovereignty over the territories they claim as theirs. Pressures now exist and will continue to mount for devising a definition of self-determination that includes territorial separation. The current principle which affirms the territorial integrity of existing states contradicts such an interpretation. If this obstacle could be overcome, such sub-state identities as the Basques, Catalonians, Kurds, Palestinians, Québecois, Sikhs, Timorese and dozens of other groups might gain international recognition.

The annotations in Part II are grouped under four headings: (1) historical perspectives, including some important historical reviews that predate U.N. deliberations, as well as some literature that deals principally with the 1920s; (2) selected international documents; (3) critical examinations of some documents, focusing particularly on U.N. deliberations; and (4) a group of literature that overviews or interprets various ideological meanings of self-determination, and examines the application of self-determination, principally in the post-World War II era.

PART III - Theoretical Considerations: Identity, Territory, and Power

The material grouped in this section relates to fundamental issues that underlie desires and demands for self-determination. These issues are first, identity and relationships with a territorial base; second, reasons for the recent resurgence in expressions of group identity; third, ways and means for dealing with differences through structural accommodations; and fourth, tracing how failed accommodations cause separatism and secession.

Under international law, as currently understood, the state generally bestows identity upon people. This may be true in theory; however, many peoples offer their primary loyalty to some sub-state group, not the state, and, thus, do not subscribe to a state nationalism. There had been hopes that new transtribal identities would be forged in the newly independent African and Asian states, and that "nation" and "state" would evolve along simultaneous lines. Such a state of affairs has failed to materialize. Ethnic or national homogeneity exists neither in Europe nor in the former colonial territories. Most states contain plural societies with several minorities. In the past, this was called a national minorities problem. Currently, the situation is that the sub-state regional identities of a people are in discord with their state (or, in some instances, as with the Kurds, states). Such groups may desire and actively seek self-determination.

The problem is old, the contemporary terminology new. The current key root word is "ethnic." Inspired by the recent "discovery" of ethnicity – the character and quality of an ethnic group – many social scientists, led by political scientists and sociologists, have jumped onto the ethnic studies bandwagon and been surprised by what they found, that is, the mid-century reemergence, revival or resurgence of many "ethnic" identities, which as "ethnoregional movements" have called for "ethnic autonomy" and "ethnic separatism" as a result of "ethnic conflict." The words "tribal" and even "nation" seem to have lost favor to "ethnic," although the former concepts often tend to be defined loosely and similarly. Alternate terms have been proposed for essentially the same phenomenon, including "ethnonationalisms," "autonomist nationalisms," "subnationalisms," and "mininationalisms." These phrases have their uses, although some researchers ignore sub-state group identities that are neither nationalist, ethnic nor ethnonational in character, and yet may actually or potentially challenge state structures.

A more inclusive and less evocative phrase than the above is Knight's "group territorial identities" (see annotation numbers 103 and 141). This term has flexibility of scale. It can be applied to any level in the hierarchy of attachments to territory, from a small group or a parochial localism to a broader (but still sub-state) regionalism, and to a nationalism (which may also be sub-state in areal focus), and possibly even to an internationalism. But whatever terms are used, the potentially most divisive level in this hierarchy of attachments is sub-state regionalism. Its adherents may possess a profound sense of "self" and can establish "self-determination" goals to such a degree that the host state's structure is threatened. The question remains, why should such identities persist, and why has there been a recent resurgence of these sub-state regionalisms?

The phrase sub-state regionalisms is being used here purposely. Regionalism — the awareness of a people's togetherness in a relatively large area — is recognizable only when it represents but a part of a whole. In this context, the latter unit is generally the territory of a state. When a regionalism that is clearly linked to a group's identity finds political expression, then the process may be termed a group's politico-territorial identity. Regionalism may develop into sectionalism, which means that the inhabitants consider regional political concerns to be more important than those pertaining elsewhere in the state. Ultimately, if accommodation fails, representatives of such sub-state regionalisms may seek and achieve secession, and create new states in accordance with the self-determination wishes of the people involved. At that point, the movement would cease to be a regionalism, however, because its people would then enjoy a new territorial identity in their own state. If a close areal concordance existed between nation and state, then the combination could be referred to as a nation-state. Clearly, unless managed within existing state structures by some means or other, the activities of sub-state minorities can precipitate the breakup of numerous states. What protective alternatives are available to existing states?

National political leaders who are pressured by sub-state regional groups and anticipate the growth of separatist movements can react in several possible ways: violent suppression; relocation; assimilation, encouraged by state action; the implementation of some form of local sociocultural autonomy; language accommodation for the minority group; or political involvement, ranging from local controls to adequately developed forms of autonomy, including provincial self-government within federal structures, authority devolution, various forms of consociational democracy, minority vetoes, proportional representation, power sharing, and so on. All of these solutions can be accommodated within existing state structures. By these means, "self-determination" demands can be met without necessarily disrupting the currently constituted international state system. Other structural possibilities also are available, including internationalized or incorporated territories, and associate statehood. The options are numerous. But so too are the insistent pressures issuing from certain groups for the attainment of sovereignty. In these instances, self-determination clearly means secession. What processes promote secession, and what are the international legal views on such separation?

The items included in this section of the bibliography relate to the above issues. Much of what is included deals with the very heart of the matter, that is, attempting to understand and interpret why and how group identities exist within and yet apart from the state. The listings selectively identify the range of debate on, for instance, nationalism, one possible approach to the issue of identity. The items in the various sections have been selected because they provide contrasting interpretations which, when combined, are instructive.

PART IV - Worldwide Regional Perspectives and State Case Studies

The annotations in this seven-part group relate specifically to the following world regions: Africa, the Americas, Asia and the Pacific, the Middle East, U.S.S.R. and Eastern Europe, Western Europe: comparative studies, and Western Europe: case studies. The items include detailed analyses of interpretations and applications which had been examined more generally or comparatively in Parts II and III. Some of the studies included in this section are continental in scope, others are either regional or specifically state-based.

PART V - The Fourth World: Indigenous Peoples

The Fourth World occupies a unique position in the community of nations. For centuries, indigenous peoples have been denied their rightful place within that community, and subjected to colonization and genocide. Indigenous peoples have consistently resisted their exclusion from the international arena and continue to this day to claim their rights as "peoples," including the right to self-determination. Many observers view these claims as a major challenge to the international legal status quo. Indeed, indigenous peoples' claims are now a significant aspect of the process whereby the definition of the concept of self-determination is being expanded.

Indigenous peoples are distinct from ethnic minorities, a fact most recently confirmed by a special report on the definition of minorities submitted to the U.N. In some instances, they outnumber the other populations within the territories they inhabit (for example, Guatemala), yet are denied the right to fully control their lives. Indigenous peoples view themselves as being distinct nations subjected to alien domination and colonization against their will. This perspective constitutes a theoretical, practical and philosophical challenge to the international community. The indigenous perspective is beginning to find support within the U.N. system. For example, the 1983 Martinéz-Cobo Report to the U.N. asserted:

> Much of their land has been taken away and whatever land is left to them is subject to constant encroachment. Their culture and their social and legal institutions and systems have been constantly under attack at all levels, through the media, the law and the public educational systems. It is only natural, therefore, that there should be a resistance to further loss of their land and rejection of the distortion or denial of their history and culture and defensive/offensive reaction to the continual linguistic and cultural aggressions and attacks on their way of life, their social and cultural integrity and their very physical existence. They have a right to continue to exist, to defend their lands, to keep and transmit their culture, their language, their social and legal institutions and systems and their way of life, which have been illegally and unjustifiably attacked. (U.N. E/CN.4/Sub.2/1983/21 add.8, p. 49).

The establishment of the U.N. Indigenous Populations Working Group in 1981 to investigate the plight of indigenous peoples globally, as well as to delineate specific standards in the form of a declaration or covenant, represents an important milestone. The International Labour Organization's current revision of the assimilationist Convention on Tribal and Indigenous Populations (No. 107) is further evidence of this trend. International coalitions of indigenous peoples are active participants in these developments and have submitted draft declarations and covenants to the U.N. Working Group. Three of the drafts are included in Part V, Section 16.

A burgeoning literature by indigenous and non-indigenous scholars asserts the importance of the restoration of rights to the Fourth World including, in particular, the right to self-determination. Just what structural form this right might take varies from people to people, and from state to state. The formulation of firm recommendations is well advanced among some peoples. The annotations are grouped into three sections: general and theoretical statements; a representative range of North American material; and a small literature sample from elsewhere.

PART VI - Future Directions

The final grouping of annotations in Part VI is but a minor representation of views that can be regarded as being future-oriented. Numerous annotated works included in many other sections of this volume also pertain directly or indirectly to future problems. The few studies included in this part serve as a reminder that the final stage of societal and territorial organization has not been reached. Changes to the worldwide politico-territorial structuring will continue, and so will the diversity in how peoples' identities, goals and ideals can find legitimate expression. Some attempts to attain self-determination will involve violence. Peaceful or not, self-determination promises to remain a powerful socio-political force for decades and perhaps centuries to come.

PART II

PRACTICE AND INTERPRETATIONS

Historical Perspectives

1. ALAPURO, Risto. "Finland: An Interface Periphery." *The Politics of Territorial Identity.* Eds. Stein Rokkan and Derek W. Urwin. London, Beverley Hills and New Delhi: Sage Publications, 1982, pp. 113-64.
   Claims that the formation of the Finnish nation, situated between Sweden and Russia, had two important effects: firstly, it consolidated a bourgeois national culture in the 19th century; and second, the Finnish state developed between one economically and culturally dominant country, and one that was politically dominant but economically backward. Considers nationalism a dual phenomenon – an expression of national self-assertion in response to uneven development, and a "civic religion" binding the population with the modern territorial state. Outlines three important European-type characteristics of Finnish development: (1) the autonomous Finnish state predated the rise of nationalism by some decades; (2) Finland was relatively over-developed within the Russian empire; and (3) St. Petersburg exercised political domination, whereas the Swedish-speaking upper class wielded economic and cultural control. Finnish nationalism intertwined with these dual aspects and bred a unified bourgeois culture in which nation and class combined to create a specifically Finnish national identity. Traces contemporary regional inequalities in Finland to the country's national development as an interface periphery.

2. AUN, K. "The Cultural Autonomy of National Minorities in Estonia." *Yearbook of the Estonian Learned Society in America,* I (1951), 26-41.

Outlines the structure of institutional safeguards for the cultural autonomy of national minorities in 1920s' and 1930s' Estonia. Notes that Estonia granted its nationalities two special rights: cultural and welfare self-government, and ethnic self-determination on the basis of personal (*i.e.* non-territorial) autonomy. This system operated on a voluntary basis through enrollment in the Nationality Register; it aimed at creating respect for individuality, and sought to win the loyalty of all minorities to Estonia, but discouraged cultural separatism.

3.   BARROS, James. *The Aland Islands Question: Its Settlement by the League of Nations.* New Haven: Yale University Press, 1968.
Establishes the lengthy nature of Swedish-inhabited Åland Island's "servitude" under Swedish, Russian and Finnish rule. Indicates pre-World War I Swedish concerns over possible Russian fortification of the islands, which would have violated an 1856 demilitarization agreement. Traces the considerable interaction during World War I between the Swedish and Russian governments on the issue of fortification, and explains the types of fortifications constructed. When Finland became independent in 1917, the Ålanders had demanded the right to national self-determination, and Sweden desired a plebiscite. A League commission of rapporteurs ruled that the autonomous state of Finland had always included the Åland Islands, and that the principle of self-determination should not apply to them. The League thereupon had recognized Finland's sovereignty over the islands, but recommended far-reaching minority guarantees for the Ålanders. Concludes that the compromise had satisfied some of Sweden's legitimate demands: neutralization of the island group and extensive guarantees to the Ålanders.

4.   BROWN, Philip Marshall. "The Aaland Islands Question." *The American Journal of International Law*, XV (1921), 268-72.
Asserts that, from the perspective of international law, the Åland Islands case warranted consideration and study. Situated at the entrance to the Gulf of Bothnia, the islands were separated from Sweden by 50 kilometers and from Finland by 70 kilometers. From 1157 A.D. until the early 18th century the islands had been part of the Swedish Kingdom. Occupied by Russia in 1809, the islands and Finland were incorporated into the Russian Empire. The islands formed part of Finland when the latter became independent in 1917. A majority of Åland

islanders thereafter sought reunion with Sweden; the Council of the League of Nations was approached to decide the issue. The International Commission of three jurists, appointed in July 1920, reported two months later that Ålanders lacked an absolute right to self-determination, and it confirmed an 1856 agreement on the demilitarization of the islands. Argues that the Commission failed to "appreciate the nature of a negative servitude" the islanders had suffered.

5. BURGHARDT, Andrew F. *Borderland: A Historical and Geographical Study of Burgenland, Austria.* Madison: University of Wisconsin Press, 1962.
Explores the emergence, since 1922, of Burgenland, a self-conscious Austrian province adjacent to the westernmost frontier of Hungary. Examines the post-World War I ideal of self-determination by analyzing the composition of the region's linguistic and religious minority groups, and explains how territorial partitionings, population transfers, and frontier delimitations had occurred in response to the application of self-determination by an Allied boundary commission.

6. CHASZAR, Edward. "The Problem of National Minorities Before and After the Paris Peace Treaties of 1947." *Nationalities Papers*, IX (1981), 195-206.
Contrasts the League of Nations system of minority protection with the lack of a similar regime within the United Nations framework, and traces recent attempts to remedy this shortcoming. Explains that the basis of the League of Nations system consisted of a series of treaties, declarations, and conventions, whereby particular states accepted provisions relating to the treatment of minority groups and recognized the League as guarantor. National minority provisions protected the rights of individual ethnics, and of members of minority groups. Contends that the 1947 Paris Peace Conference had deinternationalized the minority problem, by insisting that minorities be protected through "the defence of human rights and not national rights." The 1966 Covenant of Civil and Political Rights at last provided legal protection for minorities. Reviews recent efforts to create a more binding international minority rights convention.

7. COBBAN, Alfred. *National Self-Determination.* London: Oxford University Press, 1945.

Blames the practical failure of self-determination on a theoretical inadequacy. Traces the principle of self-determination according to the relative influence of power politics or idealism until President Wilson, who had transformed the phrase into an imperative action principle. At Versailles, however, self-determination had proved to be practically inapplicable, because the 1919 peace treaty contradicted itself. The Treaty permitted a nation to constitute an independent state and determine its own government, but it denied that rights were either absolute or could be attributed to a collective body such as a nation. Maintains that a compromise between the right to absolute sovereignty and the right to secession was impossible; abandonment of the notion of absolute sovereignty would reconcile nationalism with democracy, and self-determination would imply a truer and more subjective conception of nationality. Contends that any attempt to make the centralized, culturally united nation-state the sole basis of legitimate political organization was theoretically and practically untenable. Attributes European attempts to achieve self-determination to European influence. Ventures that federalism might prevail outside of Europe, where the conception of national sovereignty was new and not deeply rooted.

8. COBBAN, Alfred. *The Nation-State and National Self-Determination*. New York: Thomas Crowell, 1970.
    Nearly completed revision (death intervened) of his classic 1945 *National Self-Determination*, with a 1944 essay on the nation-state included. Notes that self-determination was supposed to end imperialism and the oppression of colonies. Observes, instead, the proliferation of tiny states. Explores the underlying bases for this development. Concludes that if every nation were to become a sovereign state, international chaos might result, causing wars, and preventing the development of world government.

9. FRIEDLANDER, Robert A. "Autonomy and the Thirteen Colonies: Was the American Revolution Really Necessary?" *Models of Autonomy*. Ed. Yoram Dinstein. New Brunswick, NJ: Transaction Books, 1981, pp. 135-49.
    Claims that granting autonomy to a dissident population did not frustrate independence movements or offset secessionist pressure. American colonials had established a pattern of separation later practiced by other subject peoples. Observes that the American experience was unique, in that many of the

Colonies were self-regulated by their founders, only to lose their customary rights as international trade and commerce developed. Concludes that autonomy had been useful only in a transitional sense, but could not permanently resolve the tenuous relationship between self-regulation and self-rule.

10. GRAS, Solange. "Regionalism and Autonomy in Alsace since 1918." *The Politics of Territorial Identity.* Eds. Stein Rokkan and Derek W. Urwin. London, Beverley Hills and New Delhi: Sage Publications, 1982, pp. 309-54.

Traces the emergence and retreat of Alsatian autonomist movements since 1918. Locates the roots of the rapid autonomist upsurge following World War I in the previous success of German rule, as well as the ferment of ideas spawned by the war. France had encountered numerous problems integrating Alsace during the interwar years, despite a centralized bureaucracy and exceptional control. Delineates three autonomist Alsatian forces: a clerical right wing, which championed ancient rights, culture, language and religion; a communist faction which depicted the Alsatian situation as colonial; and a moderate "radical" component, concerned above all with the economy, Alsatian civil service and the use of dialect. Autonomists had played a major role in the apparent acceptance of German occupation during World War II. Outlines several factors ensuring the decline of autonomism after World War II. Autonomists were largely discredited because of Nazi collaboration. Autonomy had lost its popular foundation because it was abandoned by the communists and churches. Concludes that, although autonomist demands had sharply declined since World War II, cultural and linguistic demands remained strong.

11. ISAAK, Robert. "Wilson: The Nation-State and International Organization." *Individuals and World Politics.* Ed. Robert Isaak. Second Edition. Monterey, CA: Duxbury Press, 1981, pp. 65-87, 165-66 and 179.

Identifies the rigid idealism of Woodrow Wilson as reflecting his cultural, academic and Protestant background. Suggests that Wilson's notion of self-determination was tied to collective security, a concept which implied a universal alliance without the competitive alignments that characterized the balance of power system.

12. KILLEN, Linda. "Self-Determination Versus Territorial Integrity: Conflict within the American Delegation at Paris over Wilsonian Policy Toward the Russian Borderlands." *Nationalities Papers*, X (1982), 65-79.
Claims that at the 1919 Paris Peace Conference, President Wilson and Robert Lansing had supported Russian territorial integrity, while most of the American delegation adopted the principle of national self-determination for the Russian borderlands. Investigates why these differences developed, how they manifested themselves at the peace conference, and why the discrepancies were not corrected. Wilson and Lansing had feared alienating the nationalistic Russians, who might turn to the Bolsheviks as symbols of Russian nationalism. Argues that this policy contradicted Wilson's ideals of self-determination and internationalism. Explains why Wilson and Lansing had disagreed with most of the American delegation. Self-determination had abstract intellectual and popular appeal, but proved difficult to enforce, whereas territorial integrity was commendable in principle but un-Wilsonian when applied to an empire composed partly of captive nations.

13. KLUKE, Paul. *Selbstbestimmung: Vom Weg einer Idee durch die Geschichte* (Self-Determination: The Path of an Idea throughout History). Göttingen: Vandenhoeck & Ruprecht, 1963.
Historical exploration of self-determination.

14. LANSING, Robert. "Self-Determination," *The Peace Negotiations: A Personal Narrative.* Boston: Houghton Mifflin, 1921, pp. 93-105.
Considers the phrase self-determination to be loaded with dynamite. Objects to the application of self-determination, because it would raise hopes which could never be realized. Fears that it would cause misery and cost thousands of lives. Suggests that ultimately it would be discredited, be called the dream of Woodrow Wilson, an idealist who had failed to realize the danger until too late to curtail those who attempted to put the principle in force. Asserts that considerations of national safety, historic rights and economic interests should all enjoy preference over the principle of self-determination.

15. LENIN, V. I. "The Right of Nations to Self-Determination." *Questions   of   National   Policy   and   Proletarian*

Internationalism. Moscow: Progress Publishers, 1970, pp. 45-104.

Ascribes the historical-economic basis of national movements to the victory of capitalism over feudalism, whereby the bourgeoisie captured the home market, and developed politically united territories with linguistically homogeneous populations. Defines national self-determination as the process which could politically separate nations from alien national bodies and create separate national states. Distinguishes between two capitalist periods: (1) the collapse of feudalism, which had bred bourgeois-democratic national movements; and (2) definitely formed capitalist states nearing the eve of the downfall of capitalism. Explains that Russia was still passing through the first period, necessitating the inclusion of the "self-determination" clause in the Communist Party program. Urges the proletariat to support the nationalist bourgeoisie, but only conditionally. Any oppressed nation's bourgeois nationalism was to be directed against oppression, and thus also merited support. Cites Norway's 1905 secession from Sweden as an example of this type of national self-determination. Claims that working class interests demanded worker unity among all nations and resistance to bourgeois nationalist policy.

16. LUXEMBURG, Rosa. *The National Question: Selected Writings by Rosa Luxemburg.* Ed. Horace B. Davis. New York and London: Monthly Review Press, 1976.

The editor explains Luxemburg's ideas on the question of national self-determination. Luxemburg had opposed the Polish Social-Democratic party's demands for Polish independence, because the formula "the right of nations to self-determination" ignored a fundamental theory of social classes. The national question had to be subordinated to class interests. She rejected federalism as reactionary feudal or petit bourgeois nationalism, both of which opposed capitalism, upon which the proletarian revolutionary class struggle depended. Luxemburg had denied the "right" of nations to self-determination, which could only harm the international workers' movement in the long run.

17. MACARTNEY, C. A. *National States and National Minorities.* London: The Royal Institute of International Affairs, 1934; reissued, New York: Russell and Russell, 1968.

Discusses the problem of reconciling the rights of national minorities with the will of majorities. Focuses on the problem of national minorities in eastern and central Europe, where the League of Nations granted minorities rights to special protection. Compares the origin and development of western Europe's "political" nationality with eastern and central Europe's "personality" nationality. Contends that numerous national minorities were being denied the opportunity to exercise self-determination and prevented from forming their own states. Identifies the national state philosophy as being the basic flaw of the international minority protection structure. Suggests some possible solutions to the minority problem, including territorial or demographic alterations to national states, the development of "un-national" states, and the treatment of minorities as an international problem.

18. MASARYK, Thomas G. *The Making of a State.* London: George Allen and Unwin, 1927.
     Questions whether self-determination applied only to a whole people or if it was valid also for segments. Maintains that even a big minority was not necessarily a nation, and that self-determination did not imply unconditional rights to political independence. Asserts that individual rights were not the sole governing factors in the question of whether a whole, or parts of the whole, should be independent; the rights of others also entered into the question, including economic rights, no less than claims "of race and tongue."

19. MUNCK, Ronnie. "Otto Bauer: Towards a Marxist Theory of Nationalism." *Capital and Class*, XXV (1985), 84-98.
     Assesses Bauer's contribution to a Marxist theory of nationalism. Explains Bauer's writings on Austrian social democratic nationalism, which operated within a multinational state. The 1899 Social Democratic Brünn program sought to resolve national tensions by allowing each national component to present its own cultural demands, while the economic struggle would be waged at the supranational state level. Bauer based the national-cultural autonomy concept on the personality principle rather than on territorial determinations, and urged nationalities to administer their own cultural affairs regardless of territory, thus ensuring the Austrian state's integrity. Describes Bauer's tracing of nationalism from economic development, social change, and class articulation. Analyzes the nature of national and class phenomena, and Bauer's dis-

tinction between the "social roots of national struggles" and the "national content of the class struggle."

20. MURRAY, Gilbert. "Self-Determination of Nationalities." *Journal of The British Institute of International Affairs*, I (1922), 6-13.
   Explains the German origins of the term, and identifies its liberal and socialist ideals at the close of World War I. Notes that Woodrow Wilson had never exactly committed himself to the phrase. Traces the issue through the Balkan states and the Åland Islands. Explores the problems that arose when the principle was put into practice, including curtailing the territorial limits of the unit that was to exercise self-determination; what to do with minorities that were not geographically distinctive; and how to take into consideration the strategic interests of large countries.

21. PHILLIPS, Walter A. "Self-Determination." *Encyclopaedia Britannica*. London: Encyclopaedia Britannica Co., Ltd., 1922, XXXII, 391-5.
   Notes that after the March 1917 Russian Revolution "self-determination" had come into sudden prominence as a political term. American President Wilson had crystallized the principle of governments deriving "all their just powers from the consent of the governed" in the term "self-determination," when he presented his 8 January 1918 Fourteen Points address to the United States Congress. Notes that Wilson considered the application of the principle conditional. Claims that in practice, self-determination had proved largely illusory, due to "tentative and timid" applications. Reviews European approaches and evasions, successes and rejections. Identifies peoples in the world "not yet capable to self-government."

22. POMERANCE, Michla. "The United States and Self-Determination: Perspectives on the Wilsonian Conception." *American Journal of International Law*, LXX (1976), 1-27.
   Argues that many of the difficulties Wilsonian era foreign policy-makers encountered resembled current problems concerning the principle of self-determination. Identifies three general perspectives of the Wilsonian conception dominating the literature: the "idealist," the "realist," and the "radical." Various strands of prewar, wartime and postwar thought on self-determination allegedly revealed a fusion and confusion of

several ideas and demonstrated numerous ambiguities and inconsistencies. All versions stressed democratic ideals and universal peace. Some interpreted self-determination to mean freedom from "alien" sovereignty (external self-determination), others as freedom to select one's own government (internal self-determination), or the principle of one nation-one state. Considers Wilsonian self-determination a peculiar blend of several interconnected strands of thought upon which were engrafted further ideas which had evolved in response to developments during and immediately after the war. Asserts that attempts to define "self" objectively had always resulted in question-begging solutions.

23. SHAHEEN, Samad. *The Communist (Bolshevik) Theory of National Self-Determination.* The Hague: W. van Hoeve Ltd., 1956.
Traces the development of the Communist (Bolshevik) theory of nationality up to the October Revolution. Argues that in Bolshevist strategy, self-determination had almost exclusively tactical significance. Aware of the centrifugal forces in Russia, Lenin had sought a theory that would recognize nationalist sentiment, without conflicting with the doctrinal and organizational premises of Bolshevism. Tsarist "Russification" had heightened nationalist aspirations among various groups, sentiments which Lenin had sought to capture for revolutionary purposes. Lenin rejected Social-Democratic regional autonomy, the Jewish Bund's extraterritorial cultural autonomy, and the Austrian thesis of cultural-national autonomy and the federal state. Considers Stalin's argument against cultural-national autonomy as an inconsistent reformulation of Lenin's thesis.

24. TOYNBEE, Arnold J. "Self-Determination." *The Quarterly Review*, CCCCLXXXIV (1925), 317-38.
Examines the "right" to self-determination in the light of historical examples elucidating the "fact" of self-determination. Contends that the utility of self-determination exercised by certain populations on certain occasions did not necessarily imply the morally valid and practically expedient existence of an absolute right to self-determination. Identifies at least three unknown quantities of self-determination, including the definition of a "people," its internal relations, and its corporate relations with other peoples. Envisages the alleged right of states to sovereignty and the supposed right of peoples to self-

determination as being essentially relative claims. Suggests devolution as an expedient compromise of self-determination. Considers the League's Åland Islands decision an example of peaceful settlement involving conflicting claims to the mutual satisfaction of all parties concerned.

25. WAMBAUGH, Sarah. *A Monograph on Plebiscites, With a Collection of Official Documents.* New York: Oxford University Press, 1920.
Explores the history of plebiscites relating to changes of sovereignty between 1791 and 1905. Explains that suffrage was frequently limited to delegates, instructed as a rule by *ad hoc* assemblies, as in the French Revolution, in Moldavia and in Wallachia. In some cases, as in the Italian plebiscites of 1848, 1860, 1866 and 1870, the suffrage incorporated practically the entire male Italian population. Emphasizes that the study of plebiscites rightly belonged within a discussion of self-determination doctrine.

26. WAMBAUGH, Sarah. *Plebiscites Since the World War.* Washington, DC: Carnegie Endowment for International Peace, 1933, 2 vols.
Volume I traces the World War I emergence of self-determination as a popular ideal and official policy. Compares and contrasts the history of twelve plebiscites during the Peace Conference and the decade following. Volume II documents these plebiscites.

27. WILKINSON, H. R. *Maps and Politics: A Review of the Ethnographic Cartography of Macedonia.* Liverpool: University of Liverpool Press, 1951.
Includes seventy-three ethnographic maps, dating from 1730 to 1946, of Macedonia, a region subject to many claims and counter-claims regarding its national affiliation. In 1919, the peace treaty had allocated it to Yugoslavia. Discusses the University of Belgrade geographer Jovan Cvijić's "revolutionary" maps, and the major role they performed in legitimizing Serbian, and subsequently Yugoslavian, claims on Macedonia.

28. WINDASS, Stan. "The League and Territorial Disputes." *The International Regulation of Frontier Disputes.* Ed. Evan Luard. London: Thames and Hudson, 1970, pp. 31-85.

Discusses territorial disputes that could arise when the principle of self-determination was applied. Examines several case studies, including the Åland Islands of Finland (where a League of Nations commission decision thwarted the Ålanders' expressed desire to be reunited with Sweden), the city of Vilna (where the League proposed a plebiscite, but the city ended up in the hands of the Lithuanian occupiers), the Mosul region (in what is now northern Iraq, disputed by Turkey), Albania (where Great Britain supported vigorous self-assertion), Chaco (where scattered Indian bands were ignored when Paraguay defeated Bolivia), and Leticia (where a territory exchange from Peru to Columbia resulted more from power-structures than League mediations). Believes that these disputes were often resolved in accordance with power structures, but that the resolutions did not necessarily contravene justice. Maintains that power situations were to some extent based on rights, which gave rise to other rights. Implies that self-determination could be applied only when power structures permitted its application.

29. WOOLSEY, Theodore S. "Self-Determination." *American Journal of International Law*, XIII (1919), 302-5.
Discusses the use of plebiscites in determining popular consent to proposed territorial cessations and loss of sovereignty between 1791 and 1917. Analyzes President Wilson's Fourteen Points. Believes the theory of self-determination was founded upon the doctrine of popular sovereignty. Argues that the object of self-determination was to avoid subjecting a people to alien control against its will. Defines a people as a unit of sufficient size to be capable of independent existence. Fears that a proliferation of small political state units would create instability and invite aggression. Concludes that self-determination ought to be applied with due regard to results and minimal size limits.

30. YAPOU, Eliezer. "The Autonomy That Never Was: The Autonomy Plans for the Sudeten in 1938." *Models of Autonomy*. Ed. Yoram Dinstein. New Brunswick, NJ: Transaction Books, 1981, pp. 97-123.
Although doomed by the Nazi conspiracy to destroy Czechoslovak independence, the 1938 negotiations between the Czechoslovak government and the Sudeten German Party leaders regarding the "Settlement of the Nationalities Questions" provided a unique case history of a proposed autonomy. Both sides had envisaged reforms that would trans-

form the Sudeten German status from a minority problem into a "co-inhabiting nationality." The comprehensive autonomy system exceeded a mere minority protection system because the Sudeten Germans comprised more than one-quarter of Czechoslovakia's population, and resided in compact and defined areas. Under Nazi pressure and threats of irredentism, the Czechs had gone to extreme limits of offering concessions compatible with the preservation of the country's unity.

Selected International Instruments

31. United Nations. *Declaration on Principles of International Law Concerning Friendly Relations and Co-operation Among States in Accordance with the Charter of the United Nations.* General Assembly Resolution 2625 (XXV) of 24 October 1970.

With regard to the principle of equal rights and self-determination of peoples, the Declaration proclaims that:

"By virtue of the principle of equal rights and self-determination of peoples enshrined in the Charter of the United Nations, all peoples have the right freely to determine, without external interference, their political status and to pursue their economic social and cultural development, and every State has the duty to respect this right in accordance with the provisions of the Charter.

Every State has the duty to promote, through joint and separate action, realization of the principle of equal rights and self-determination of peoples, in accordance with the provisions of the Charter, and to render assistance to the United Nations in carrying out the responsibilities entrusted to it by the Charter regarding the implementation of the principle in order:

(a) to promote friendly relations and co-operation among States; and

(b) To bring a speedy end to colonialism, having due regard to the freely expressed will of the peoples concerned; and bearing in mind that subjection of peoples to alien subjugation, domination and exploitation constitutes a violation of the principle, as well as a denial of fundamental rights, and is contrary to the Charter.

Every State has the duty to promote through joint and separate action universal respect for and observance of human rights and fundamental freedoms in accordance with the Charter.

The establishment of a sovereign and independent State, the free association or integration with an independent State or the emergence into any other political status freely determined by a people constitute modes of implementing the right of self-determination by that people.

Every State has the duty to refrain from any forcible action which deprives people referred to above in the elaboration of the present principle of their right to self-determination and freedom and independence. In their actions against, and resistance to, such forcible action in pursuit of the exercise of their right to self-determination, such peoples are entitled to speak and to receive support in accordance with the purposes and principles of the Charter.

The territory of a colony or other Non-Self-Governing Territory has, under the Charter, a status separate and distinct from the territory of the State administering it; and such separate and distinct status under the Charter shall exist until the people of the colony or Non-Self-Governing Territory have exercised their right of self-determination in accordance with the Charter, and particularly its purposes and principles.

Nothing in the foregoing paragraphs shall be construed as authorizing or encouraging any action which would dismember or impair, totally or in part, the territorial integrity or political unity of sovereign and independent States conducting themselves in compliance with the principle of equal rights and self-determination of peoples as described above and thus possessed of a government representing the whole people belonging to the territory without distinction as to race, creed or colour.

Every State shall refrain from any action aimed at the partial or total disruption of the national unity and territorial integrity of any other State or country."

32.　United Nations. *Declaration on the Granting of Independence to Colonial Countries and Peoples.* General Assembly Resolution 1514 (XV) of 14 December 1960.
　　　"The General Assembly,

　　　Mindful of the determination proclaimed by the peoples of the world in the Charter of the United Nations to reaffirm faith in fundamental human rights, in the dignity and worth of the human person, in the equal rights of men and women and of nations large and small and to promote social progress and better standards of life in larger freedom,

Conscious of the need for the creation of conditions of stability and well-being and peaceful and friendly relations based on respect for the principles of equal rights and self-determination of all peoples, and of universal respect for, and observance of, human rights and fundamental freedoms for all without distinction as to race, sex, language or religion,

Recognizing the passionate yearning for freedom in all dependent peoples and the decisive role of such peoples in the attainment of their independence,

Aware of the increasing conflicts resulting from the denial of or impediments in the way of the freedom of such peoples, which constitute a serious threat to world peace,

Considering the important role of the United Nations in assisting the movement for independence in Trust and Non-Self Governing Territories,

Recognizing that the peoples of the world ardently desire the end of colonialism in all its manifestations,

Convinced that the continued existence of colonialism prevents the development of international economic cooperation, impedes the social, cultural and economic development of dependent peoples and militates against the United Nations ideal of universal peace,

Affirming that peoples may, for their own ends, freely dispose of their natural wealth and resources without prejudice to any obligations arising out of international economic cooperation, based upon the principle of mutual benefit, and international law,

Believing that the process of liberation is irresistible and irreversible and that, in order to avoid serious crises, an end must be put to colonialism and all practices of segregation and discrimination associated therewith,

Welcoming the emergence in recent years of a large number of dependent territories into freedom and independence, and recognizing the increasingly powerful trends towards freedom in such territories which have not yet attained independence,

Convinced that all peoples have an inalienable right to complete freedom, the exercise of their sovereignty and the integrity of their national territory,

Solemnly proclaims the necessity of bringing to a speedy and unconditional end colonialism in all its forms and manifestations;

And to this end

Declares that:

1.   The subjection of peoples to alien subjugation, domination and exploitation constitutes a denial of fundamental human rights, is contrary to the Charter of the United Nations and is impediment to the promotion of world peace and cooperation.

2.   All peoples have the right to self-determination; by virtue of that right they freely determine their political status and freely pursue their economic, social and cultural development.

3.   Inadequacy of political, economic, social or educational preparedness should never serve as a pretext for delaying independence.

4.   All armed action or repressive measures of all kinds directed against dependent peoples shall cease in order to enable them to exercise peacefully and freely their right to complete independence, and the integrity of their national territory shall be respected.

5.   Immediate steps shall be taken, in Trust and Non-Self-Governing Territories or all other territories which have not yet attained independence, to transfer all power to the peoples of those territories, without any conditions or reservations, in accordance with their freely expressed will and desire, without any distinction as to race, creed or colour, in order to enable them to enjoy complete independence and freedom.

6.   Any attempt aimed at the partial or total disruption of the national unity and the territorial integrity of a country is incompatible with the purposes and principles of the Charter of the United nations.

7.   All States shall observe faithfully and strictly the provisions of the Charter of the United Nations, the Universal Declaration of Human Rights and the present Declaration on the basis of equality, non-interference in the internal affairs of all States, and respect for the sovereign rights of all peoples and their territorial integrity."

33.   Conference on Security and Cooperation in Europe. *Final Act.* United Nations: Helsinki, 1975.

"Questions Relating to Security in Europe:

1.   (a) Declaration on Principles Guiding Relations Between Participating States.

VIII.   Equal Rights and Self-Determination of Peoples.

The participating States will respect the equal rights of peoples and their right to self-determination, acting at all times in conformity with the purposes and principles of the Charter of the United Nations and with the relevant norms of international law, including those relating to territorial integrity of States.

By virtue of the principle of equal rights and self-determination of peoples, all peoples always have the right, in full freedom, to determine, when and as they wish, their internal and external political status, without external interference, and to pursue as they wish their political, economic, social and cultural developments.

The participating States reaffirm the universal significance of respect for effective exercise of equal rights and self-determination of peoples for the development of friendly relations among themselves as among all States; they also recall the importance of the elimination of any form of violation of this principle."

34.   United Nations. *Human Rights: A Compilation of International Instruments.*   New York: United Nations, Document ST/HR/1/Rev.2, 1983.
Documents included in Section C (pp. 20-1) dealing with self-determination are: The Declaration on the Granting of Independence to Colonial Countries and Peoples and General Assembly resolution 1803 (XVII) on the Permanent Sovereignty over Natural Resources.

35.   United Nations. *International Covenant on Civil and Political Rights.* Adopted and opened for signature, ratification and accession by General Assembly Resolution 2200 A (XXI) of 16 December 1966. Entry into force: 23 March 1976, in accordance with article 49.

PREAMBLE
"The States Parties to the present Covenant,

Considering that, in accordance with the principles proclaimed in the Charter of the United Nations, recognition of the inherent dignity and of the equal and inalienable rights of all members of the human family is the foundation of freedom, justice and peace in the world.

Recognizing that these rights derive from the inherent dignity of the human person,

Recognizing that, in accordance with the Universal Declaration of Human Rights, the ideal of free human beings enjoying civil and political freedom and freedom from fear and want can only be achieved if conditions are created whereby everyone may enjoy his civil and political rights, as well as his economic, social and cultural rights,

Considering the obligation of States under the Charter of the United nations to promote universal respect for, and observance of, human rights and freedoms,

Realizing that the individual, having duties to other individuals and to the community to which he belongs, is under a responsibility to strive for the promotion and observance of the rights recognized in the present Covenant,

Agree upon the following articles:

PART I

Article I

1.   All peoples have the right of self-determination. By virtue of that right they freely determine their political status and freely pursue their economic, social and cultural development.

2.   All peoples may, for their own ends, freely dispose of their natural wealth and resources without prejudice to any obligations arising out of international economic co-operation, based upon the principle of mutual benefit, and international law. In no case may a people be deprived of its own means of subsistence.

3.   The States Parties to the present Covenant, including those having responsibility for the administration of Non-Self-Governing and Trust Territories, shall promote the realization of the right of self-determination, and shall respect that right, in conformity with the provisions of the Charter of the United Nations."

36.   United Nations. *International Covenant on Economic, Social and Cultural Rights.* Adopted and opened for signature, ratification and accession by General Assembly Resolution 2200 (XXI) of 16 December 1966. Entry into force: 3 January 1976, in accordance with article 27.

PREAMBLE

"The States Parties to the present Covenant,

Considering that, in accordance with the principles proclaimed in the Charter of the United Nations, recognition of the inherent dignity and of the equal and inalienable rights of all members of the human family is the foundation of freedom, justice and peace in the world,

Recognizing that these rights derive from the inherent dignity of the human person,

Recognizing that, in accordance with the Universal Declaration of Human Rights, the ideal of free human beings enjoying freedom from fear and want can only be achieved if conditions are created whereby everyone may enjoy his economic, social and cultural rights, as well as his civil and political rights,

Considering the obligation of States under the Charter of the United Nations to promote universal respect for, and observance of, human rights and freedoms,

Realizing that the individual, having duties to other individuals and to the community to which he belongs, is under a responsibility to strive for promotion and observance of the rights recognized in the present Covenant,

Agree upon the following articles:

PART I

Article I

1. All peoples have the right of self-determination. By virtue of that right they freely determine their political status and freely pursue their economic, social and cultural development.

2. All peoples may, for their own ends, freely dispose of their natural wealth and resources without prejudice to any obligations arising out of international economic co-operation, based upon the principle of mutual benefit, and international law. In no case may a people be deprived of its own means of subsistence.

3. The States Parties to the present Covenant, including those having responsibility for the administration of Non-Self-Governing and Trust Territories, shall promote the realization of the right of self-determination, and shall respect that right, in

conformity with the provisions of the Charter of the United Nations."

37. United Nations. *Permanent Sovereignty Over Natural Resources.* General Assembly Resolution 1803 (XVII) of 14 December 1962.

"**The General Assembly,**

Recalling its resolutions 523 (VI) of 12 January 1952 and 626 (VII) of 21 December 1952,

Bearing in mind its resolution 1314 (XIII) of 12 December 1958, by which it established the Commission on Permanent Sovereignty over Natural Resources and instructed it to conduct a full survey of the status of permanent sovereignty over natural wealth and resources as a basic constituent of the right to self-determination, with recommendations, where necessary, for its strengthening, and decided further that, in the conduct of the full survey of the status of the permanent sovereignty of peoples and nations over their natural wealth and resources, due regard should be paid to the rights and duties of States under international law and to the importance of encouraging international co-operation in the economic development of developing countries,

Bearing in mind its resolution 1515 (XV) of 15 December 1960, in which it recommended that the sovereign right of every State to dispose of its wealth and its natural resources should be respected,

Considering that any measure in this respect must be based on the recognition of the inalienable right of all States freely to dispose of their natural wealth and resources in accordance with their national interests, and on respect for the economic independence of States,

Considering that nothing in paragraph 4 below in any way prejudices the position of any Member State on any aspect of the question of the rights and obligations of successor States and Governments in respect of property acquired before the accession to complete sovereignty of countries formerly under colonial rule,

Noting that the subject of succession of States and Governments is being examined as a matter of priority by the International Law Commission,

Considering that it is desirable to promote international co-operation for the economic development of developing countries, and that economic and financial agreements between the developed and the developing countries must be based on the principles of equality and of the right of peoples and nations to self-determination,

Considering that the provision of economic and technical assistance, loans and increased foreign investment must not be subject to conditions which conflict with the interests of the recipient State,

Considering the benefits to be derived from exchanges of technical and scientific information likely to promote the development and use of such resources and wealth, and the important part which the United Nations and other international organizations are called upon to play in that connexion,

Attaching particular importance to the question of promoting the economic development of developing countries and securing their economic independence,

Noting that the creation and strengthening of the inalienable sovereignty of States over their natural wealth and resources reinforces their economic independence,

Desiring that there should be further consideration by the United Nations of the subject of permanent sovereignty over natural resources in the spirit of international co-operation in the field of economic development, particularly that of the developing countries,

Declares that:

1.　The right of peoples and nations to permanent sovereignty over their natural wealth and resources must be exercised in the interest of their national development and of the well-being of the people of the State concerned.

2.　The exploration, development and disposition of such resources, as well as the import of the foreign capital required for these purposes, should be in conformity with the rules and conditions which the peoples and nations freely consider to be necessary or desirable with regard to the authorization, restriction or prohibition of such activities.

3.　In cases where authorization is granted, the capital imported and the earnings on that capital shall be governed by the terms thereof, by the national legislation in force, and by international law. The profits derived must be shared in the proportions freely agreed upon, in each case, between the investors and the recipient State, due care being taken to ensure that there is no impairment, for any reason, of that State's sovereignty over its natural wealth and resources.

4.　Nationalization, expropriation or requisitioning shall be based on grounds or reasons of public utility, security or the national interest which are recognized as overriding purely individual or private interests, both domestic and foreign. In such cases the owner shall be paid appropriate compensation, in accordance with the rules in force in the State taking such measures in the exercise of its sovereignty and in accordance with international law. In any case where the question of compensation gives rise to a controversy, the national jurisdiction of the State taking such measures shall be exhausted. However, upon agreement by sovereign States and other parties concerned, settlement of the dispute should be made through arbitration or international adjudication.

5. The free and beneficial exercise of the sovereignty of peoples and nations over their natural resources must be furthered by the mutual respect of States based on their sovereign equality.

6. International co-operation for the economic development of developing countries, whether in the form of public or private capital investments, exchange of goods and services, technical assistance, or exchange of scientific information, shall be such as to further their independent national development and shall be based upon respect for their sovereignty over their natural wealth and resources.

7. Violation of the rights of peoples and nations to sovereignty over their natural wealth and resources is contrary to the spirit and principles of the Charter of the United Nations and hinders the development of international co-operation and the maintenance of peace.

8. Foreign investment agreements freely entered into by or between sovereign States shall be observed in good faith; States and international organizations shall strictly and conscientiously respect the sovereignty of peoples and nations over their natural wealth and resources in accordance with the Charter and principles set forth in the present resolution...."

38. United Nations. *Provisions of the Charter of the United Nations.*

1. Article 1, paragraph 2: "To develop friendly relations among nations based on respect for the principle of equal rights and self-determination of peoples...."

2. Article 55: "With a view to the creation of conditions of stability and well-being which are necessary for peaceful and friendly relations among nations based on respect for the principle of equal rights and self-determination of peoples, the United Nations shall promote...."

3. Chapter XI, Declaration Regarding Non-Self-Governing Territories, Article 73: "Members of the United Nations which have or assumed responsibilities for the admission of territories whose peoples have not yet attained a full measure of self-government recognize the principle that the interests of the inhabitants of these territories are paramount, and accept as a sacred trust the obligation to promote to the utmost, within the system of international peace and security established by the present Charter, the well-being of the inhabitants of these territories, and, to this end:....

b. to develop self-government, to take due account of the political aspirations of the peoples, and to assist them in the progressive development of their free political institutions, according to the particular circumstances of each territory and its peoples and their varying stages of advancement."

4. Chapter XII, International Trusteeship System, Article 76: "The basic objectives of the trusteeship system, in accordance with the Purposes of the United Nations laid down in article 1 of the present Charter, shall be:....

b. to promote the political, economic, social, and educational advancement of the inhabitants of the trust territories, and their progressive development towards self-government or independence as may be appropriate to the particular circumstances of each territory and its peoples and the freely expressed wishes of the peoples concerned, and as may be provided by the terms of each trusteeship agreement;

c. to encourage respect for human rights and for fundamental freedoms for all without discrimination as to race, sex, language, or religions, and to encourage recognition of the independence of the peoples of the world."

Examination of Some International Instruments

39. BARBER, Hollis W. "Decolonisation: The Committee of Twenty-Four." *World Affairs*, CXXXVIII (1975), 128-51.
During political transition periods, previously accepted norms of behavior or laws often conflicted with new perceptions of the rules that ought to apply. In international law, the authoritative rules must be based on international practice rather than on formal legislation. Explains that the United Nations Committee of Twenty-Four was formulating new rules of interna-

tional practice that some day might harden into accepted law. The Committee had championed numerous principles which conflicted with orthodox international practice. It had condemned colonialism, advocated the granting of material and moral support to liberation movements, and had urged the U.N. to recognize these movements, sometimes on the same basis as sovereign states. The Committee had helped develop the "principle" of self-determination into an assumed "right." For years, the Committee had assumed that the purpose of its activity was to grant independence to *all* existing colonies; it now conceded that independence and self-determination were not interchangeable concepts, and recognized that not all people desired political independence, nor would they all be able to manage sovereignty even if they had it. Claims that the Committee had not been effective in forcing imperialists to dismantle their empires, and that its confrontation policies were sometimes damaging.

40.   BLUM, Y. Z. "Reflections On the Changing Concept of Self-Determination." *Israel Law Review*, X (1975), 509-14.
Focuses primarily on the juridical aspects of an alleged political concept. Explains that self-determination, in essence the right of secession, could be reconciled with sovereignty, which sought to preserve territorial integrity. Believes that this contradiction might be resolved theoretically, but not politically, and that any attempt to convert self-determination into a legally recognized right would legitimize revolution by absorbing it into the international juridical system. Explains that the U.N. Charter considered self-determination as one of the desiderata of the charter rather than as a legal right. States that although various U.N. declarations and other instruments purportedly converted self-determination into one of the basic rules of contemporary international law, in practice self-determination had only been invoked in the context of gaining independence for colonial territories in Africa and Asia from European colonial masters. Lists two factors that had enabled self-determination and sovereignty to exist peacefully side by side: (1) self-determination depended on the ability of a people to implement its right to self-determination; and (2) self-determination was usually accepted for application only with reference to a total overseas colonial territory.

41.   CASSESE, Antonio.   "The Helsinki Declaration and Self-Determination." *Human Rights, International Law and the*

Helsinki Accord. Ed. T. Buergenthal. New York: Allanheld Osmun/Universe Books, 1977, pp. 83-110.

Examines the evolution of the principle of self-determiantion within the U.N. Describes the tension between Socialist and Western interpretations of the doctrine. Points out that U.N. action in this respect had focused essentially on external self-determination, but at the same time enjoyed priority. As a result, the U.N. had favored established governments at the expense of the rights of peoples. Argues that the Helsinki Accords had expanded and added depth to the U.N. concept of self-determination. Notes in particular that the right was explicitly defined to be perpetual, and to have internal and external applications. Concludes that, although ambiguous legal status of the agreement had created certain problems in terms of impact, signatory states were accountable for breaches of compliance and could not deny the validity of the content. Argues that signatories had political and moral duties in this regard.

42. CASSESE, Antonio. "The Self-Determination of Peoples." *The International Bill of Rights: The Covenant on Civil and Political Rights.* Ed. Louis Henkin. New York: Columbia University Press, 1981, pp. 92-113.

Interprets the terms and concepts enshrined in Article 1 of the Covenant as they related to the self-determination of peoples. Maintains that, clearly, the people belonging to a national component in a multinational state, as well as those living in territories that had not attained political independence, enjoyed the right to self-determination under Article 1, provided that the national entity was not embroiled in a majority/minority group situation, and that the national or ethnic group was recognized constitutionally, having a distinct legal status within the host state's constitutional framework. Self-determination also applied to the people of a sovereign state living under foreign domination. Considers the content of the right in the context of "internal" and "external" self-determination. Examines the two-fold link which the Covenant established between the self-determination of peoples and the civil and political rights of individuals. Claims external self-determination to be a necessary precondition for the enjoyment of individual rights, and international self-determination as the synthesis and *summa* of civil and political rights. Discusses the problem of implementing self-determination and disposition of natural wealth and resources. Maintains that, although international instruments subsequent to the drafting of the Covenant could not affect the obligations of the parties to it, they might pertain to the interpretation and implementation of Article 1.

43.   CHOWDHURY, Subraty R.   "The Status and Norms of Self-
         Determination in Contemporary International Law."
         Netherlands International Law Review, XXIV (1977), 72-84.
Considers self-determination a legal status, based on General Assembly resolutin 2625 (1970), the "Declaration on Principles of International Law Concerning Friendly Relations and Cooperation among States in Accordance with The Charter of the United Nations." Maintains that the resolution had established binding rules according to article 31(3)(a) of the Vienna Convention of the Law of Treaties. Enumerates four norms of self-determination: The first norm concerned the beneficiaries of the right and manner of exercise. The beneficiaries of the right were the people, not the territory, and a majority had the right within an accepted political unit to exercise power. The second norm pertained to territories and situations, wherever applicable. Contends that the rule was not confined to colonial or trust territories, but was universal in application. The third norm outlined the modes of implementation, which included a full sovereign state, free association with an independent state, or any other political status freely determined by a people. The fourth norm established a correlation between the people's right to self-determination and the duties of the state to promote the realization of this right in good faith.

44.   CRISTESCU, Aureliu. *The Right to Self-Determination; His-
         torical and Current Development on the Basis of United Na-
         tions Documents.* New York: United Nations Publication
         E/C.N. 4/Sub.2/404/rev.1, 1981.
Examines the evolution of the right to self-determination through United Nations instruments and documents, as established in Article 1, paragraph 2 of the United Nations Charter. Complains that although the right to self-determination had become a universal rule and a fundamental human right according to conventional and customary international law, it was being denied in various parts of the world. Considers territorial integrity still a paramout principle governing states. Suggests that the right of secession existed only when peoples became subjugated in defiance of international law. Defines the duties and privileges of peoples, nations and states reflected in the right to political and economic self-determination. Relates the cul-

tural aspect of the right to self-determination to the social-economic conditions that encouraged a people to engage in creative material and spiritual activity. Believes that colonial domination, racial discrimination and apartheid, neo-colonialism, aggression, foreign occupation or imperialism violated the right to self-determination and threatened world peace. Stresses that self-determination promoted the realization of other human rights. Urges the United Nations and affiliated organizations to encourage the right to self-determination for all peoples.

45. EAGLETON, Clyde. "Excesses of Self-Determination." *Foreign Affairs*, XXXI (1952-53), 592-604.
Notes that the "wild rush" to grant self-determination to colonized peoples involved the United Nations in entanglements. Expresses concern for the limits that had been placed on interpretations and applications. Suggests that not only was self-determination difficult to define, but that it was a double-edged concept which could disintegrate as well as unify. Discusses U.N. prescriptions and questions how "desire" for self-determination was to be ascertained and measured. Discusses various interpretations, and concludes that due to the variety of expectations, self-determination had lost all meaning. Examines some U.N. expectations, and declares that many recognized states could not measure up to the standards. Discusses problems related to stated expectations. Suggests that "self-determination" had reached the age of responsibility. Declares that it should not be granted to any group for the sole reason that the group chose to claim it. Urges the U.N. to provide pertinent criteria for measuring possible successes before permitting self-determination to be granted.

46. EAGLETON, Clyde. "Self-Determination in the United Nations." *American Journal of International Law*, XXXXVII (1953), 88-93.
Argues that United Nations discussions and actions had proven self-determination to be a term of practical importance and immediate urgency, and badly in need of legal definition. Believes that noble utterances on behalf of lofty principles could not be transformed into responsible action by states. Suggests criteria to test a state's readiness for independence, because independence did not necessarily suit a particular group.

47.   EL-AYOUTY, Yassin. *The United Nations and Decolonization:
        The Role of Afro-Asia.* The Hague: Martinus Nijhoff,
        1971.
        Examines the contribution of the Afro-Asian bloc to the inter-
        pretation of the United Nations Charter's concept of dealing
        with Non-Self-Governing Territories (NSGTs).   Reports that
        the Afro-Asian states considered the United Nations the main
        guardian of indigenous inhabitants' interests in all dependent
        territories, and therefore they opposed the Charter's distinctions
        between NSGTs (Chapter XI, which did not specifically state
        these groups' rights to independence), and Trust Territories
        (Chapters XII and XIII, which did).   Blames the ever-changing
        international political climate and the vague terminology for the
        conflict involving interpretations of the Charter.   Explains the
        slow process of making the Charter an effective instrument for
        the protection of NSGTs.   However, the General Assembly's
        "Declaration on the Granting of Independence" established in-
        dependence as the best way to achieve decolonization.

48.   ENGERS, J. F.   "From Sacred Trust to Self-Determination."
        Netherlands International Law Review, XXIV (1977), 85-91.
        Traces the evolution of the concept of sacred trust from the
        League of Nations to the Charter.   Notes the gap between the
        law (as embodied in the Charter) and current political reality
        (best exemplified by the decolonization of Africa).   Contends
        that this gap had been filled by General Assembly Resolutions
        1514 (1960) and 2625 (1970).   Considers these resolutions
        technically *communis opinio* and thus not law, but U.N. mem-
        bers could not disregard these obligations, because they repre-
        sented the current norms of International Law pertaining to
        non-self-governing territories.   Discusses the two principal ob-
        jections to the doctrine: (1) subordination of good government
        to self-government, and (2) selective rather than universal
        application.   Concludes that the substance of international law
        relating to non-self-governing territories had been reversed due
        to the decision of the General Assembly to accept "reality."

49.   EYASSU, Gayim.   "Reflections on the Draft Articles of the
        International Law Commission on State Responsibility:
        Articles 14; 15; and 19 in the Context of the Contemporary
        International Law of Self-Determination." *Nordisk
        Tidsskrift For International Ret,* LIV (1985), 85-111.
        Points out that maintenance of international peace and security,
        the development of friendly relations among nations and the

effective enjoyment of basic human rights required respect for the principle of self-determination, a dynamic principle affecting all the major elements of relations involving states. Reviews the contemporary norm of self-determination through resolutions of the U.N. General Assembly. Analyzes draft articles 14, 15 and 19 of the International Law Commission. Suggests that article 19 reflected the contemporary development of international law by recognizing special categories of international rules requiring a separate regime of international responsibility. States that violation of the rules on self-determination could arise under article 19, possibly a positive element in implementing the purposes of the U.N. in this context. Argues that article 15, dealing with insurrectional movements, and Article 14, addressing the conduct of organs of an insurrectional movement, failed to consider contemporary norms relating to self-determination. Concludes that, unlike article 19, articles 14 and 15 were not "in tune with the march of time."

50. FINGER, Seymour Maxwell and Gurcharan SINGH. "Self-Determination: A United Nations Perspective." *Self-Determination: National, Regional, and Global Dimensions.* Eds. Yonah Alexander and Robert A. Friedlander. Boulder, CO: Westview Press, 1980, pp. 333-46.

During the struggle against colonialism, the anti-colonial forces at the United Nations had allegedly attacked Western colonialism by expanding the implications of Chapter 11 of the Charter and by campaigning against restrictive interpretations of self-determination. Inspired by the principle of self-determination contained in Articles 1 and 55 of the Charter, the anti-colonial forces had attempted to apply it across the board to all colonial territories. The authors consider it misleading to believe that the practical application of self-determination had been expanded beyond limits. With the demise of the old colonial empires and the emergence of new multinational and polyethnic political entities, opponents of intrastate imperialism had reincarnated the principle of self-determination in new forms. Argue that, in many cases, the principle of territorial integrity might have to yield to the principle of self-determination, or find a way to compromise with it. Urge the global community to discover how to deal with these new claims for internal self-determination.

51. GOODMAN, G. "The Cry of National Liberation: Recent
     Soviet Attitudes Towards National Self-Determination."
     International Organization, XIV (1960), 92-106.
     Considers the idea of national self-determination of Western
     origin.   Examines Soviet attempts to manipulate this idea,
     particularly in the United Nations. Defines Western-style self-
     determination as a desirable ideal that might be applied in var-
     ying circumstances, but which could not be reduced to a simple,
     concrete formula. Defines Soviet self-determination as the right
     of every dependent people to terminate this status through the
     formation of its own independent national state.   Describes
     Soviet attempts to get its concept of self-determination in the
     draft Covenant, and the Western response to this strategy. Ar-
     gues that the Soviets had used the idea of national self-
     determination as a tool of ideological warfare. Bases this view
     on the USSR's negative reaction to the 1956 General Assembly
     Resolution in response to the Hungarian Revolt, a resolution
     which the Soviet Union branded a violation of article 2(7) of the
     U.N. Charter. Contends that this was a test case of the appli-
     cation of national self-determination inside the Soviet Bloc.

52. GROS ESPIELL, Hector. *The Right to Self-Determination
     Implementation of United Nations Resolutions.* New York:
     United Nations Publication E/CN.4/Sub.2/405 Rev.1,
     1980.
     Deals with the right applying to peoples under "colonial and
     alien domination." Defines its application to include any kind
     of domination, but indicates that "it does not exist where a
     people lives freely and voluntarily under legal order of a state
     whose territorial integrity must be respected." Examines poli-
     tical, economic, social and cultural aspects of the right, and de-
     scribes implementation of U.N. resolutions.   Considers the
     U.N. very successful in this regard. Notes that certain colonial
     situations (notably in South Africa) still required resolution.
     Warns that, although traditional colonialism was on the wane,
     economic neo-imperialism and new forms of colonialism, dam-
     aging in particular to developing countries, posed a serious
     problem.   Provides a comprehensive list of specific situations
     which had been or were being dealt with by the U.N. Recom-
     mends that breaches of the obligation to recognize the right to
     self-determination be deemed an international crime with
     appropriate sanctions. Considers self-determination the *sine
     qua non* for the existence of human rights and freedoms.

53. GUNTER, Michael M. "Self-Determination or Territorial Integrity: The United Nations in Confusion." *World Affairs*, CXXXXI (1979), 203-16.

Analyzes United Nations documents dealing with the confusion and conflict involving adherents of self-determination and territorial integrity, and considers future implications. Argues that the norms of self-determination and territorial integrity had been seriously threatened recently in Belize, the Falklands Islands and Gibraltar, and even overturned in the Western Sahara and East Timor. The doctrine of territorial integrity might now be construed as permitting a state to claim neighboring territories, especially when, as in the cases of Belize, the Falkland Islands and Gibraltar, these territories were susceptible to the charge that they were presently occupied by settler populations; the implications of this interpretation for the state of Israel, as well as irredentist claims throughout the world, were profound. Attributes the inability of the United Nations to uphold its norms to the voting power of the Third World majority and the military power of the norm-breakers.

54. HIGGINS, R. *The Development of International Law through the Organs of the United Nations.* New York: Oxford University Press, 1963.

Discusses self-determination as an international right within the context of the United Nations.

55. KAY, David A. "Politics of Decolonization: The New Nations and the U.N. Political Process." *International Organization*, XXI (1967), 786-811.

Reviews the evolution of the United Nations' approach to the developing nations beginning in 1955 and culminating in 1960, when the organization turned from the problems and conflicts of the creator states to the central focus of the new nations, that is, securing a speedy and complete end to Western colonialism. Illustrates the employment of two principal mechanisms: the creation of a Special United Nations Committe on colonial problems, which avoided the necessity of "kowtowing" to the administration of the Trusteeship Council and encouraged innovative solutions, as demonstrated by Rhodesia; and the transformation of the United Nations' traditional preoccupation with individual human rights into concern for national independence and self-determination as the right of political groups. Contends that, in essence, self-determination had been added to the roster of human rights to be used as a weapon against colonialism and not to enhance the rights of all persons against all governments.

56. KOHN, Hans. "The United Nations and National Self-Determination." *Review of Politics*, XX (1958), 526-45.
Considers the modern concepts of national self-determination and the United Nations contradictory to a degree: the United Nations envisaged an international or supranational order at a time when nationalism had for the first time in history become a world-wide phenomenon. The Anglo-American ideas of trusteeship and self-government laid the foundations for a conscious and evolutionary growth of self-determination and political liberty throughout the politically and economically dependent or underdeveloped parts of mankind. The United Nations did not interpret national self-determination in the narrow sense as independence but as the attainment of a status of self-government and equality in conformity with the freely expressed wishes of the peoples involved. For the first time in history, all races and civilizations could meet on a footing of legal equality. Recommends that the United States follow a policy of positive sympathy with the forces of freedom and self-determination to effectively counter the threat of communist totalitarianism.

57. MITTELMAN, James H. "Collective Decolonisation and the UN Committee of 24." *Journal of Modern African Studies*, XIV (1976), 41-64.
Examines the role of the United Nations Committee of 24 in facilitating the implementation of the Declaration on the Granting of Independence to Colonial Countries and Peoples. During the era of mandates and trusts, the administering powers had encountered relatively little collective challenge. Collective decolonization in the postwar period referred to mutually sponsored efforts to co-ordinate indigenous resistance against external domination. Considers the chief contributions of the Committee: it assembled hard core evidence on the activities of foreign interests in non-self-governing territories; it monitored specialized agencies, regional organizations, and other international institutions, and encouraged compliance with General Assembly resolutions; it exerted constant pressure on those forces which impeded rapid implementation of the Resolution; and it performed a standard-setting function in defining permissible and impermissible behavior on colonial issues.

58. NAWAZ, M. K. "The Encounter Between Colonialism and Self-Determination in Historical and Legal Perspective: Lessons for the Future." *Ausgewählte Gegenwartsfragen zum Problem der Verwirklichung des Selbstbestimmungsrechts der Völker* (Selected Contemporary Questions Regarding the Problem of Establishing the People's Right to Self-Determination). Ed. Kurt Rabl. München: Verlag Robert Lerche, 1965, pp. 43-62.
Challenges some scholars' belief (for example, Rupert Emerson) that self-determination did not belong in the province of law. Acknowledges a political dimension, but claims that it would serve no useful purpose to pit law against politics. Reviews the impact of the U.N. Charter, and concludes that the principle of self-determination related not only to states and governments, but also to groups and individuals. Foresees problems of colonialism and neocolonialism.

59. NAWAZ, M. K. "The Meaning and Range of the Principle of Self-Determination." *Duke Law Journal*, LXXXII (1965), 82-101.
Challenges the view that self-determination had no place in the province of law, arguing that it, like other United Nations charter concepts, belonged as much in the realm of law as of politics. Explains the operational context of self-determination and outlines the juridical aspects of the doctrine. Surveys the historical perspective of self-determination, discusses Wilson's efforts to institutionalize the doctrine in the League of Nations, and analyzes the performance of self-determination in the United Nations. Examines United Nations resolutions and practices, especially the cases of Angola and Malaysia regarding self-determination. Identifies self-determination as one of the modern principles of international law that derived principally from the Charter of the United Nations, which did not, however, define the concept.

60. NINČIĆ, Djura. "Domestic Jurisdiction, Sovereignty and the Right of Peoples to Self-Determination." *The Problem of Sovereignty in the Charter and in the Practice of the United Nations.* Ed. Djura Ninčić. The Hague: Martinus Nijhoff, 1970, pp. 219-59.
Considers the right of peoples to self-determination one of the basic democratic principles of current international life. Claims that the inclusion of the right in the United Nations charter had made it part of a universal, multilateral international treaty, and

thus a source of definite and universally valid legal rights and obligations. Explains that United Nations practice had developed along two lines: First, it attempted to define and clarify the concept, and then to ensure the application of the principle, particularly in colonial and dependent territories. Reviews case studies involving the right to self-determination brought before the U.N., notably Indonesia, Tunisia, Morocco, Algeria, Cyprus and Angola. Identifies the anti-colonial struggle as a conflict of authority between domestic jurisdiction and self-determination. Considers self-determination a collective and individual right, exercised by peoples (or nations) as well as individuals.

61. POMERANCE, Michla. *Self-Determination in Law and Practice: The New Doctrine in the United Nations.* The Hague, Boston and London: Martinus Nijhoff, 1982.
Outlines the various post-World War I interpretations of the term self-determination, a concept initiated by Woodrow Wilson. Discusses problems and inconsistencies in implementation, and examines how the United Nations had dealt with the ensuing political controversies. Considers the legal premises for the recently conceived right to self-determination as *jus cogens* weak, and earlier dilemmas and ambiguities unsolved. Urges the United Nations to create objective criteria for defining a "people" and "colonial and alien domination." Discusses the rival claims of self-determination and territorial integrity, and contrasts the principles of non-intervention and sovereign equality with self-determination. Considers self-determination a moral rather than a legal right.

62. REISMAN, Michael. "Coercion and Self-Determination: Construing Article 2 (4)." *American Journal of International Law*, LXXVIII (1984), 642-45.
Focuses on the application of Article 2 (4) of the U.N. Charter in a contemporary political context. Believes the article was designed to operate as part of a complex collective security system. Argues that Article 2 (4) did not operate as intended in the context of "bloody" world politics. Owing to the difference between the letter of 2 (4) and political reality, urges lawyers to develop criteria for appraising the lawfulness of unilateral resort to coercion. Each application of 2 (4) must also enhance opportunities for self-determination. Article 2 (4) was based on two assumptions inconsistent with current political reality: all usurpation threats against the right to political independence

were external, overt invasion; and the article had failed to en-
vision division between two contending public order systems.

63. ROSENSTOCK, R. "The Declaration of Principles of International Law Concerning Friendly Relations: A Survey."
American Journal of International Law, LXV (1971),
713-35.
Examines the U.N. Special Committee's difficulties in drafting
the Declaration Concerning Friendly Relations. Outlines opposing viewpoints encountered in the areas of self-
determination. Points out significant progress in the acceptance
of self-determination by states as a positive obligation to promote that right. Commends the Committee for providing
alternative modes of implementation in addition to independence.

64. SHUKRI, Muhammad Aziz. *The Concept of Self-
Determination in the United Nations.* Damascus: Al
Jadidah Press, 1965.
Reviews the concept of self-determination, and stresses U.N.
documents and the varied interpretations.

65. SINHA, S. P. "Has Self-Determination Become a Principle of
International Law Today?" *Indian Journal of International
Law*, XIV (1974), 332-61.
Explains that prior to World War II, states did not support the
notion of self-determination as a "principle" of international
law. Examines self-determination in the U.N. Charter and in
state practice. Refers to Charter Articles 1 (2) and 55, Chapters
XI, XII and XIII. Lists three Charter limitations – lack of definition, subservience to other purposes outlined in the Charter,
and application only within existing states which raised doubts
about the legal value of the concept. Asserts that although state
practice had legitimized the principle of self-determination, its
application within the U.N. had been limited to colonial peoples. Notes that states had yet to view the principle of self-
determination as obligatory, and that an emerging norm had
not yet crystallized into law.

66. SOHN, Louis B. "Models of Autonomy Within the United
Nations Framework." *Models of Autonomy.* Ed. Yoram
Dinstein. New Brunswick, NJ: Transaction Books, 1981,
pp. 5-22.

Examines Articles 73 and 76 of the United Nations Charter, relating, respectively, to non-self-governing territories and the trusteeship system. Unlike the concept of independence, which implied the right of separation from another political entity, the concept of self-government meant that for important political or economic reasons a particular area would remain within the territorial jurisdiction of another political entity, but would regulate certain of its own affairs unimpeded.

67. SUREDA, A. Rigo. *The Evolution of the Right of Self-Determination: A Study of United Nations Practice.* Leiden: A. W. Sijthoff, 1973.

Examines the evolution of the principle of self-determination from a political concept into an international legal right. Clarifies its meaning and scope by reviewing specific cases, such as British Togoland, British Cameroons, Ruanda-Urundi, Algeria, Oman, the Cook Islands, French Somaliland, Cyprus, West Irian, Gibraltar, the Spanish Sahara, Morocco, Tunisia, Mauritania, Southern Rhodesia, Eritrea, Goa, Fiji, Aden's offshore islands and Muscat. Building on the work of the League of Nations with regard to the Åland Islands case and the Palestinian question, discusses United Nations competence over self-determination in trust, non-self-governing, and mandated territories. Traces the delimitation of the right to self-determination, the volatility of the content of the principle due to political structures, and the legitimate means of substantiating claims through plebiscites, elections, commissions of inquiry, or the use of force. Suggests that the League of Nations had diluted the general principle of self-determination as proclaimed by Woodrow Wilson, and merely implied it with regard to mandated territories. Points out that the United Nations had limited the application of self-determination to colonies, and that territorial integrity and existing boundaries would usually determine whether or not a people was entitled to external self-determination, even though all peoples had that right. Suggests that the emphasis on colonial independence as the content and subject of self-determination combined with the political concept of a nation had resulted in the neglect of the relevance of internal self-determination, which caused much upheaval in former colonies with multiracial societies. Judges the United Nations as having been unsuccessful in matching collective and individual dimensions of self-determination when striving to create free and plural political units.

68. TRAVERS, P. J. "The Legal Effect of United Nations Action in Support of the Palestine Liberation Organization and the National Liberation Movements of Africa." *Howard University International Law Journal*, XVII (1976), 561-80.
Notes the resemblance between General Assembly resolutions urging the United Nations to cooperate with the PLO, and those regularly adopted assisting national liberation movements' struggles against colonial and white supremacist regimes in several African territories. Examines the legal effects of both activities, and compares them with respect to the proposition that such measures could guide the formation of binding rules of customary international law. Concludes that, although the U.N.'s activities in support of African movements had encouraged rules of international law requiring similar support for those movements by individual states, recent activities in favor of the PLO had not engendered such legal obligations.

69. TWITCHETT, Kenneth J. "The Colonial Powers and the United Nations." *Journal of Contemporary History* (special issue on "Colonialism and Decolonization"), IV (1969), 167-86.
Identifies the United Nations as the focal point of the anticolonial movement in the 1950s. The newly emerged Afro-Asian U.N. members, supported by a wide anticolonial bloc, had interpreted and employed the ambiguous Charter provisions as legal and moral justifications for their crusade. Attributes the success of the anti-colonial U.N. majority in challenging the European colonial powers, especially with regard to strengthening the machinery of the Charter, to three factors: the relative decline of Western Europe's global power; the steady diminution in the political will and ability of the metropoles to preserve their colonial empires intact; and the growth of liberal Western sentiment. Believes that despite its militancy, the U.N. had enhanced international stability by assisting territories to achieve independence.

70. United Nations. *Action in the Field of Human Rights.* New York: United Nations, Document ST/HR/2/Rev.2, 1983.
Outlines U.N. measures to ensure people's right to self-determination, including provisions of the U.N. Charter regarding self-determination as a human right, the Declaration on the Granting of Independence to Colonial Countries and Peoples, and the Declaration on Principles of International Law

Concerning Friendly Relations and Co-operation among States in Accordance with the U.N. Charter.

71. VAN DYKE, Vernon. "Self-Determination and Minority Rights." *Human Rights, the United States, and World Community.* Ed. Vernon van Dyke. New York: Oxford University Press, 1970, pp. 77-104.
Considers the terms "self-determination" and "minority rights" extremely vague. Although some of the controversy surrounding them had been settled in the United Nations General Assembly, they would likely remain sources of trouble and conflict, because governments endorsed the notions of internal and external self-determination, minority rights, and economic self-determination only when they suited their interests. Explains that the notion of external self-determination had been very effective in fragmenting large empires, and might also terminate heterogeneous states. Believes that the United Nations would be in a far better position if self-determination had never been called a right and the limits of its application had been more clearly specified from the beginning.

General Overviews and Interpretations

72. ALEXANDER, Yonah and Robert A. FRIEDLANDER, eds. *Self-Determination: National, Regional, and Global Dimensions.* Boulder, CO: Westview Press, 1980.
Fourteen essays explore three questions: (1) Is self-determination truly a necessary precondition to international peace and stability? (2) Is self-determination a basic international human right and part of the guaranteed fundamental freedoms proclaimed by the world community? and (3) What will the effect of self-determination be upon the remaining decades of the twentieth century?

73. ARZINGER, Rudolf. *Das Selbstbestimmungsrecht in allgemeinen Völkerrecht der Gegenwart* (Self-Determination in General Contemporary International Law). Berlin (East): Staatsverlag, 1966.
A contemporary Marxist explores interpretations and applications of the universal right to self-determination.

74. BIBO, Istvan. *The Paralysis of International Institutions and the Remedies: A Study of Self-Determination, Concord among the Major Powers, and Political Arbitration.* Hassocis, Sussex (England): Harvester Press Ltd., 1976.
Acknowledges that sovereignty, territorial integrity and independence ensured peace and stability, and that the right to self-determination of peoples safeguarded national boundaries and restricted abuses of power. Concedes that the practical application of these principles had been difficult, because they might represent conflicting interests. Blames the ineffectiveness of international negotiations and conflict resolution on often diametrically opposed self-interest and morality. Traces the principle of self-determination to the demise of monarchic-feudal legitimacy. Explains that the post-World War II world emphasized colonial self-determination, but that the colonial powers retained political and economic influence, and in some cases maintained former dependencies in a semi-colonial state.

75. BOKOR-SZEGŐ, Hanna. *New States and International Law.* Budapest: Akadémiai Kiadó, 1970.
Traces the process of colonial independence through self-determination, a principle proclaimed by the bourgeoisie as a political tool to end feudalism and thereby expand its markets. Currently, self-determination served as an international legal right claimed by dependent nations living under the rule of colonial powers, including trust and non-self-governing territories. Explains that internal self-determination referred to a nation's autonomy within the state, whereas external self-determination pertained to the right of a nation to decide its own international destiny, without posing a threat to international peace and security. Points out, however, that international law inherently operated in contradiction to the principle of self-determination. Concludes that many Third World countries' continuing ties with colonial powers limited the exercise of external self-determination.

76. BOWETT, D. W. "Self-Determination and Political Rights in the Developing Countries." *Proceedings of the American Society of International Law*, 60th Session, 1966, 129-35.
Analyzes three respects in which self-determination proved an issue in interstate relations: territorial settlements, prohibition of intervention and decolonization. Suggests that the principle of self-determination had achieved substantial recognition as a norm for the settlement of territorial disputes. Points out that

the link between self-determination and protection of minorities was clear. Stresses the political nature of the right to self-determination and suggests that the principle of non-intervention was paramount. Stresses the problem created by the lack of concern for individual rights once independence had been achieved through the application of self-determination as a human right.

77.   CASSESE, Antonio. "Political Self-Determination: Old Concepts and New Developments." *UN Law/Fundamental Rights.* Ed. Antonio Cassese. Alphen aan den Rijn: Sijthoff and Noordhoff, 1979, pp. 137-65.
States that self-determination could be either "external" or "internal." Defines "external" self-determination as the ability of a people or a minority to choose its actions freely in international relations, whether opting for independence or union with other states. Defines "internal" self-determination as the freedom a people in a sovereign state enjoyed to elect and maintain the government of its choice or an ethnic, racial, religious or other minority's right within a sovereign state not to be oppressed by the central government. Examines the various international instruments that outline the principle of self-determination. Notes a shift of emphasis from "external" to "internal" political self-determination since 1945, although economically, "external" self-determination still played an important role. Notes a shift from an all-embracing and generic concept of "internal" self-determination to a notion that closely linked this collective right to the human rights and fundamental freedoms of individuals, thus conceiving political self-determination as the right of peoples or minorities to be free from any form of authoritarian oppression.

78.   CHEN, Lung-Chu. "Self-Determination as a Human Right." *Toward World Order and Human Dignity.* Eds. W. Michael Reisman and Burns H. Weston. New York: The Free Press, 1976, pp. 198-261.
Contends that self-determination is deeply rooted in the notions of human rights and human dignity. Focuses on self-determination involving separation. Suggests that the prevailing system of nation-states is rendered rigid by the principle of territorial integrity. Notes that self-determination can guide groups as they seek to maximize community values. Notes that without the allegiance of the people living in the territory, "territorial integrity" is an empty phrase. Concludes that re-

cognition of self-determination and the right of secession may contribute to the optimal realization of human dignity.

79. CONNOR, Walker. *The National Question in Marxist-Leninist Theory and Strategy*. Princeton: Princeton University Press, 1984.
Utilizes the elements of Lenin's precepts concerning self-determination to examine the successes and failures of the Soviet, Chinese, Vietnamese and Yugoslav experiences, as well as other interwar and post-World War II variations. In the four main examples, Communists had assumed power in states with numerically and/or strategically located ethnic minorities, and had sought their support by promising self-determination, including the right to secede. Once in power, however, all four had denied the right of secession to the minorities, and had ostensibly introduced regional cultural autonomy. Party strategy had followed Lenin's policy of institutionalizing the form but not the content of nationalism. Examines these countries' strategies for resolving the contradiction of supporting the blossoming of national cultures with the object of preparing the way for their withering and combining into a single, common socialist culture: "the dialectical route to transnational fusion." Compares these ideas with the experiences of implementing cultural, economic and political "national equality" in the communist countries. Finds discrepancies and state-wide variations of application, and cites the numerous anomalies involved. Explains the numerous weaknesses in Leninist nationality strategy and brands it a failure, because it had failed to quell nationalism. Defends the Hegelian view of nations as the effective social units, supported by historical experience. Considers the Marxian historial dialectic a flawed view.

80. CONNOR, Walker. "Self-Determination: The New Phase." *World Politics*, XX (1967), 30-53.
Explains that political developments since World War II had clearly demonstrated the growth of national consciousness as a political force. Believes that, although African and Asian independence movements had been launched in the name of self-determination, they were, in fact, demands for political independence at variance with ethnic distributions. Outlines the positions of scholarly detractors and supporters of multinationalism, examines African, Asian and European experiences, and notes an increasing trend toward political consciousness along the lines of nationality. Notes that within

typical multinational states, the centrifugal forces of national aspirations were proving more powerful than the centripetal forces of transnationalism. Asserts that governments had been underestimating the resistance of distinct nationalities to assimilation, and had become less democratic in response to the growing threat of nationalist movements.

81.   CRAWFORD, J. *The Creation of States in International Law.* Oxford (England): Clarendon Press, 1979.
Analyzes self-determination in several contexts, including *jus cogens*, the laws of war, statehood, the use of force, colonial enclaves and the mandate system. Concludes that international law recognized the principle of self-determination with particular application to trust and mandated territories and states, but that it was not a right directly applicable to all people desiring independence or self-government. Maintains that it was a legal principle which applied as a matter of right only after the unit of self-determination had been determined through the application of appropriate rules.

82.   EMERSON, Rupert. *From Empire to Nation.* Cambridge: Harvard University Press, 1960.
Examines the rise of Asian and African peoples to self-assertion. Develops the following core theme: the rise of non-European nationalisms, resulting from the global extension of Western civilization; the emphasis on freedom and democracy after World Wars I and II; the failure to apply these principles to the colonies; the influence of material advancements, education and sophisticated administrative structures on the native peoples; and their refusal to accept good government as a substitute for self-government. Discusses the anatomy of a nation, including the elements of territory, state, language, culture, religion and economics. Considers the right to self-determination a revolutionary proposition. Despite attempts to translate it from an ethnical and political precept into a binding legal norm, it had yet to find a stable place in the international legal structure or to be accepted by states as a consistent policy. Explains that in politically united societies divided by race, language, religion or historical development, nationalism frequently served to emphasize inner cleavages. Outlines the virtues and dangers of nationalism, uncertain whether nationalism would cause war or peace, chauvinism or internationalism.

83. EMERSON, Rupert. "Self-Determination." *American Journal of International Law*, LXV (1971), 459-76.
    Examines the concept of self-determination within the framework of three sets of overlapping and interrelated questions: (1) What was the status of self-determination under international law? (2) Who might legitimately claim to exercise the right and under what circumstances? and (3) What were the rights and obligations of other states and international organizations in relation to self-determination, and how might they be strengthened to bring a potentially explosive procedure under control? Maintains that due to the existence of a substantial body of doubt and opposition regarding the general principles and scope of United Nations lawmaking powers, the existence of a rule of international law could not be automatically assumed. Discusses the question of whether the right to self-determination included the right of secession. Differentiates between "internal" and "external" self-determination, and maintains that internal self-determination, as contrasted with the positive action implied by external self-determination, was essentially negative. Believes that, although the U.N. had accepted non-intervention as one of its highest principles, a still higher concept bade all states to completely eliminate racial discrimination and colonialism.

84. EMERSON, Rupert. "Self-Determination." *Proceedings of the American Society of International Law*, 60th Session, 1966, 129-35.
    Describes self-determination as one aspect of the right to launch a revolution. Analyzes the gradually changing perceptions regarding the applicability of the concept. Believes the essence of self-determination to be its anti-colonial mandate. In this context, the phrase "all peoples" meant all existing states or colonies, rather than nations. Proposes that order and stability could be achieved only if self-determination was limited to the first round of the establishment of states in a closely defined situation.

85. EMERSON, Rupert. *Self-Determination Revisited in the Era of Decolonization.* Cambridge: Harvard University Center for International Affairs, 1964.
    Identifies anticolonialism as a new higher concept in international law, engendered by the currently widespread condemnation of colonialism. Explains, however, that self-determination had encountered widespread opposition in

the post-colonial era.   Reviews several cases illustrating key problems involving self-determination in the post-colonial era, including Sudan, Somalia, West Irian and Malaysia. Concludes that as a generalized right, self-determination could be incorporated into an orderly international system only when the peoples to whom it applied were rigidly defined. "The right of all people to self-determination" in its present interpretation meant that all overseas colonial peoples had the right to be liberated from the overlordship of their alien white masters.

86.   FRANCK, T. M. and P. HOFFMAN.   "The Right of Self-Determination in Very Small Places." *New York University Journal of International Law and Politics*, VIII (1975-76), 331-86.
The authors discuss self-determination from Woodrow Wilson to the present, and concentrate on four examples of decolonization: Western Sahara, East Timor, Belize and French Somaliland (Djibouti). Describe the political situation in each of the four cases as well as the role of the United Nations in general, the Special Committee of the United Nations and, where applicable, the Organization of African Unity. Conclude that in the East Timor and Western Sahara cases the decolonization process had resulted in large numbers of refugees and destabilizing precedents. Fear that the rise of historic and ethnic irredentist claims and the downgrading of self-determination and the sanctity of established boundaries might cause further disorder and injustice. Observe that in each of the four cases, neighboring states had designs on smaller countries. In each case, the former made the following assertions to justify the denial of self-determination to the territories: pre-colonization title; strong ethnic or socio-cultural affinities; geography and topography; and charges of interference by colonial powers.   Discuss two cases where self-determination had been denied – Gibraltar and the Falklands Islands. Conclude that the apparent demise of carefully constructed norms of self-determination, state legitimacy and the inviolability of boundaries posed a threat to the territorial integrity of states that lacked the military capability to resist their more powerful neighbors' expansionist and irredentist aspirations.

87.   FRIEDLANDER, Robert A.   "Proposed Criteria for Testing the Validity of Self-Determination as It Applies to Disaffected Minorities." *Chitty's Law Journal*, XXV (1977), 338-39.

Defines self-determination as the right of a people to shape its own political, cultural and economic destiny. States that self-determination had always been a basic doctrine of the United Nations, which currently provided juridical justification for new states and a legal rationale for revolution within established politics. Considers the principles of self-determination as conflict-promoting, and in need of a precise, definable standard. Proposes definitions for "people" and "nation" as possible tools in an evaluation of the self-determination principle. Suggests that this approach might provide a means for legitimizing the revolutionary process as a compromise between national aspirations and international law.

88.   FRIEDLANDER, Robert A.   "Self-Determination: A Legal-Political Inquiry." *Self-Determination: National, Regional, and Global Dimensions.* Eds. Yonah Alexander and Robert A. Friedlander.   Boulder, CO: Westview Press, 1980, pp. 307-31.

Argues that self-determination had never been universally applied and was more an ideological weapon than a practical political device. Originally proposed as a philosophical principle, self-determination had become transformed after World War I into a political remedy, primarily utilized by the victors as justification for legitimizing their newly formed eastern European client states. After World War II, the United Nations had transformed the concept of self-determination into a universal human right, implying an international guarantee of popular sovereignty. It countered the staggering disintegrative possibilities of this formulation with the irreconcilable principle of territorial integrity. Once independence had been achieved through decolonization, the danger of further political disintegration owing to racial, cultural, economic and religious antagonisms placed self-determination in a new and disadvantageous light. The principle of self-determination had apparently evolved into selective self-determination, to be applied only in non-African or perhaps non-Third World situations. Asserts that, whatever the value of self-determination as a moral force, its legal validity now would have to be questioned.

89.   GOMEZ-QUINONES, Juan. "Critique on the National Question, Self-Determination, and Nationalism." *Latin American Perspective,* IX (1982), 62-83.

Considers the question of self-determination within a materialist framework and outlines the basic debates and literature on the "national question." Contrasts the positions of Marx, Engels, Lenin, Stalin, Luxemburg, Trotsky and the Austrian Marxists. Notes that the literature distinguished between "nations with history" and "nations without history" as the basis of valid self-determination claims, while maintaining that in principle the proletarian had no fatherland, only membership in the international working class. Investigates prevailing theories of national consciousness and nationalism, and traces the strategic formulations for national and social revolutions. Stresses that the practice, the line and strategy in factual political situations had outpaced theory. In principle, self-determination had resolved the contradictions of imperialism: the presence of oppressed and oppressed nations. However, the dialectic of self-determination and proletarian internationalism was itself subject to the contradiction of the concurrent centripetal and centrifugal capitalist political and economic processes of global historical development, a trend continuing under socialism. Refutes the economic and idealistic Marxist formulation on nationalism, defining it as a collective phenomenon historically rooted in economic and social relations developed over time, entailing the will to collective national power, political self-determination, and the need for self-realization and self-identification through national collective consciousness and work.

90.   GORDON, David C.   *Self-Determination and History in the Third World.* Princeton: Princeton University Press, 1971. Examines the concept of history – its uses and abuses, embodiment in myths, propagation through propaganda and education – of peoples in the process of self-determination. Draws examples from the Middle East and North African Arab states, India, Greece and Turkey, some African states, and Black Nationalists in the United States. Outlines three approaches to the role of the past in spurring the contemporary struggle for self-determination: "futurism," or history must be exorcised and transcended; "apologism," or salvation and power demanded a return to a specific past tradition; and "reconstructionalism," or a progressive future must draw on a reinvigorated past. Utilizes the notion of a "Copernican" revolution to suggest the need of a colonized people to rewrite its own history in order to liberate itself from the paralyzing myths of the colonizer. Considers this stage to be a temporary one in the process toward a greater maturity characterized by modernity and ecumenicalism.

91. GROSS, Leo. "The Right of Self-Determination in International Law." *New States in the Modern World.* Ed. Martin Kilson. Cambridge: Harvard University Press, 1975, pp. 136-57.
Analyzes the status or concept of self-determination in the sense of the right of an ethnic or national entity to establish itself as an independent state. Claims the right to be well-established in international law, although the scope and range had not been precisely defined. Suggests that the right to self-determination in the legal sense would prosper through the authority or competence of U.N. organs, particularly the General Assembly. Maintains that the U.N. Charter had not established the right to self-determination. Evaluates the criteria of customary international law, and concludes that the right to self-determination was "not yet" based on customary law. Insists that the General Assembly lacked law-making competence generally, or with specific reference to self-determination. Argues that the effectiveness of the principle of self-determination depended less on right than upon political pressure in and out of the United Nations.

92. GROS ESPIELL, Hector. "Self-Determination and *Jus Cogens.*" *UN Law/Fundamental Rights.* Ed. Antonio Cassese. Alphen aan den Rijn: Sijthoff and Noordhoff, 1979, pp. 167-73.
Examines debates in the U.N. and international diplomatic conferences to prove the transformation of self-determination into *jus cogens,* that is, into a "peremptory norm of general international law."

93. HACHEY, Thomas E. "Self-Determination: British Perspectives." *Self-Determination: National, Regional, and Global Dimensions.* Eds. Yonah Alexander and Robert A. Friedlander. Boulder, CO: Westview Press, 1980, pp. 97-131.
During World War I, the rulers of ethnically heterogeneous empires had not fully comprehended the implications of endorsing the principle of self-determination. Argues that the twentieth-century Irish experience had exercised a profound influence upon Great Britain's perception of and attitudes regarding self-determination, and had inspired contemporary self-determination movements elsewhere in the United Kingdom. Distinguishes within the Commonwealth between imperialistic crown colonies and settler colonies enjoying incre-

ments of political self-determination. The British policy of establishing trusteeships in Africa and Asia following World War II was meant to be a compromise to appease both imperialists and anti-imperialists.

94.   HEALY, Sally. "The Principle of Self-Determination: Still
      Alive and Well." *Millennium*, X (1981), 14-28.
      Shows how the concept of self-determination had retained its vitality in the 1980s, despite its varied and at times contrasting interpretations throughout the 20th century. Examines the application of the principle to the post-World War II anti-colonial movement and to the aspiration of peoples with a common nationality to statehood. In pressing their demands on the basis of anti-colonialism, the movements in the African Horn recognized the orthodox view that colonial populations, whether or not "nations" in the cultural sense, were the legitimate claimants of the right to self-determination. They departed from the orthodox view, however, in asserting that colonialism not be limited to overseas territories.

95.   HENKIN, L., R. PUGH, O. SCHACHTER and H. SMIT, eds.
      International Law: Cases and Materials. St. Paul, MN:
      West Publishing, 1980, pp. 209-16.
      The authors outline the different positions adopted on issues relating to the definition of "self," and explain how the right to self-determination was to be effected. Discuss the U.N.'s role in ascertaining the "will of the people," and in gaining international "recognition" of national liberation movements.

96.   HULA, Erich. "National Self-Determination Reconsidered."
      Social Research, X (1943), 1-21.
      Distinguishes between the principle of self-determination and national self-determination. Whereas the former guided the application of democratic postulates where the altering of territorial boundaries was deemed necessary, the latter so-called nationality principle had come to stand for the idea that every nationality should have a right to form its own state. The Atlantic Charter recognized concrete historical rights to territory, but failed to proclaim abstract national rights. Argues that the slogan of national self-determination thrived on ideas suggested by the phrase, but was alien to the principle itself. The term sounded like an assertion of the free will of man, but was essentially a determinist doctrine promising peace and order, while actually intensifying national feeling and precipitat-

ing a permanent revolution. It presented itself as the crowning of democracy, but substituted for the rights of man the rights of ethnic collectivities. Examines the problems of national self-determination in east and central Europe during World War I.

97. JOHNSON, Harold S. "Self-Determination: Western European Perspectives." *Self-Determination: National, Regional and Global Dimensions.* Eds. Yonah Alexander and Robert A. Friedlander. Boulder, CO: Westview Press, 1980, pp. 81-96.

Locates the rise of the concept of self-determination in the development of nationalism and the nation-state in 18th- and 19th-century Europe, in response to the internal social and political forces in each state. Links self-determination to democracy and popular sovereignty. Discerns a shift from external to internal self-determination: from focusing on the sovereign equality of states to stressing the status of self-governing people. The strengthening of ethnonationalist movements in Western Europe had resulted in quests for regional autonomy. Sovereignty within the European Community represented a relationship governing various authorities at the supranational, national and community levels. Argues that Western Europe had maintained a democratic base in its concept of self-determination, and emphasis on individual human rights had enabled safeguarding of the status of the individual in relation to governments at all levels.

98. JOHNSON, Harold S. and Baljit SINGH. "Self-Determination and World Order." *Self-Determination: National, Regional and Global Dimensions.* Eds. Yonah Alexander and Robert A. Friedlander. Boulder, CO: Westview Press, 1980, pp. 349-59.

The authors regard self-determination as the process by which a people determined its own sovereign status. Locate the central issue as being which nations the international community had been willing to recognize as sovereign. Contend that it was one thing to claim that self-determination of peoples should govern inter-state relations, but another to suggest that it must govern relations between a people and its government. The United Nations had extended sovereignty in dependent areas directly to the inhabitants by establishing a self-determination claim on behalf of their territories. United Nations support for national liberation movements had legitimized intevention in the domestic affairs of a state in such cases. Consider modern nationalism a disintegrative force, because it pledged loyalty to non-state units. The focus of self-determination had shifted from territorial to national: from permitting a people of a given territory to determine its own government to the assertion by a people possessing a national identity of its right to determine its own sovereignty.

99. JOURNAL OF CONTEMPORARY HISTORY, IV, 1 (1969).
This special theme issue on colonialism and decolonization includes discussions on the application of "external" self-determination.

100. KLÖSS, Heinz, ed. *Beiträge zu einen System des Selbstbestimmungsrechts* (Contributions on a System of Self-Determination Rights). Wien: Wilhelm Braumüller, 1970.
Twenty-two papers explore many facets of the right to self-determination.

101. KNIGHT, David B. "Geographical Perspectives on Self-Determination." *Political Geography: Recent Advances and Future Directions.* Eds. P. J. Taylor and J. W. House. London: Croom Helm, 1984, pp. 168-90.
Maintains that the concept of self-determination was inherently geographic, inasmuch as it involved people, sense of place and bounded space. It was also a legal concept, because notions of sovereignty and recognition were involved; thus, focusing on self-determination necessarily involved an examination of international law. Reviews the concept of self-determination as it had evolved through time, and shows that the concept remained a dynamic one, which would engender further restructuring of the world's political division of territory.

102. KNIGHT, David B. "Self-Determination as a Geopolitical Force." *Journal of Geography,* LXXXII (1983), 148-52.
Identifies self-determination as a geopolitical force, yet notes that geographers had largely ignored it. Outlines the historical development of the "revolutionary proposition," notes ideological differences, identifies the issues of decolonization versus secession, discusses the disruptive aspect of the principle, and questions whether there need be only one course to resolve pressures resulting from calls for self-determination. Suggests some of the many alternatives available for accommodating de-

mands. Concludes that the world's state system would continue to change because the politico-territorial evolution continued.

103. KNIGHT, David B. "Territory and People or People and Territory?: Thoughts on Postcolonial Self-Determination." *International Political Science Review*, VI (1985), 248-72.
Traces the development of international law, whereby entire populations of states and their governments, rather than sub-state groups, received preferential recognition. Explains that self-determination might be legitimately imposed on an entire population in a colonial territory (external self-determination). Notes, however, that since self-determination could be granted only once within such a territory, parts of the population within parts of the territory could legitimately be denied any subsequent claims to self-determination. Indicates that many such sub-state groups found this international legal limitation unacceptable, especially when they desired secession. Notes that the latter process might disrupt the international state system. Indicates that not all sub-state groups demanded secession, some desired a form of internal self-determination. Identifies possibilities for sub-state groups to be permitted a degree of international recognition through participation in certain fora.

104. MACMILLAN, W. M. *The Road to Self-Rule*. London: Faber and Faber, 1959.
Directs attention to the neglected history of the British Empire's less mature colonial peoples, in order to highlight the weaknesses hindering these peoples from standing firmly alone in the modern world. The American Revolution had taught that colonial control became unworkable in a politically self-conscious community. The newly-freed slaves of the West Indies were unready to carry such a responsibility. Traces the evolution of British colonialism throughout Africa. Maintains that the central colonial question in South Africa was to legally establish the peaceful coexistence of diverse peoples. Emphasizes that, throughout Africa, the responsibility for colonial development had shifted from a "white man's burden" to a "black man's burden" in the postwar period.

105. MURPHY, John F. "Self-Determination: United States Perspectives." *Self-Determination: National, Regional and Global Dimensions*. Eds. Yonah Alexander and Robert A.

Friedlander.   Boulder, CO: Westview Press, 1980, pp. 43-61.

Considers self-determination an ambiguous concept. The principle of self-determination, as manifested in international law, was being contradicted by an overriding concern for territorial integrity. The United States was reluctant to recognize the right to secession, and had treated the problem of minority rights as a function in the human rights field, separate and distinguishable from that of self-determination.   Argues that the principle of self-determination should not be so defined as to permit the right of secession. Self-determination did not necessarily mean the creation of a separate state, but could also mean free association or integration with a sovereign state.   Favors United States opposition to the unilateral use of armed force undertaken in the name of self-determination.   Recommends that other means of protecting and promoting self-determination, such as human rights programs, be made available and utilized more effectively.

106.   MUSTAFA, Zubeida.   "The Principle of Self-Determination in International Law." *International Lawyer*, V (1971), 479-87.

Discusses the internal and external aspects of self-determination and the Åland Islands case. Argues that lack of a precise definition of self-determination as a human right made it difficult to believe that the U.N. Charter intended to introduce a new principle of international law, rather than to uphold the principle as a political and moral force. Asserts that Resolution 1514 and the two international covenants did not conclusively establish self-determination as a right in positive international law. States the need for a scientific and objective definition of the word "peoples."   Believes that a clearer concept of self-determination had emerged in the Special Committee on Principles of International Law, which resulted in broad agreement that self-determination was not a license for secession to disrupt the national unity and territorial integrity of sovereign states. Deems self-determination a political principle that was difficult to enforce as a legal right.

107.   NOVOGROD, J. C.   "Indirect Aggression." *A Treatise on International Criminal Law*.   Eds. C. M. Bassiouni and V. P. Nanda.   New York: Charles C. Thomas Publisher, 1973, I, 199-237.

Discusses the fundamental principle of the U.N. Charter: any change in the world's power structure should be peaceful and orderly. Charges that currently states were conducting external attacks disguised as internal change through "rebel" forces located within a target state. Defines self-determination as the genuine self-direction of a people in establishing its own internal order. Asserts that all internally organized resistance to an incumbent élite could not be regarded as a legitimate manifestation of self-determination. Concludes that self-determination itself might be threatened if a foreign state should assist a rebel group not reflecting the genuine demands of the majority population.

108. PAUST, Jordan J. "Self-Determination: A Definitional Focus." *Self-Determination: National, Regional and Global Dimensions.* Eds. Yonah Alexander and Robert A. Friedlander. Boulder, CO: Westview Press, 1980, pp. 3-18.
Examines the concept of self-determination as manifested in the United Nations Charter. Links self-determination with human rights. Includes the free determination of a people's political status as a definitional feature, and also economic, social and cultural rights. A people was entitled to pursue its own social and cultural determination, whether or not it had separate political or territorially-based status. A state that complied with the principle of equal rights and self-determination possessed a government with authority vested in the will of the people. Defines self-determination as the right of all peoples to participate freely and fully in the sharing of all values, and political self-determination as the collective right of peoples to pursue their own political demands, to share power equally, and, as the correlative right of the individual, to participate freely and fully in the political process.

109. PETERS, F. "The Right of Nations to Auto-Determination." *World Justice,* II (1961), 148.
Rejects the theory that nations and peoples were entitled to self-determination as a right.

110. RABL, Kurt. *Das Selbstbestimmungsrecht der Völker: Geschichtliche Grundlagen. Umriss der gegewärtigen Bedeutung* (The Peoples' Right to Self-Determination: Historical Foundations. An Outline of Contemporary Meaning). Köln: Böhlau Verlag, 1973.

Attempts to integrate the issue of self-determination into the general system of modern international relations. Considers the historical, legal and political factors, and examines the application of the principle following World War I and II, as well as the interwar period. Analyzes pertinent resolutions of U.N. bodies and endeavors to explain the particular relationship between a group's right to self-determination and the individual rights of the group's members. Maintains that the League of Nations had conceived self-determination as a "right," but that the U.N. Charter in 1945 reduced it to a mere "principle." After 1945, the United Nations had transformed it into a "right" again. Explains that the mutual relationship between self-determination as a collective right and individual freedoms and liberties had been clarified and confirmed. The rules were (1) no people should be forced to live, as a whole or in part, under territorial and/or constitutional-administrative arrangements made or maintained by, or in the preponderant interest of, a non-indigenous power or authority, if it rejected these arrangements; and (2) every nation or people was entitled to live in its own territory in political unity, external freedom, and internal liberty. Defines "people" as an indigenous ethnic community permanently settled within a given territory, or a multitude of tribes, religious groups and racial units living in a given territory, whether or not their frontiers were arbitrarily drawn during colonial times, provided that these tribes, groups and units were willing and able to build a nation through joint endeavor. The act of self-determination might aim at (1) the establishment of an independent State; (2) at the amalgamation with an independent state; (3) at the continuation within the state either in the same or in a new position; or (4) at the restoration of a preexistent independent and unified state.

111.   RABL, Kurt, ed. *Ausgewählte Gegenwartsfragen zum Problem der Verwirklichung des Selbstbestimmungsrechts der Völker* (Selected Contemporary Questions on the Problem of Realizing the Right of Peoples to Self-Determination). München: Verlag Robert Lerche, 1965.
Five conference papers on self-determination, with group discussions recorded, from a variety of perspectives, including an ethnic entity's or group's theoretical basis for self-determination.

112.   RONEN, Dov. *The Quest for Self-Determination.* New York and London: Yale University Press, 1979.

Regards society at a dynamic point in relation to the quest for individual self-determination. Considers self-determination as the aspiration to rule one's self and not to be ruled by others. Explains that self-determination had emerged as a sociopolitical force during the French Revolution, and nationalism, Marxism, Wilsonian self-determination, African and Asian decolonization, and ethnonationalism were successive manifestations of this quest. Denies the existence of a basic group identity, but believes that individuals entered into functional aggregations for the sake of survival. The "self" in self-determination was the singular, individual human being, but because the institutionalization of individual self-determination was unworkable, the aggregation had been substituted. Human beings formed conscious aggregations and activated one or more of their identities when they no longer perceived the government as intermediary to the achievement of aspirations, but as an obstacle. Asserts that the identity did not create the quest for self-determination; the quest created the identity. Proposes that complementary centrifugal and centripetal trends were mutually reinforcing and challenged all aspects of the state monopoly over public life. Because the centrifugal trend claimed for itself the economic and normative functions, whereas the centripetal trend claimed the social and political functions, the emerging alternative system was to be composed of a large number of interdependent sociopolitical entities within wider economic-normative ones.

113. ROTHCHILD, Donald. "The Two Senses of Ethnonational Self-Determination." *Africa Report*, XXVI, 6 (1981), 56-8. Reviews the volume on self-determination by Dov Ronen, and the collections edited by Ndiva Kofele-Kale and by Yonah Alexander and Robert A. Friedlander. Distinguishes between two types of ethnonational self-determination: "external," solely concerned with state independence, and "internal," identified with various forms of autonomous integration within the state. Reviews these books in light of this distinction. Asserts that, because of the ambiguity surrounding the concept, self-determination was only relevant to powerful states, whereas the remaining peoples had few options but to accommodate themselves to existing multiethnic states. Furthermore, doubts whether existing states or the United Nations would ever accept the notion of external self-determination when it implied secession. Concludes that the multiethnic state would remain for some time, and Africa would have to accommodate itself to the

former colonial state borders, while searching for new formulas of internal self-determination.

114.   SCHOENBERG, Harris O.   "Limits of Self-Determination."
         Israel Yearbook on Human Rights. Ed. Yoram Dinstein.
         Tel Aviv: Tel Aviv University, Faculty of Law, 1976, VI,
         91-103.
         Reviews the many instances of denials of self-determination,
         and concludes that despite U.N. General Assembly
         pronouncements, all peoples did not automatically possess the
         right to self-determination.

115.   SELASSIE, Bereket H.   "The Evolution of the Principle of
         Self-Determination." *Horn of Africa*, I, 4 (1978), 3-9.
         Traces the notion of self-determination to primordial biological
         needs.   Credits the idea of self-determination with playing a
         central role in the emancipation of humanity.   Although the
         concept had been invoked under differing conditions, in all
         cases one oppressive nation or class dominating another had
         been the common denominator.   Maintains that self-
         determination had become so charged with symbolic signif-
         icance that it governed peoples' conduct.   Identifies two basic
         aspects of self-determination in the United Nations Charter: (1)
         political, involving nations or peoples; and (2) economic. Poli-
         tically, African states were caught between the imperative of
         stability and nation-building on one hand, and the
         moral/philosophical imperative of self-determination as a uni-
         versally accepted principle, on the other hand.   Theoretically,
         the Third World had begun to reject economic development
         theories imposed by the West, and devise alternative models.
         At the political/organizational level, the Third World had begun
         advocating a new international economic order. Urges the cre-
         ation of a system involving collective self-reliance.

116.   STARUSHENKO, G.   *The Principle of National Self-*
         Determination in Soviet Foreign Policy. Moscow: Foreign
         Languages Publishing House, 1960.
         Explains that in Marxist-Leninist theory, self-determination
         was formulated as a demand to recognize every nation's right to
         self-determination up to and including secession and formation
         of an independent state. Declares that no U.S.S.R republic had
         ever seceded from the Union, because the main merit of the
         principle of self-determination lay in the fact that its recognition
         helped to create conditions in which no nation wanted to secede.

With respect to colonized peoples who desired self-determination, the decisive factor was the will of the self-determining people who sought an end to their colonial status, not the interests of the administering power or other states. Considers national liberation wars by oppressed peoples to be legitimate. Claims that the Soviet Union sought no privileges for itself; it wanted the United Nations to find solutions for oppressed peoples.

117. SUZUKI, T. "Self-Determination and World Public Order." *Virginia Journal of International Law*, XVI (1976), 779-862. Argues that territorial separation was legitimate and essential for "human dignity" when secession by cohesive groups with strong senses of separate identities demanded it.

118. THÜRER, Daniel. *Das Selbstbestimmungsrecht der Völker* (The Peoples' Right to Self-Determination). Bern: Verlag Stämpfli, 1976. Reviews the concept of self-determination.

119. TUBIANA, Joseph. "The Linguistic Approach to Self-Determination." *Nationalism and Self-Determination in the Horn of Africa.* Ed. I. M. Lewis. London: Ithaca Press, 1983, pp. 23-30. Examines the role of language in the desire for self-determination fulfilment. Considers language, the conventional system for conveying information encompassing the totality of culture, as part of the patrimony a community sought to control for the sake of its constituent people. Language was crucial to individual self-identification, to identifying one's position in society, and in the development of group consciousness. Stresses the importance of language use in individual-state relations. Cultural factors, such as history, religion, political organization, laws and education played decisive roles in cultural conflict and desire for self-determination, so that language was not a prime differential. However, it remained the simplest component to define and the easiest to grasp, embodying the entire culture, so that "all that threatens the language, threatens the culture as a whole." Considers it a rare situation to find a wish for self-determination evolving in the absence of a common language. Summarizes the language situation in the Horn of Africa, without commenting on its political ramifications. Wonders whether communities speaking distinct languages constituted "nations" or "nationalities." Urges politicians to

pay heed to living languages and to linguistic approaches to
nationalities problems.

120. UMOZURIKE, U. O. *Self-Determination in International
      Law*. Hamden, CT: Archon Books, 1972.
      Examines the evolution and development of the principle of
      self-determination, tracing the origin of the term to antiquity,
      expressed as the desire of a people to be free from external or
      internal domination. The notion of popular government had
      been added over time. The American and French Revolutions
      as well as World War I had been fought on this basis. Notes
      that Woodrow Wilson had transformed self-determination into
      a popular concept, if not a peremptory norm for world peace.
      Maintains that, whereas after World War I self-determination
      had manifested itself in secession and the formation of in-
      dependent states, soon the smaller minorities had become sub-
      ject to a more restrictive interpretation. Discusses the
      provisions related to League of Nations' mandated territories,
      in which self-determination had been merely implied. Assesses
      the positive contribution of the United Nations to the concept
      of self-determination. Refers to the U.N. attitude and practice
      regarding non-self-governing and trust territories. Contrasts
      American, Soviet, British and French practice in the develop-
      ment of the principle of self-determination, now widely recog-
      nized as a fundamental right in international law. Analyzes the
      effects of economic self-determination, citing many violations.
      Argues that a resident people ought to decide the destiny of a
      territory, and that ameliorating the violation of basic human
      rights, such as genocide, must supersede the principle of terri-
      torial integrity. Examines the challenges presented by the
      Somalis, the Kashmiri, the Nagas, the Afro-Americans, the
      Québecois, the Namibians and Biafrans. Does not consider
      self-determination to be an absolute right, because it had to be
      reconciled with other fundamental principles of international
      law and factual situations. A denial of the right to self-
      determination, however, must become a proper matter of inter-
      national concern if peace and security were threatened.

121. WESTON, B., R. FALK AND A. D'AMATO, eds. *Interna-
      tional Law and World Public Order: A Problem-Oriented
      Casebook*. St. Paul, MN: West Publishing Co., 1980.
      The authors place the question of self-determination within the
      context of sociopolitical justice, and link self-determination to
      minority rights.

122. WHITE, Robin C. A. "Self-Determination: Time for Re-Assessment?" *Netherlands International Law Review*, XXVIII (1984), 147-70.
Analyzes claims to self-determination within the typology established by Professor J. Moore ("Towards an Applied Theory for the Regulation of Intervention," *Law and Civil War in the Modern World*, ed. J. Moore, 1974). The five types are (1) the colonial situation; (2) situations where a government denied a people within a state participation in the government of that state; (3) situations whereby a state or people sought to join with another state or people of similar ethnic, linguistic or religious affiliation; (4) situations in which a people sought to secede from a state in order to establish a separate national identity; and (5) situations involving demands for a particular type of political organization within an existing state. Argues that most of the claims to self-determination considered attempted to remedy breaches to that right. Suggests that these were more concerned with *how* to assert that right than with its definition. States that self-determination encompassed a "bundle" of rights relating to peoples as collectivities. Defines "group" as peoples sharing ethnic, religious, cultural or national origins. Notes that the right included preservation of group identity, which imposed a positive obligation on states to respect cultural heritages and religious customs. Argues that breaches of the right to self-determination must be persistent and gross to attract international attention. Perceives a need for international institutions to assess claims to self-determination.

123. WIBERG, Hakan. "Self-Determination as an International Issue." *Nationalism and Self-Determination in the Horn of Africa*. Ed. I. M. Lewis. London: Ithaca Press, 1983, pp. 43-65.
Reviews the history, theory and practice of the concepts of the nation-state and national self-determination, and notes the recent intermittent nature of the application of self-determination. Discusses the relationship between political ideas and change, and explores how it was being analyzed. Questions the nature of "people," when and how the right to self-determination applied, and the Marxist-Leninist approach to self-determination. Views the U.N.'s role in supporting peoples' quests for self-determination in existing states pessimistically. Studies the number, method and histories of autonomous geopolitical units from 1815 to 1980. Urges an improved linkage between a better methodology and a more developed theoretical framework in

order to arrive at accurate conclusions in the social scientific analysis of national self-determination. Suggests that the history of the ideas of "nation," "self-determination," and the key concepts of state, class and ethnicity be considered.

124.   YOUNG, Crawford. "Decolonization in Africa." *Colonialism in Africa 1870-1960.* Eds. L. H. Gann and Peter Duignan. Cambridge (England): Cambridge University Press, 1970, II, 450-502.

Examines the decolonization of British, French and Belgian possessions in Africa, and locates the primary impulses for decolonization in the changes wrought by World War II. The end of colonial rule in Asia had two major repercussions in Africa: (1) the continued success of nationalist movements in the colonial world appeared to be inevitable; and (2) the emergence of Arab and Asian groups vigorously asserting the rights of oppressed peoples created an entirely new factor in international affairs. Regards the United Nations as an important agency for hastening decolonization. The U.N. Charter had established a Trusteeship Council with more extensive powers of supervision and a composition less benevolent toward colonial powers than had ever been the case with the earlier Permanent Mandates Commission of the League of Nations. The U.N. Visiting Missions were critical of the sedate pace of political development charted by the trust powers, and pressed for the establishment of firm deadlines for independence. The General Assembly provided a forum for the enunciation of nationalist demands. Argues that rapid postwar social and economic change in the colonies had engendered a favorable environment for political mobilization. Nationalism gained a major organizational weapon with the emergence of mass parties. Educated African élites became increasingly aware of the vast gap between metropolitan democratic theory and colonial practice. Examines the impact of metropolitan politics on the pace of the decolonization process.

PART III

THEORETICAL CONSIDERATIONS: IDENTITY, TERRITORY AND POWER

Basic Issues: Identity, Territory and Power

125. BLAUT, J. M. "Nationalism As An Autonomous Force." *Science and Society*, XXXXVI (1983), 1-23.
Dismisses recent Marxist and neo-Marxist arguments that nationalism or national struggles differed from class struggles. Traces such concepts to conservative theoreticians, particularly Hegel, who developed two concepts of nationalism. One related to the idea of state or nation as a unique entity, whereas the second pertained to the notion of language groups as distinct national identities. After Hegel, a broader representation removed the concept from the special privilege accorded monarchies, and democratized it into the "collective consciousness." Nation became the "will" of the people. Raises penetrating questions regarding national struggles relating to class struggle, particularly the Leninist proposition that "the idea of the nation cannot be divorced from the idea of the state and the struggle for state power."

126. BRASS, Paul and Pierre L. VAN DEN BERGHE. "Ethnicity and Nationalism in World Perspective." *Ethnicity*, III (1976), 197-201.
The authors identify two sources of the new interest in ethnicity, nationality and nationalism, including the recent theoretical concern with national integration: (1) the contemporary flowering of social movements among previously dormant ethnic and nationality groups; and (2) the rise of ethnic assertiveness and political demands among minority groups in the United States. The papers in this special issue adopt a sociostructural

view of ethnicity, placing it in the broad context of the social
structure of broad society.

127. BREUILLY, John. *Nationalism and the State.* Chicago:
     University of Chicago Press, 1982, 1985.
     Considers nationalism a form of politics that arises in oppo-
     sition to the modern state and asserts that from that perspective
     nationalisms were appropriate for advancing the interests of
     élites, social groups and foreign governments against the state.
     Challenges the conventional view that nationalism emerged
     from a cultural sense of national identity, and shows that
     nationalism served to create a sense of identity useful for mobi-
     lizing popular support.   Examines this thesis in a number of
     national settings, including discussions on anti-colonial and
     separatist nationalisms.

128. BURGHARDT, Andrew F.   "The Bases of Territorial
     Claims." *Geographical Review*, LXIII, 2 (1973), 225-45.
     Maintains that virtually all states and empires had treated
     territory as being good of itself, and that international law had
     favored stability within the state system.   Arranges all terri-
     torial claims in one or more of the following categories: (1)
     effective control; (2) historical; (3) cultural; (4) territorial integ-
     rity; (5) economic; (6) élitist; and (7) ideological. The first four
     categories were the strongest and conservative; the remaining
     three tended to be dynamic.   Concedes that territorial disputes
     had been almost always settled by force.

129. CANADIAN REVIEW OF STUDIES IN NATIONALISM
     (Charlottetown: University of Prince Edward Island,
     Canada.   Ed. Thomas Spira).
     Most important scholarly journal devoted to study of ethnic is-
     sues, nation, nationalism and cognate subjects.

130. CAPOTORTI, F. *Study on the Rights of Persons Belonging to
     Ethnic, Religious and Linguistic Minorities.* New York:
     United Nations E/CN.4/Sub.2/384/Rev.1, 1979.
     Explains the international protection of minorities by analyzing
     the concept of a minority, international protection since 1919,
     and particularly Article 27 of the International Covenant on
     Civil and Political Rights.

131. DRUMMOND, R. "Nationalism and Ethnic Demands: Some Speculations on a Congenial Note." *Canadian Journal of Political Science*, X (1977), 375-89.
Proposes a synthesis between the prevailing different approaches to the study of nationalism. Argues that "nationalism" comprised differentation and ethnic identity as well as a relationship between the ethnic group and the state. Views the interaction of ideology, strategy and resources as a cyclical process. Provides tables outlining "varieties of nationalist ideology" and "possible outcomes of transactional ethnic group contact given particular nationalist ideologies."

132. EMERSON, Rupert. "The Problem of Identity, Selfhood, and Image in the New Nations: The Situation in Africa." *Comparative Politics*, I (1969), 297-312.
Claims that colonialism and rapid decolonization had caused an uncertain and unstable sense of identity and image of society for many Africans. Identifies three basic propositions relating to African self-determination: (1) that all colonial peoples wanted to abandon colonialism as speedily as possible; (2) that each colonial territory as established by the imperial powers constituted a nation whose aspirations to become an independent state had unchallengeable validity; and (3) that the political independence and territorial integrity of the states thus created must be safeguarded against attack from within or without. Delineates three levels of African identity: tribal, state and Pan-African. Considers the roots of African nationalism shallow, thanks to post-colonial power struggles and tribal differentiations that stirred up tribal animosities. However, notes a sense of "Africanness" in reponse to contact with the outside world. Expects the new states to consolidate their positions as the key political actors in Africa.

133. GELLNER, Ernest. *Nations and Nationalisms*. Ithaca, NY: Cornell University Press, 1983.
Interprets nationalism in terms of its social roots located in industrial social organization. Asserts that a society's affluence and economic growth depended on innovation, occupational mobility, the effectiveness of the mass media, universal literacy, and an all-embracing educational system based on a shared standard idiom. These combined factors governed the relationship between culture and the state. Political units that did not conform to the principle of "one state, one culture" felt the strain in the form of centrifugal nationalistic activities.

134.   GOTTMANN, Jean.   "Geography and International
       Relations." *World Politics*, III (1951), 153-73; *idem*, "The
       Political Partitioning of Our World: An Attempt at Anal-
       ysis." *Ibid.*, IV (1952), 512-9.
       Establishes the geographical foundation for understanding the
       international structuring of space, and the meanings attributed
       to territory by national societies.

135.   GOTTMANN, Jean.   *The Significance of Territory.*
       Charlottesville: The University Press of Virginia, 1973.
       Traces the evolution of the concept of territory through the
       centuries. Rejects a narrow interpretation of the concept to
       mean the extent of land and water delimited by agreed-upon
       lines. Asserts that territory more appropriately designated the
       relationship established in a community of politically organized
       people and its space, which had a material, concrete, and defi-
       nite character, and a "psychosomatic" nature. Investigates the
       themes of the physical and psychological relationship between
       people and their land through a historical review of the
       development of the Western world's concepts of sovereignty and
       the nation-state.   Discusses the extension of the concept of
       territory to the non-Western parts of the world, the partitioning
       of coastal waters and air space, and the limitation in the use of
       outer space and seabeds. Speculates on the future of the con-
       cepts of territory and sovereignty. Believes that despite "mod-
       ern fluidity," sovereign territory would remain an important
       concept, because of its importance as an "international social
       function" (the capacity to be a member of the world commu-
       nity), and also because of the strength of the popular concept
       of land as the basic resource for survival, and of territory as the
       "sacred land of our ancestors."

136.   HOROWITZ, Donald L. "Ethnic Identity." *Ethnicity: Theory
       and Experience.*   Eds. Nathan Glazer and Daniel P.
       Moynihan. Cambridge: Harvard University Press, 1975,
       pp. 111-40.
       Explores problems relating to definitions and parameters of
       identity, including the issue of identity change as a result of the
       imposition of political boundaries.

137.   HOWARD, Peter. "The Definition of a Nation: A Discussion
       in 'Voprosy Istorii'." *Central Asian Review*, XV (1967),
       26-36.

Summarizes and draws conclusions from the discussion on how to define a nation that appeared in the Soviet periodical 'Voprosy Istorii' (1966). Despite the importance of the discussion in the U.S.S.R., an agreement regarding the definition of a nation had failed to emerge. The rise of national consciousness among the non-Russian nations of the Soviet Union had led to a reappraisal of Stalin's definition. An overstatement of the "psychological" features of a nation may give rise to "radicalism" and "chauvinism." Two main divergent opinions existed: those who saw national statehood as inseparable from the development of a nation, and those who followed the Party line more closely by envisaging the imminent "drawing together" and "merging" of Soviet nations.

138. INTERNATIONAL SOCIAL SCIENCE JOURNAL, XXX, 1 (1978).
Special issue on the politics of territoriality.

139. ISAACS, Harold R. "Basic Group Identity: The Idols of the Tribe." *Ethnicity: Theory and Experience.* Eds. Nathan Glazer and Daniel P. Moynihan. Cambridge: Harvard University Press, 1975, pp. 29-52.
Analyzes the fundamental elements in group identity, *i.e.*, the identity derived from belonging to an "ethnic group." Identifies its composition as "primordial affinities and attachments" distinct from all the other multiple and secondary identities people acquired.

140. JENNINGS, R. Y. *The Acquisition of Territory in International Law.* Manchester, NH: Manchester University Press, 1963.
Outlines the rules of international law governing the acquisition of territorial sovereignty. Discusses the nature of territorial sovereignty and various aspects of acquiring valid title. Notes that traditional rules of international law had not played a central role in actual territorial changes. Discusses the question of legal versus political claims. Refers to the importance of self-determination as a generally recognized political principle. States that, although it was sanctioned by the United Nations and had legal overtones, self-determination remained essentially a useful guide in *political* decision-making.

141. KNIGHT, David B. "Identity and Territory: Geographical Perspectives on Nationalism and Regionalism." *Annals,*

Association of American Geographers, LXXII (1982), 514-31.

Claims group politico-territorial identities to be potent realities. Discusses elements and processes involved in identifying such territorially-bound identities, stressing questions of scale and perception. The "legitimacy" of a group's politico-territorial identity depended upon the peoples' scale of abstraction and upon the definer's perspective. The main problem lay in defining "nation." At one level of abstraction a nation was only a type of region; yet many groups accepted the nation as fact. Discusses related concepts to demonstrate the interplay between these points, including priorities in the hierarchy of belonging, nationalism, common territory, state, ethnic separatism, secession, and, notably, self-determination. Identifies different responses to the question of whether groups with distinct territorially-based identities should have a right to separate territorial and political independence.

142. KOHN, Hans. *The Idea of Nationalism: A Study of Its Origins and Background.* New York: Macmillan, 1944.
      Major historical examination of the development of nationalism.

143. LEWIS, I. M. "Pre- and Post-Colonial Forms of Polity in Africa." *Nationalism and Self-Determination in the Horn of Africa.* Ed. I. M. Lewis. London: Ithaca Press, 1983, pp. 67-76.
      Examines the concepts of nation and tribe regarding pre- and post-colonial African polity forms. Discusses the appropriateness of the prevailing view of "nations" as civilized, progressive units and "tribes" as parochial, backward units in etymological and realistic terms. Demonstrates that many features of African society, particularly the predominance of tribe, were effects of colonialism. Reviews the work of social anthropologists in discovering Africa's pre-colonial political framework. These findings had led to analysis of sets of polities, some hierarchically organized and others systems of "minimal government" based on segmentary linkage organizations, some based on ethnic identity, others on cultural pluralism. Linkage of the idea of political cohesion to cultural identity helped to distinguish three distinct groups in Africa: culturally plural states, heterogeneous "empires," and homogeneous states, as well as several transitional stages.

144. LOWENTHAL, David. "The West Indies Chooses a Capital."
     Geographical Review, XXXXVIII (1958), 336-64.
     Examines group identities that are deeply rooted in particular
     places. Intergroup behavior can be powerfully influenced by
     such identities, especially when one's own group is viewed posi-
     tively while all other groups are viewed negatively and with
     suspicion. Marked intergroup discord can result from "incor-
     rect" perceptions and resulting jealousies. The paper examines
     these points as the West Indies Federation sought a site for a
     capital city. The powerful group island-based identities were so
     strong that the selection process was marked with discord and
     conflict.

145. MORSE, S. J. "National Identity from a Social Psychological
     Perspective: Two Brazilian Case Studies." *Canadian Review
     of Studies in Nationalism*, IV (1976), 52-76; *idem*, "National
     Identity from a Social Psychological Perspective: A Study
     of University Students in Saskatchewan." *Ibid.*, VII (1980),
     299-312. Also see S. J. Morse, J. W. Mann and E. Nel.
     "National Identity in a 'Multi-National' State: A Compar-
     ison of Afrikaners and English-Speaking South Africans."
     Ibid., IV (1977), 225-46.
     Social-psychological exploration into identifications with na-
     tion. Identifies levels of attachments. Demonstrates that the
     sample of Saskatchewan students had strong identification with
     the Canadian "nation" as part of a "constellation of social atti-
     tudes and cognitions," and, importantly, that regional, sub-
     group and local attachments in Saskatchewan did not mitigate
     against, but might even have reinforced, attachments to Can-
     ada.

146. NIELSSON, Gunnar P. "States and 'Nation-Groups': A Global
     Taxonomy." *New Nationalisms of the Developed West.*
     Eds. Edward A. Tiryakian and Ronald Rogowski. Boston:
     Allen and Unwin, 1985, pp. 27-56.
     Considers the methodological problems with studies of ethnicity
     and cultural pluralisms to be that they lacked (1) comparability
     across cases; (2) balance between conflictual and cooperative
     experiences; and (3) a general framework for global, systematic
     comparative analysis. Constructs taxonomies for future
     comparative analyses of ranking states according to the classi-
     fication schemes developed. The state-centric taxonomy, with
     its five categories of ethnic fragmentation within states, con-
     tained the ethnic-centric taxonomy with five categories, accord-

ing to the extent of the nation-group's dispersion in different states. The subsequent section combines the two taxonomies into a matrix, within which the global state system is analyzed. Discusses the international regional distribution of states in the two-taxonomy matrix.

147.   SACK, R[obert] D. "Human Territoriality: A Theory." *Annals of the Association of American Geographers*, LXXII (1983), 55-74.
Defines territoriality as the attempt to affect, influence or control actions, interactions, or access by asserting and attempting to enforce control over a specific geographic area. Presents territoriality as a means of enhancing or impeding interaction. Develops a theory of territoriality that contains ten potential consequences and fourteen primary combinations of consequences to territorial strategies, some of which involved large groups. Hypothesizes that any instance of territoriality would draw from among these. Indicates that specific consequences and combinations were likely to occur in particular sociohistorical contexts.

148.   SACK, Robert D. "Territorial Bases of Power." *Political Studies from Spatial Perspectives*. Eds. A. D. Burnett and P. J. Taylor. Chichester: John Wiley, 1981, pp. 53-72.
Contends that traditional geographic analyses of the roles which physical space and spatial relations played in human actions have neglected the essential role of territoriality. Defines territoriality as the attempt to affect, influence or control actions and interactions by asserting and attempting to enforce control over a specific geographic area. Claims that this definition would point to the role of territoriality as a principle of space in causality. Suggests that the simple "control of area" definition of territoriality should be replaced by a more dynamic focus on particular actions and strategies in space. Outlines a series of functions which determined how, why and under what conditions a person or group used a territorial strategy to control other people, objects or relationships.

149.   SATHYAMURTHY, T. V. *Nationalism in the Contemporary World: Political and Sociological Perspectives*. London: Frances Pinter (Publishers), 1983.
Argues that postwar nationalist movements be viewed in their international context as well as against their particular historical background. Maintains that nationalism could not be ex-

plained in terms of cultural atavism or psychological factors alone. Invariably, its political dynamic was derived from a complex intermeshing of conflictual ethnic, religious, communal, linguistic and cultural dimensions, all of them rooted more or less directly in the concrete economic circumstances of deprived peoples. Indicates a close connection linking national autonomy and global political economy.

150. SETON-WATSON, Hugh. *Nations and States.* London: Methuen, 1977.
Considers national identities and state sovereignties the basic realities of history and current politics. Suggests that, although they overlapped and influenced each other, they were different realities. Explores the differences and similarities, as well as interactions, using thematic and regional approaches. Distinguishes between states and nations. Concludes that the survival of human civilization depended on the recognition that neither absolute state sovereignty nor the abolition of national identities was possible, and that a balance had to be struck between national cultures and interstate cooperation, no less than a balance between class interests and interclass cooperation within nations, if destructive civil wars and nuclear holocausts were to be avoided.

151. SHAFER, Boyd C. *Faces of Nationalism, New Realities and Old Myths.* New York: Harcourt Brace Jovanovich, 1972.
Examines nationalism, including perspectives from history and the social sciences, and refers to European, North American and Third World experiences.

152. SMITH, A. D. "Ethnic Identity and World Order." *Millennium,* XII (1983), 149-61.
Considers nationalism not an ideology on its own, but rather an attempt to imbue the state with cultural identity. Discerns more in ethnic identity than the balanced combination of interest and effect; often ethnic identity presented itself as a non-rational, primordial, exclusive and overriding compulsion. Urges examination of myths regarding the historical experience of the community, including the myth of origins, descent, the heroic age, and decline and rebirth. When combined with the more recent tradition of self-determination, these myths of descent of historic communities forged ethnic groups into dynamic political forces.

153. SMITH, A. D.   "States and Homelands: The Social and
      Geopolitical   Implications   of   National   Territory."
      Millennium, X (1981), 187-202.
      Identifies some of the broader implications of demanding or
      possessing a national homeland within a preexisting system of
      territorial states; and particularly shows how the drive for "na-
      tional congruence," or co-extensiveness linking state, nation
      and territory had exacerbated interstate tensions, threatened to
      destabilize them and remould them in a new pattern. Considers
      the nation a territorial unit that required a recognized "home-
      land" by virtue of a historic association and origin. Delineates
      four dimensions of territory relating to the antagonism between
      nation and state: habitat, folkways, extent and location.
      Nationalists viewed territory as a "homeland," encompassing
      four further dimensions: boundary, history, self-sufficiency,
      and nation-building.   Argues that the two processes of the
      "hardening of space" and the "abstraction of land" had
      complicated the possibilities of evolving a stable world order
      based on a simple unit of population classification.

154. SYMMONS-SYMONOLEWICZ, Konstantin.   "Collective
      Sentiments and Their Social Hierarchies." *Canadian Re-
      view of Studies in Nationalism*, X (1983), 267-297.
      Asserts that nationalism, although a dominant force, was not
      the only loyalty that people proclaimed. Conflict with other
      values, such as loyalty to a religious faith or to a particular so-
      cial philosophy, also existed.   Notes two historical develop-
      ments: (1) the growing sentiment favoring ever larger human
      communities; and (2) the stubborn survival of certain sentiments
      associated with earlier human groupings. Identifies at least four
      human collectivities that during certain periods had com-
      manded people's supreme loyalty: kinship, ethnic, religious and
      national loci of sentiments.   Denies the permanence of the
      hierarchical structure.   Collectivities which could inspire an
      overriding commitment, including nationalism, might be clas-
      sified as groups of supreme loyalty. However, other loyalties,
      such as urban, regional, imperial or class had never achieved
      such a universal or intense hold.

155. TAJFEL, Henri. *The Social Psychology of Minorities*. London:
      Minority Rights Group, Report No. 38, 1978.
      Discusses the meaning of minority "group" from a social-
      psychological point of view, and urges the study of relations
      between social groups to consider both the "objective" condi-

tions (the economic, political, social and historical circumstances) and the "subjective" definitions of these circumstances through belief systems, identifications, likes and dislikes and related behavior. Identifies the social-psychological criteria for distinguishing a minority group: "they are self-conscious units of people who have in common certain similarities and certain social disadvantages." Reviews the variety of issues involved in minority-group membership in terms of "internal" and "external" criteria, and analyzes the relationship between them. Argues that only modest claims about the "psychological effects" of minority-group membership could be proposed presently because generalizations often applied only to some members of some minorities. Explores the patterns of acceptance and rejection of minority groups in society within the context of the two major post-World War II social processes: interdependence and differentiation. Emphasizes the concepts of perceived stability and legitimacy in majority-minority relations.

156. TUAN, Yi-Fu. "Attachment to Homeland." *Space and Place: The Perspective of Experience.* Ed. Yi-Fu Tuan. Minneapolis: University of Minnesota Press, 1977, pp. 149-60.
Asserts that attachment to one's homeland could be intense. Notes that human groups nearly everywhere tended to regard their own homeland as the center of the world, and claimed, implicitly, the ineluctable worth of their locality. Discusses the issue of rootedness by drawing from a range of examples.

157. WILLIAMS, Colin H. "Conceived in Bondage – Called unto Liberty: Reflections on Nationalism." *Progress in Human Geography*, IX (1985), 331-55.
Highlights some general interpretive issues, and assesses recent developments in theories of nationalism. The issues of realism-relativism, holism-individualism and freedom-determination figured strongly in these theories. Contends that geographical work on nation-formation and nationalism had tended to be apolitical and teleological. Comparatively little attention had been paid to the influence of scale in determining the mobilization and success of nationalist movements. Identifies several promising strands of current research on nationalism of interest to geographers, including the national construction of social space; uneven development and nationalism; the secular intelligentsia; structural preconditions and triggering factors;

and ecological analysis. Considers comparative contextual analysis tied to the triggering factors of interest-group ideology, élite mobilization, and economic development to be the most profitable direction for political-geographic analysis of nationalism.

Understanding Recent Identity Resurgences

158. AGNEW, John A. "Structural and Dialectical Theories of Political Regionalism." *Political Studies from Spatial Perspectives.* Eds. A. D. Burnett and P. J. Taylor. Chichester: John Wiley, 1981, pp. 275-89.
Proposes a dialectical alternative to the dominant structural approach to understanding political regionalism. Structural reasoning postulates political behavior as the direct result of structural conditions. According to dialectical theorizing, political consciousness was not invariably monolithic. Links political regionalism to regional environments in complex ways that a simple cultural-economic domination theory could not explain; as manifested by electoral behavior, it could be deepseated or epiphenomenal. Dialectical reasoning did not reify political regionalism, but regarded it as meaningful only in its situational or regional contexts. The dialectical theorist did not accept a one-way view of causality, but adopted a "generative" perspective requiring the investigation of all possible links.

159. ALVERSON, H. S. "The Roots of Time: A Comment on Utilitarian and Primordial Sentiments in Ethnic Identification." *Ethnic Autonomy: Comparative Dynamics.* Ed. Raymond Hall. New York: Pergamon Press, 1979, pp. 13-7.
Discusses and contrasts two major schools of thought on ethnic group formation. Outlines Frederik Barth's view that ethnic groups arose and persisted by virtue of "boundary creation and maintenance," which emphasized the "adoptive" nature of identification. Reviews the work of scholars such as De Vos and Deveraux, who saw ethnicity not as a force that arose because it was "adaptive," but as one that persisted despite sometimes devastating ecological and social costs to the group. Suggests that the key to this apparent contradiction lay in the discrep-

ancy of understanding the meaning of ethnic identity. This contradiction might arise because of differing emphases shaped by the two major approaches to social sciences: *Verstehen* and positivism. The resolution might arise in a melding of these two strands of thought.

160. ASANTE, M. K. "Systematic Nationalism: A Legitimate Strategy for National Selfhood." *Journal of Black Studies*, IX (1980), 115-28.
Defines nationalism as a relationship connecting people having a common heritage and expectations. Argues that systematic nationalism did not depend on land. Contends that Afro-Americans, like others, such as Palestinians, constituted nations when they achieved political and spiritual solidarity. Systematic nationalism was activist in character and viewed race and class as twin evils. Identifies the philosophical base of this movement as emancipatory politics.

161. BERTELSEN, Judy. "An Introduction to the Study of Non-state Nations in International Politics," and "The Nonstate Nations in International Politics: Some Observations." *Nonstate Nations in International Politics: A Comparative Systems Analysis*. Ed. J. S. Bertelsen. New York: Praeger, 1979, pp. 1-5 and 245-57.
Explains that a nonstate nation (NSN) generally entered the international system as a sovereign power without being recognized as a sovereign entity. Analyzes the impact of NSNs on international politics from the theoretical perspective of the NSN. Describes seven NSNs in terms of five categories: (1) the decision-maker, and for each decision-maker; (2) goals; (3) resources — assets controlled by the decision-maker influencing outcomes; (4) environment — conditions not controlled by the decision-maker altering outcomes; and (5) components or missions — the decision-maker's projects undertaken to achieve goals. Considers durability and audibility in the international system the NSN's key goals. Cites the diffusion and increasing international visibility of NSNs and the varieties of national autonomy goals these groups pursued. Examines the varieties of their impact upon the international order. Urges research into situations that would accommodate a NSN's needs for more national self-determination short of complete independence, while avoiding the fragmentation of small states into non-viable units.

162.   BIRCH, Anthony H.   "Minority Nationalist Movements and
        Theories of Political Integration." *World Politics*, XXX
        (1978), 325-44.
        Explains that the recent growth of minority nationalist move-
        ments posed the conceptual question of testing the validity of
        social science theories dealing with national integration, and the
        practical question of assessing the options open to governments
        faced with nationalistic agitations and demands for secession.
        Older theories predicting the decline of ethnic and cultural con-
        flicts had been challenged by the theory of internal colonialism
        and by a group of theories stressing the durability of ethnic
        loyalties.   Considers the theory of internal colonialism unhelp-
        ful.   Accepts the durability of ethnic loyalties; advances four
        propositions to explain the growth of minority nationalist
        movements.   Suggests that this was a rational development in
        view of recent changes in the international order.   Canadian and
        British experience demonstrated that governments found it
        diffiult to prevent demands for secession from arising.   How-
        ever, the growth of interdependence had reduced the signif-
        icance of secession.

163.   CLAVAL, P.   "Idéologie territoriale et ethnologénèse" (Terri-
        torial Ideology and Ethnology).   *International Political
        Science Review*, VI (1985), 161-70.
        Challenges the view that ethnic groups were naturally stable and
        immutable.   Suggests and illustrates that group identification
        had an evolutionary and changing character.   Finds shared
        language to be a major but not exclusive factor in ethnicity.
        Considers the role of ideology in linking individuals to
        collectivities.   Reviews the interactions between religious and
        spatial ideology and collective identity; between universalism
        and dimensions of difference; and between territorial and non-
        territorial affiliations.   Considers 19th-century nationalism to
        be a compromise between the nationalist penchant for ever
        larger   communities   and   human   tendencies   toward
        particularistic attachments.   Considers the effect the transfer of
        these dual attractions had in North America.   Deems national
        and regional loyalties a mask for a profound problem – the in-
        dispensable sense of individual space.

164.   CONNOR, Walker.   "Nation-Building or Nation-Destroying?"
        World Politics, XXIII (1972), 319-55.
        Accuses the leading theoreticians of "nation-building" of having
        slighted problems associated with ethnic diversity.   Maintains

that most states were multiethnic, and that ethnic consciousness was on the ascendancy as a political force. The increased social mobilization and communication which accompanied economic development had increased ethnic tensions and encouraged separatist demands. Advances in communications and transportation tended to increase minorities' awareness by making members more conscious of the distinctions between themselves and others. The diffusion of the self-determination doctrine had induced minorities to question the validity of present political boundaries and had served as a catalyst for ethnic movements. A favorable international climate had resulted in independence being viewed as an enduring prospect for even the weakest of units. Outlines twelve academic errors or tendencies causing gaps between theories of nation-building and reality.

165. CONNOR, Walker. "The Politics of Ethnonationalism." *Journal of International Affairs*, XXVII (1973), 1-21.
Contends that the failure of contemporary states to correspond to the principle of national self-determination was neither a measure of the popular appeal of the principle nor its political impact. Attributes the emergence of the principle of 19th-century European self-determination to two factors: (1) the rise of nations as self-conscious ethnic groups; and (2) the growing acceptance of the notion of popular sovereignty. The coining of the phrase "self-determination" did not create, but merely concisely expressed, an existing and expanding sociopolitical force; it raised the matter above the specifics of any particular case, endowing it with universal validity. Considers the principle of self-determination poorly reflected on the global political map, primarily because of governmental resistance and the inability of national groups to coordinate efforts and overcome internal divisions. Governmental responses to the threat of ethnonationalism had included genocide and expulsion, the granting of cultural and/or political autonomy, and assimilation. Doubts whether ethnonationalism could be managed or accommodated within existing political structures.

166. DOFNY, J. and A. AKIWOWO. *National and Ethnic Movements*. Palo Alto, CA: Sage Publications, 1980.
A collection of seventeen articles in English and French concerning ethnic and national movements in Europe, North America, Asia, Africa and Latin America.

167. ENLOE, Cynthia H. "Internal Colonialism, Federalism and Alternative State Development Strategies." *Publius: The Journal of Federalism*, VII, 4 (1977), 145-60.
Argues that the analysis of ethnic politics within a federalist system should not be confined exclusively to federal relationships; rather, federalism was best understood as one conflict management strategy among many. Proposes eight prevalent ethnic conflict management formulas, including "divide and rule," "displacement," "internal colonialism," "sub-machine," "consociational democracy," "federalism," "vanguard assimilation," and "vanguard assimilation-cum-pluralism." The three principal variables which determined the feasibility and viability of particular conflict management formulas were the level of demand for state mobilization capacity, the levels of political development of relevant ethnic groups, and the state élite's varying perceptions of the need to mobilize the resources of certain groups. These three factors varied over time and within a single society; likewise, the ensemble of management strategies utilized by political élites varied in composition over time. Claims the simultaneous growth of all these conditions in multiethnic countries.

168. ESMAN, Milton J., ed. *Ethnic Conflict in the Western World.* Ithaca, NY: Cornell University Press, 1977.
The contributors examine the reemergence of ethnic conflict in Western societies via fifteen essays focusing on specific European and Canadian regions.

169. FISCHER, Eric. *Minorities and Minority Problems.* Chicago: Vantage Press, 1980.
Finds that despite great diversities regarding minorities, three types could be distinguished: (1) states that took shape before the emergence of modern nationalism and that inherited minorities from the former non-national political bodies, whether created by conquest, dynastic inheritance, subinfeudation or any other way. Most European and Asian states belonged to this category; (2) states in which the minorities originated through voluntary or involuntary immigration, such as the United States and Argentina; and (3) states in which minorities evolved from some other form of social organization, such as tribes or ideological groups, as in many African countries. In type 1, minorities preceded the modern national state. In types 2 and 3, the formation of the state preceded that of minorities. Combinations also existed.

170. GORDENKER, Leon. "Self-Determination Yesterday and Today." *Resolving Nationality Conflicts: The Role of Public Opinion Research.* Eds. W. Phillips Davidson and Leon Gordenker. New York: Praeger, 1980, pp., i-xiv.
Asserts that devoting more attention to mass attitudes could materially assist in resolving at least some conflicts based on demands for self-determination. Offers examples of case studies with varying characteristics, representing different stages of conflict or accommodation, including the Harijans of India, the Basques of Spain, the Arabs of Israel, the Muslims of the Philippines, the French in Canada, Northern Ireland, Puerto Rico and Belgium. Reveals several common insights into issues concerning self-determination: (1) ethnic divisions frequently involved dual loyalties, with individuals often identifying themselves both with their minority group and with the national state; (2) violence could be sustained in the name of a nationality or religious group even though the overwhelming majority of its members opposed violence; (3) many minority group members opposing the use of violence perpetrated in its name refused to oppose this violence actively and often sympathized with the aims of the violent minority; (4) physical proximity (as opposed to geographical separateness), did not necessarily promote interethnic understanding; (5) rapid social change appeared to link closely with the development of nationalistic ideas; and (6) economic expectations and satisfactions coincided with ethnic identification and conflict.

171. HECHTER, M[ichael]. *Internal Colonialism.* London: Routledge & Kegan Paul, 1975.
Accounts for the animosities which separate England from the Celtic fringe through a discussion of the types of conditions which promoted national development in culturally heterogeneous societies. Presents two alternative models of national development: (1) the diffusion model, which suggests that sustained contact between the core and periphery would spread national development and lead to greater commonalities; and (2) the internal colonialism model, which did not predict national development following industrialization, but suggested that structural inequalities between the core and periphery would increase. Ethnic change was the critical process in national development, and referred to the willingness of a culturally subordinate group to redefine its ethnic identity to be congruent with that of the culturally dominant group. Describes the essentially colonial process by which English insti-

tutions and markets expanded, and the development of the "cultural division of labour" in the Celtic fringe. By the 19th century, the existence of Celtic culture had become a weapon that could be used as a basis for anti-English mobilization in traditionally disadvantaged regions.

172.   HECHTER, Michael. "Internal Colonialism Revisited." *New Nationalisms of the Developed West.* Eds. Edward A. Tiryakian and Ronald Rogowski. Boston: Allen and Unwin, 1985, pp. 17-26.

Claims that the argument of *Internal Colonialism* was not so much incorrect as it was incomplete. It failed to recognize the possibility of segmental cultural divisions of labor in addition to hierarchical ones, and thus took too narrow a view of the conditions that promoted common material interests among culturally distinct populations. Furthermore, the text was also incomplete because it failed to attend to organizational mechanisms that were necessary to solve the "free-rider" problem. The mere existence of common material interests was not a sufficient condition for the establishment of group solidarity or collective action, although it was a necessary one. First, nationalist organizations must gain sufficient resources to make their members more dependent on them than on rival political organizations. Second, to be successful, such groups must have the means of monitoring their members' compliance to the movements' goals and procedures.

173.   HECHTER, Michael and Margaret LEVI. "The Comparative Analysis of Ethnoregional Movements." *Ethnic and Racial Studies*, II (1979), 260-74.

The authors consider the cultural division of labor a necessary condition for the development of ethnoregionalism. Note two major obstacles to the elaboration of an adequate explanation of ethnoregionalism: the need to derive better measures of ethnic solidarity; and the need to analyze the difficulties of separating the effects of the process being studied from its varying social contexts. Identify two dimensions of the cultural division of labor leading to reactive group formation: the hierarchical mechanism (*i.e.*, the extent to which group membership determined individual life chances); and the segmental mechanism (*i.e.*, the extent to which members interacted wholly within the boundaries of their own group). Suggest that the intensity of an ethnoregional movement largely depended on the existence of the ethnoregion's culture. The central state's tolerance of cultural diversity not only ensured the continued existence of the culture, but also vouchsafed the organizational infrastructure the social movement required. Link the timing of ethnoregional movements to changes in state policy and structural alterations in the global system.

174. INTERNATIONAL POLITICAL SCIENCE REVIEW, VI, 2 (1985).
Special issue on ethnicity and regionalism, with papers on territorialism and ethnogenesis, the Scottish National Party and voting patterns of support, the case of Friuli, religious ethnicity in the world of Islam, secessionist attempts in Tuvalu in the Pacific, and post-colonial self-determination.

175. KILSON, Martin, ed. *New States in the Modern World.* Cambridge: Harvard University Press, 1975.
Ten essays consider the new (principally African) states in relationship to their effect on world political order. Includes discussions of cultural pluralism within states, nationalism and separatism, and self-determination.

176. KNIGHT, David B. "The Dilemma of Nations in a Rigid State Structured World." *Pluralism and Political Geography: People, Territory and State.* Eds. Nurit Kliot and Stanley Waterman. London: Croom Helm, 1983, pp. 114-37.
Examines concepts of territory, territorial attachments, large group allegiances, and the issues of self-determination and legitimacy as a means for discussing the dilemmas which substate groups with distinct regional identities encountered within the existing rigid international state system. Focuses on Canada, with its several types of group-territorial identities, and discusses how their needs might be met by internal space restructuring, but then also notes how successful secessionist thrusts in several parts of the present state would cause its disintegration. Presents several future scenarios. The Canadian case was not unique. Predicts that large group sub-state territorial identities would continue causing conflict, with territorial consequences, in many parts of the world.

177. LEVI, Margaret and Michael HECHTER. "A Rational Choice Approach to the Rise and Decline of Ethnoregional Political Parties." *New Nationalisms of the Developed West.* Eds. Edward A. Tiryakian and Ronald Rogowski. Boston: Allen and Unwin, 1985, pp. 128-46.

The authors consider three questions to be crucial in the formulation of a theory of ethnoregionalism, one concerning its geographical distribution, another its timing, and the third concerning the future of ethnoregional movements. Develop a set of testable hypotheses that account for variations in location, size and timing of ethnoregional movements. The key to understanding the geographical distribution of ethnoregional parties lay in the cultural division of labor. The more segmental or hierarchical it was, the greater the potential for the politicization of ethnic distinctions; the more sites of interaction it created, the easier it would be to mobilize potential followers. Predict that ethnoregional party membership would increase: as more individuals found that membership in the party was their only or main avenue of advancement; and as benefits increased, especially the selective incentives, offered by the party. Voters were most likely to be attracted to an ethnoregional party when seeking changes that a vote for the party might help to effect. The demand for change was predicated on a dissatisfaction with the current government and on the political salience of ethnic and ethnoregional identity. Deny any necessary connection between ethnoregionalism and industrialization, or the expansion of national markets.

178. LINZ, Juan. "From Primordialism to Nationalism." *New Nationalisms of the Developed West.* Eds. Edward A. Tiryakian and Ronald Rogowski. Boston: Allen and Unwin, 1985, pp. 203-53.
     Argues that ethnic peripheral nationalism would move from emphasizing primordial elements (*i.e.*, common descent, race, language, cultural tradition or religion) to a definition based on territoriality (*i.e.*, "living and working" in an area, or a willingness to identify with that community, or both). This hypothesis had emerged out of the analysis of data from surveys of the Spanish and French Basque country and, to some extent, was confirmed by data from Catalonia and Galicia. The data suggests that the stronger the nationalist sentiment in a region, the more likely a territorial definition of national identity would be articulated. In the Basque case, the progressive supplanting of a primordial conception of Basque identity by a territorial one was clearly linked to political changes, to efforts at mobilization, and to generational change. The analysis was complicated by the fact that a significant proportion of the population in the Spanish and French Basque territories and Catalonia was either immigrant or descended from recent

immigrants. Where a nationalist movement aspired to govern within an ethnically heterogeneous territory, the saliency of class alignments led to the incorporation of those who did not share the primordial characteristics, and therefore, to an emphasis on a territorial rather than a primordial conception of the nation. Primordialism might be the original source of nationalism, but ultimately nationalism's political implications were incompatible with primordialism; they required loyalty to the new emerging community, irrespective of cultural, linguistic or other characteristics.

179. MIKESELL, Marvin W. "The Myth of the Nation State." *Journal of Geography*, LXXXII (1983), 257-60.
Dispells the myth of the nation state, that is, the notion that the world consisted of political states, the boundaries of which coincided neatly with the homelands of cultural groups whose national goals and aspirations were manifest in those states. Boundaries of almost every state encompassed (in part or in total) the homelands of several groups which might or might not have a common political allegiance. Through careful treatment of the "nation" and "state" concepts, lays the groundwork for a structural approach to the examination of cultural conflict. Notes that dissident groups within states often had well-defined aims. Suggests that two patterns could be discerned, depending on whether the unhappy group "wants in" or "wants out" of a larger "national society." The first aspiration was often expressed by a progression of key words: "recognition," "access," "participation." Failure to achieve these goals was often expressed by a different set of diagnostic terms: "autonomy," "separation," "independence." Raises pedagogical issues.

180. ORRIDGE, Andrew W. "Separatist and Autonomist Nationalisms: The Structure of Regional Loyalties in the Modern State." *National Separatism*. Ed. Colin H. Williams. Cardiff: University of Wales Press, 1982, pp. 43-74.
Investigates the conditions under which separatist or autonomist nationalism had developed in European states over the last two centuries. Outlines three structural preconditions: (1) a core territory in which the group was concentrated in sufficiently high proportion; (2) a cultural infrastructure, such as language or religion, so that a people might conceive of itself as a national community; and (3) sizable groups closely asso-

ciated with the dominant power should be concentrated either regionally or at the top of the social hierarchy. Suggests linguistic factors and location on frontiers as highly influential factors in structural preconditions of autonomist nationalism. In addition, the ability of states to promote administrative centralization and cultural assimilation had promoted the development of the preconditions for nationalism.

181.   ORRIDGE, Andrew W.   "Uneven Development and
          Nationalism: 1." *Political Studies*, XXXIX (1981), 1-15.
       Discerns nothing in the works of Karl Marx that might be re-
       garded as a general theory of the emergence and importance of
       nationalism.   Attributes the origins of the term "uneven
       development" to the Marxian theories of imperialism associated
       with Bukharin, Luxemburg, Hilferding and Lenin.   They had
       located and analyzed an antagonism that could be construed as
       an explanation of national or ethnic conflicts.   Nationalism
       allegedly functioned as a reaction to imperialism. Post-World
       War II formulations of neo-imperialism and neo-colonialism
       had freed the theory of imperialism from its connection with
       political imperialism, and thus had made the former more suit-
       able as a basis for a general theory of nationalism.   Notions of
       internal colonialism and the work of Marxists such as Andre
       Gunder Frank had begun to transform the theory of
       imperialism into a general theory of uneven development by
       extending it to span the entire globe and influence relationships
       within as well as among countries.

182.   ORRIDGE, Andrew W.   "Uneven Development and
          Nationalism: 2." *Political Studies*, XXXIX (1981), 181-90.
       Criticizes the theory primarily associated with Tom Nairn that
       nationalism had arisen as a response to uneven development.
       Contends that the theory could not accommodate instances of
       nationalism unaccompanied by great differences in develop-
       mental level from their surroundings, and conversely, instances
       of uneven development without the attendance of pronounced
       nationalism. Argues that the theory could not account for some
       of the main features of nationalism. It explained global political
       fragmentation, but not the nature and composition of the frag-
       ments. Considers development uneven in the sense that it did
       not follow the same course wherever it occurred, and involved
       much more than simply variations in the level of development.
       The theory did not clarify the relationship between uneven
       development and pre-existing ethnic identity in the genesis of

nationalism. Identifies ethnic and religious differences, not uneven development, as the primary factors in the creation of a sense of nationality. Asserts that development as such, and not its unevenness, had converted ethnic and religious identities into the modern sense of nationality.

183. ORRIDGE, Andrew W. and Colin H. WILLIAMS. "Autonomous Nationalism: A Theoretical Framework for Spatial Variations in Its Genesis and Development." *Political Geography Quarterly*, I (1982), 19-39.
The authors propose a theoretical framework which separated preconditions from triggering factors in the analysis of nationalism, and emphasized political events at the international state system level rather than the more traditional explanations which concentrated on the individual state level. Outline three structural preconditions for autonomist nationalism: (1) there must be some core territory in which the group was concentrated in sufficiently high proportion; (2) there must be one or more characteristics to provide the basis for separateness and community in the potential nationality, such as language or religion; and (3) if there were sizable groups in the territory closely associated with the dominant power, they should be either regionally concentrated, or located at the top of the social hierarchy. Suggest that linguistic geography and the location of territory on frontiers had highly influenced and reinforced the structural preconditions of autonomist nationalism in many European instances. In addition, the European state system and economy, especially when it promoted administrative centralization and cultural assimilation, had affected the preconditions for nationalism. Argue that theories of nationalism suffered from severe empirical problems because the factors to which they pertained, while always influential, failed to take into account the variation produced by the place in the state system that a country occupied.

184. PADDISON, Ronan. "Territorial Integration and 'Disintegration' in the Unitary State." *The Fragmented State: The Political Geography of Power.* Ed. Ronan Paddison. Oxford (England): Basil Blackwell, 1983, pp. 57-96.
Focuses on the evolution from the unitary to the compound unitary state. Sees the concept of nation as the vital construct underpinning the political integration of the state. The reemergence of peripheral nationalism evidenced cultural, political and/or economic malintegration. Finds the center-periphery

model a useful spatial framework for the analysis of economic and cultural domination. Applies an action-reaction model of center-periphery politics to the case of the United Kingdom.

185.   PRATT, Jeff.   "A Sense of Place." *'Nation' and 'State' in Europe: Anthropological Perspectives.* Ed. R. D. Grillo. London: Academic Press, 1980, pp. 31-43.
Examines how territorial identities and organizational divisions below the level of the nation-state played a prominent role in Italian life.   Claims that with the emergence of the 12th- and 13th-century Central Italian city-state, people had become territorially defined according to their town of birth and citizenship.   Despite liberal economic and administrative reform since the 16th century, anachronistic political and economic institutions seemingly at odds with the needs of a modern industrial country, as well as a strong sense of local identity, still remained.   Maintains that the idea of a local group's common interests found expression in the parochial language of *campanilismo*, and in the ideology of the Christian Democratic Party.   Local ideology was elaborated upon through the use of organic analogies, where the distinction between the governors and the governed was considered fixed and natural.   The structure and imagery of the ideology of nationalism was often a simple transposition of the ideology of local subnational identities.

186.   RA'ANAN, Uri, ed.   *Ethnic Resurgence in Modern Democratic States.* New York: Pergamon Press, 1980.
The contributors analyze the resurgence of ethnic self-assertion in the West.   The editor's introduction examines the causes and effects of ethnic resurgence.   Special studies include a conceptual and analytical approach to the problem of multiethnic states, including a discussion of models of conflict resolution; an analysis of national and ethnic conflict in an immigration society — the United States; a survey of problems and social, economic, educational, and legal remedial measures relating to the migrant labor phenomenon in northwestern Europe; a review of political "fallout" as well as the roots of an ethnic/regional movement — the new Scottish nationalism; and three country studies of "indigenous" ethnic problems in northwestern Europe, the Mediterranean and the Far East.

187.   ROTHSCHILD, Joseph.   *Ethnopolitics: A Conceptual Framework.* New York: Columbia University Press, 1981.

Focuses on the political dimension and the structural problematics of ethnicity. Considers the politicization of ethnicity a dialectical process that had preserved ethnic groups by emphasizing their singularity, and had also transformed them into effective political conflict groups for the modern political arena. Ethnicity, currently the crucial principle of political legitimation and the case for delegitimation of systems, states, regimes and governments, had become a potentially critical issue only since the French Revolution and Napoleonic Wars, as modern states sought to base their legitimacy on democratic claims and purported to be, or striven to become, nation-states expressing and enhancing specific national cultures. The postwar expansion in contacts and communications had heightened peoples' awareness of ethnic differences and imbalances. Asserts that ethnic consciousness and assertiveness had not flowed automatically out of primordial cultural or naturalistic data and differences but were the products of political entrepreneurship. Examines the impact of politicized ethnicity upon state, interstate and interethnic relations.

188. RUSTOW, D. *A World of Nations: Problems in Political Modernization.* Washington, DC: The Brookings Institution, 1967.

Argues that the nation-state had been and remained the only vehicle for political modernization. The idea of the nation included three primary ingredients for modernization: (1) identity; (2) equality of opportunity needed for intensive division of labor and cooperation; and (3) state authority as the institutional representative of the nation. Asserts that the concepts of nationalism and political development were so intertwined that the latter was often taken to mean the evolution of modern nation-statehood. Believes that the international system provided ample encouragement for state authority, so that would-be nations were on their own in their quest for identity and participation. Discusses the objective and subjective criteria for nationhood, including the importance of history and language, and the patterns of interdependence modernization demanded. Suggests that some of the more successful modernization patterns relied not only on blends of tradition and modernity but on "reinforcing dualism." Notes the inner contradictions complicating the achievement of national sovereignty, independence and power, and explains their method of diffusion through worldwide interdependence, vulnerability to penetration and susceptibility to external power. Expects the nation-state to remain the deliberate choice of statesmen, but urges that their search for nationhood be moderated by recognizing the interdependence of nations.

189. SMITH, A. D.   *The Ethnic Revival in the Modern World.* Cambridge: Cambridge University Press, 1981.

Identifies the opposition between state and community as a major source of conflict in the modern world. Despite claims about the recent "dissolution of ethnicity, the transcendence of nationalism and the internationalization of culture," the ethnic revival as the social and cultural roots of development "remains the fundamental trend of the last two centuries." Asserts that liberals had failed to appreciate the significance of the ethnic revolution, convinced that trade and industry would cement continents and erase internal barriers, with the nation-state acting as an intermediate framework. Although the world had become more interdependent and unified, ethnic ties and national loyalties had become stronger than ever. Reviews the possible causes of the ethnic revival, including uneven economic development, the negative relationship between language and community, and the role of historicism in communal regeneration. Stresses the myth of the "nation-state" and the ideology of "internationalism," which represented "the desirability of cooperation between states which claim to reflect the aspirations of 'peoples' and 'nations' within their borders." This "grid of state-nations" remained the framework for the growth of a political community, but it was relatively fragile and mutable despite the legitimization of the world order. Discusses methods used for "development" and "nation-building" that recognized the modernizing strength of a "national political culture."

190. SNYDER, Louis L.   *Global Mini-Nationalisms: Autonomy or Independence.* Westport, CT: Greenwood Press, 1982.

A wide-ranging review of "mini-nationalisms," *i.e.*, of those smaller nationalisms, or regionalisms, that had been absorbed into larger centralized states. Believing themselves to be a distinct people, members of a mini-nationalism demanded "self-determination" which could range in meaning from greater autonomy than currently enjoyed to outright independence. Outlines the existence and recent resurgence of numerous groups in all continents but South America, although stresses mostly European cases.

191. SUHRKE, A. and L. G. NOBLE. "Introduction," and "Spread or Containment - The Ethnic Factor." *Ethnic Conflict in International Relations.* Eds. A. Suhrke and L. G. Noble. New York: Praeger, 1979, pp. 1-20 and 213-32.

The authors explore the relationship between internal ethnic conflict and patterns of international conflict and cooperation in seven contemporary case studies. Outline the three main themes: (1) the role of domestic ethnic conflict in attacting outside intervention and thus developing international conflict; (2) the possible effects of facilitating international cooperation to contain or regulate them; and (3) the significance of ethnic factors in determining foreign involvement and the nature of that involvement. Examine the policy implications for the state and the ethnic groups. Establish the assumptions regarding the context and characteristics of ethnic conflict, specifying the form of involvement, the interaction process, the nature of ethnic conflict, the importance of the external parties' ethnic characteristics and cross-boundary ethnic links. Compare the results of the case studies based on two dimensions: (1) the scope of involvement; and (2) the nature of involvement (conflicting or cooperative). Discuss the cases in terms of whether they reflected competitive conflict expansion, simple conflict expansion, simple conflict containment or conflict equilibration. Summarize the most important factors: (1) the scope of external involvement; (2) the consequences of involvement on the international system; and (3) the external characteristics of the outside party. Review the policy implications for international stability and conflict regulation for parties to the domestic conflict in terms of instrumental and effective intervention. Report that their finding contradicted the presupposition that internal ethnic conflict constituted a major source of international conflict. When intervention did occur, it was usually a vehicle for outside parties to promote unrelated interests.

192. TIRYAKIAN, Edward A. and Neil NEVITTE. "Nationalism and Modernity." *New Nationalisms of the Developed West.* Eds. Edward A. Tiryakian and Ronald Rogowski. Boston: Allen and Unwin, 1985, pp. 57-86.

The authors reconceptualize the character and boundaries of nation and nationalism, to be used in a heuristic categorization of the interrelationship between nationalism and modernity. Consider the nation the core structure of society, as its societal community. It had important dynamic and voluntaristic attributes, in the sense that the nation was a historically evolving reality, and that membership in the national collectivity involved an element of subjective choice and commitment. These attributes provided essential grounding for a definition of nationalism which had comparative utility, understood as the lodging of claims in the name, or on behalf, of the nation. Propose a typology of nationalism and modernity based on four external and internal attributes: (1) claims by élites on behalf of the nation-state against either external or internal collectivities whose culture and territory differed from those of the "nation," taken as the societal community of the nation-state; (2) nationalism of the periphery: identification with the nation-state; (3) nationalism of the periphery: withdrawal (retreat) from modernity; and (4) nationalism of the periphery: overtaking modernity. Applies the typology to two concrete cases: France and Québec.

193.   VAN DYKE, Vernon. "The Individual, the State, and Ethnic Communities in Political Theory." *World Politics*, XXIX (1977), 343-69.
Considers liberal political theory and contemporary application of human rights unduly limited, because they focused mainly on the individual. Some theorists denied that ethnic communities and other groups had any moral rights as collective entities. This view reflected a preoccupation with a model of domestic politics that neglected the concept of heterogeneity. Claims that in many countries, groups identified by race, language or religion made moral claims, which were sometimes conceded. Liberals ignored the commonly held view that nations or "peoples" had a moral right to self-determination. Asserts that the question of group rights had to be explored, and the interrelationships linking the rights of individuals, groups and the state needed to be clarified.

194.   WILLIAMS, Colin H. "Ethnic Resurgence in the Periphery." *Area*, XI (1979), 279-83.
Considers the inadequacies of the core-periphery explanation of Celtic nationalism, and argues that ethnic resurgence was best understood in terms of the internationalization of capital in supra-state economies and the attempt by the ethnic intelligentsia to redefine its role vis-à-vis the state bureaucracy.

195.   WILLIAMS, Colin H., ed. *National Separatism*. Vancouver: University of British Columbia Press, 1982.

Nine essays address autonomy demands made by sub-national groups. Linguistic and cultural differences in particular regions had persisted over generations and survived despite strong pressures toward assimilation. Political leaders had recently emerged who sought more political power and varying degrees of autonomy. Considers national self-determination to be a moral right. Essays examine the bases for such claims in several European states and Canada.

196. WILLIAMS, S. W. "Internal Colonialism, Core-Periphery Contrasts and Devolution: An Integrative Comment." *Area*, IX (1977), 272-8.
Presents the idea of internal deprivation as a framework for examining regional deprivation, especially in distinct cultural environments. Associates internal colonialism with the interrelation of peripheral position and industrial development at a certain point in societal development. Concludes that devolution for Scotland and Wales might provide a long-term economically and socially just solution to regional deprivation.

Dealing with Differences: Structural Accommodations

197. ADEJUYIGBE, Omolade. *Social Considerations in the Political Territorial Organization of Society.* Ile Ife (Nigeria): University of Ife Press, Inaugural Lecture Series 45, 1982.
Highlights the general principles derived from geographical studies of the evolution, organization and cohesion of political units, and discusses their applicability to the solution of relevant problems in Nigeria. Considers "primary community" a group of people having common ownership rights, common territories, and allegiance to the same administration. Argues that such a community and its territory should be grouped in the same administration, but consideration to primary communities was often absent where political units had been created, giving rise to demands for separation and constitution of home areas into new states or local government areas. The almost total disregard for primary communities in the delimitation of the present nineteen states of Nigeria partly explained current demands for new states in that country.

198.   ALCOCK, A. E.   "A Reappraisal of Existing Theory and Prac-
       tice in the Protection of Minorities." *Minorities in History.*
       Ed. A. C. Hepburn. London: Edward Arnold, 1978, pp.
       226-41.
       Claims that the principle of "positive" rights, where ethnic
       groups had a right to decide upon all statutory measures for the
       maintenance of their ethnic character and their cultural and
       economic development, had been in decline in favor of the view
       that all countries should maintain a universal standard of hu-
       man rights for all citizens, regardless of minority status.   Be-
       cause of changes in the terms by which the majority-minority
       dialogue had been traditionally engaged since the 19th century,
       minorities had come to depend overwhelmingly upon the state
       for their protection.   Minorities had responded to the growing
       power of the modern state by making it clear that their overrid-
       ing aim was to preserve and develop their culture, by rejecting
       the idea of formal equality with the majority, and by harboring
       increasing resentment toward the central government.   Main-
       tains that the possession of a "homeland" was of chief impor-
       tance to a minority's economic power, and it was upon
       economic power that a minority's cultural power depended.
       The argument that the minority group had a legal right to its
       homeland depended on the claim that ethnic groups should be
       granted "positive" rights, and the acceptance of self-
       determination for peoples rather than exclusively for state or
       political entities.

199.   ALLEN, Philip M.   "Self-Determination in the Western Indian
       Ocean." *International Conciliation*, DLX (1966-67), 5-74.
       Surveys the imperial and colonial influences upon five islands in
       the Western Indian Ocean, noting the two streams of national
       consciousness which have developed in the area since World
       War II.   Linked to European metropoles, Madagascar,
       Mauritius, Reunion, the Comoros and the Seychelles, represent
       culturally and geographically the Afro-Asian bridge.   Outlines
       both the relatively conservative European-oriented sensibility
       devoted to modernization within the existing social, economic
       and political framework, and the anti-Establishment opposition
       subject to such international stimuli as global decolonization,
       nonalignment and communism.   Reviews arguments favoring
       prolonged colonial "protection" against claims that associate
       status with a former administering colonial power violated the
       very concept of self-determination as intepreted by those who
       called for immediate and unequivocal decolonization.   Exam-

ines the U.N.'s experiences with non-self-governing territories back to the late 1940s, reviewing the implications of the Declaration of the Granting of Independence to Colonial Countries and People. Surveys other theoretical possibilities for the territories (such as economic regionalism, regionalism, regional federation, diversification of independence, or a form of United Nations trusteeship) which might help shrink the gap between enlightened protectionists and the more moderate decolonizers who stress self-determination over "liberation."

200. ASHWORTH, Georgina, ed. *World Minorities.* London: Minority Rights Group, 1977, 1978 and 1980, I, II and III. Brief analyses of the situation of the world's numerous minority peoples and their position within their "host communities."

201. BARRY. Brian. "Self-Government Revisited." *The Nature of Political Theory.* Eds. David Miller and Larry Siedentop. Oxford: Clarendon Press, 1983, pp. 121-54.
Reconciles the characteristic doctrines of nationalism with individual ideals. Finds the individualist claim that the role of states should be confined to protecting the property and physical security of their citizens to be unduly narrow, and believes that a full-bodied conception of the state should take into account additional criteria of citizenship. Argues that ethnicity could not in itself be a basis for the composition of the state on individualist premises, because no necessary connection existed between descent, which was a matter of biology, and interest, which was a matter of the fulfillment of human needs and purposes. On the other hand, the notion that nationality should be the basis for the composition of states was unambiguously compatable with the individualist principle; firstly, given the subjective definition of nationality, it was an analytic truth that the nation-state fulfilled the aspirations of those who belonged to the nation embodied in the state; second, the presence of fellow-feeling facilitated cooperation on common projects and made redistribution within the polity more acceptable. Cultural nationalism was more problematic; to bring it within the individualist fold depended on the actual desire on the part of past and present people to pass on their culture. Concludes that disagreements within individualist moral theory about the rights and wrongs of nationalism turned on different conceptions of "interest," and on the ways of life one believed conducive to human interests.

202.   BERNHARDT, Rudolph.   "Federalism and Autonomy."
       Models of Autonomy.   Ed. Yoram Dinstein.   New
       Brunswick, NJ: Transaction Books, 1981. pp. 23-8.
       Although the institutions of federalism and autonomy shared
       certain common features, they were distinct phenomena with
       basically different underlying philosophies. Federalism referred
       to the distribution of powers between the central government
       and the constituent units which had their own organs and
       competences. Autonomy meant the legal recognition of minor-
       ities and minority rights. It excluded absolute majority rule in
       view of the special values of a minority, and thus was closely
       connected with the notions of self-determination and human
       rights.

203.   BOGDANOR, Vernon. *Devolution.* Oxford: Oxford University
       Press, 1979.
       Deals with the history of proposals for devolution in Great
       Britain, giving special attention to the issue of Irish Home Rule.
       Also considers the relevance of the debate on the experience of
       Northern Ireland.   Examines the growing demand for
       devolution in contemporary politics, and the effects which re-
       cent legislation might have had upon the structure of govern-
       ment in Great Britain.   Discusses the problems of Scotland,
       Wales and the English regions, and considers the federal sol-
       ution, reputedly the most hopeful direction of constitutional
       advance.

204.   CLAUDE, Inis L., Jr. *National Minorities: An International
       Problem.* Westport, CT: Greenwood Press, 1955.
       Maintains that the problem of national minorities arose out of
       the conflict between the ideal of the homogeneous national state
       and the reality of ethnic heterogeneity.   Notes that not only
       have national minorities not been eliminated in Europe in the
       years since 1919, but that the problem was worldwide, because
       ethnic homogeneity was the exception rather than the rule. Be-
       lieves that most states were assimilationist, whereby national
       minorities were meant to be absorbed, not perpetuated. Asserts
       that some states avowedly opposed rights for minorities, rather
       than favoring positive rights facilitating ethnic differentiation.
       Claims that the League of Nations had failed to fulfil its at-
       tempted international solution of national minority problems,
       and suggests that contemporary prospects for resolving such
       problems through United Nations actions were not good, be-
       cause of the persistence by many states that minority group

pressures for claiming recognition were a domestic matter, plus the inclination by disinterested member states to prevent the issue from becoming a genuine international responsibility.

205. DIKSHIT, Ramesh Dutta. *The Political Geography of Federalism.* New Delhi: Macmillan Company of India, 1975.
Seeks to develop some general propositions on the origins and stability of federalism. Argues that the essential nature of federalism should not be sought in the nature of societies or social diversities *per se*, but in the spatial pattern of the total complex of social, political, economic and other diversities that imparted some sense of individual identity to the various constituent regions of a federation important enough to make them forego the economics of a completely centralized government, and demand and receive some guarantee for their continued existence as organizations and as holders of power. Determines the functioning examples of federalism according to the existence of guaranteed regional autonomy.

206. DINSTEIN, Yoram, ed. *Models of Autonomy.* New Brunswick, NJ: Transaction Books, 1981.
The contributors identify and analyze past and present autonomy models, with specific references to the mandate for negotiating full autonomy for West Bank and Gaza inhabitants, as outlined in the Camp David Framework for Peace in the Middle East. Includes essays on the theoretical concept of autonomy within the U.N. framework in relation to federalism and in international law. Other essays survey various autonomy arrangements in Europe, America and Africa. A final section considers the Israeli-Egyptian autonomy negotiations. The concluding essay reflects upon the relationship linking sovereignty, autonomy and self-determination. Notes that Israel has accepted the concept of Palestinian Arab autonomy, whereas Egypt had considered autonomy as a channel to ultimate statehood. These concepts, and the potential power redistribution through the varying autonomy arrangements, must be clearly understood to facilitate a viable, long-term peace.

207. DUCHACEK, Ivo. "Antagonistic Cooperation: Territorial and Ethnic Communities." *Publius: The Journal of Federalism* (special issue on "Ethnicity and Federalism"), VII, 4 (1977), 3-30.

Considers territory the dominant characteristic of the organization of political authority everywhere. The territorial principle of political organization extended to the internal structure of states, and territorial subunits were endowed with varying degrees of local autonomy either by delegation or devolution in unitary systems or by constitutional separation of territorial powers in federal systems. Considers the present territorial fragmentation of humanity subject to two conflicting challenges: globalism and ethnonationalism. Almost all states were polyethnic, and federalism was often suggested as an appropriate device for the management of interethnic conflict; but, for various reasons, even partial ethnoterritorial federal formulas were rare. Identifies five alternate approaches to the problems of polyethnic states: elimination of polyethnicity; discriminating regulation; communal or quota systems; quasi-federal solutions (such as unitary grants of home rule or confederal associations; international inspection and supervision.

208. DUCHACEK, Ivo. *Comparative Federalism: The Territorial Dimensions.* New York: Holt Rinehart, 1970.
Compares the territorial aspects of politics, using the notion of a territorial interest group as the central concept. Locates territorial identity in politics in conflicts of territorial allegiances and territorial disintegration. Examines aspects of the territorial distribution of authority. Identifies one challenge to unitary centralism as from "above": central authorities searched for greater efficiency, flexibility, responsibility and initiative on the local level. A second challenge came from below: territorial interests pressed for institutional recognition of their right to self-expression, dignity and self-rule. Proposes ten possible yardsticks of federalism. A second important test of federalism was to compare the constitutional text with actual practice.

209. FOIGHEL, Isi. "A Framework for Local Autonomy: The Greenland Case." *Models of Autonomy.* Ed. Yoram Dinstein. New Brunswick, NJ: Transaction Books, 1981, pp. 31-52.
Examines the background and implementation of the system of local autonomy for Greenland found in the Home Rule Act of 1979. Its basic philosophy might be expressed in terms that the population of Greenland did not desire national independence, but better opportunities for strengthening and expanding the identity of Greenland through increased dependent respon-

sibility. The main purpose of home rule was to transfer certain political, economic and cultural responsibilities from Danish political authorities to those in Greenland, while maintaining Danish national unity. The Act was not based on the principle of equality between Greenland and the rest of Denmark, but on the principle of equal rights regarding responsibilities and powers concerning the future of the respective societies.

210. FORSYTH, Murray. *Unions of States: The Theory and Practice of Confederation.* New York: Holmes and Meier, 1981.
Considers the process by which states formed themselves into federal unions or confederations. Distinguishes between the concepts of federalism, federal union, and federal states, and views federal unions as an intermediary stage between normal interstate relations and normal intrastate relations. Considers confederation or federal union from three distinctive perspectives: (1) confederation for defense in theory or practices; (2) economic confederation in theory and practice; and (3) universal confederation in theory and practice. Concludes that confederation was one of three classic forms of relationship that states adopted in order to guarantee or underwrite their continued existence; the other two forms were hegemony and the balance of power.

211. HACHEY, Thomas E., ed. *The Problem of Partition: Peril to World Peace.* Chicago: Rand McNally, 1972.
The editor contends that partitioning of people and territory compounded difficult problems rather than resolved them. Believes that colonial partitions were usually provoked by religious and separatist elements which sought to establish their own nationalist state, whereas Cold War partitions, in contrast, divided existing nations and peoples without reference to either the needs or the desires of the resident populations. Different authors present six case studies: Ireland, Korea, Germany, India and Pakistan, Bangladesh, Palestine and Vietnam.

212. HALL, R., ed. *Ethnic Autonomy - Comparative Dynamics: The Americas, Europe and the Developing World.* New York: Pergamon Press, 1979.
Twenty essays are divided into five parts: conceptual overviews of ethnicity and ethnic dynamics; racial and ethnic autonomy in North America; autonomy and ethnicity in Europe; ethnicity and autonomy in the developing world; and autonomy in perspective.

213. HANNUM, Hurst and Richard B. LILLICH. "The Concept
      of Autonomy in International Law." *American Journal of
      International Law*, LXXIV (1980), 858-89.
      The authors analyze the concept of autonomy based on the data
      gathered from twenty-two case studies of non-sovereign entities
      and federal states offering a wide range of examples of varying
      degrees of governmental autonomy and internal self-
      government.   The examination of autonomy in theory and
      practice provided a description and investigation of the degree
      of independence and control over its own internal affairs that
      an autonomous entity generally enjoyed. Survey a wide range
      of intergovernmental relationships of these entities, indicating
      the distribution of executive, legislative, and judicial authority
      between the entity and central government. Functionally ana-
      lyze police and security arrangements; land and natural re-
      sources; social services; financial and economic arrangements;
      and cultural, religious, and minority group concerns. Consider
      the degree of international personality, including control over
      foreign affairs and defense which the autonomous entity en-
      joyed. Conclude that autonomy remained a useful if imprecise
      concept within which flexible and unique political structures
      might be developed to respond to the increasing complexity of
      contemporary world politics.

214. HENDERSON, Gregory, Richard N. LEBOW and J. G.
      STOESSINGER, eds.   *Divided Nations in a Divided
      World.* New York: David McKay Co., 1974.
      Eleven essays explore why certain peoples had become divided
      by political boundaries and how some states were partitioned
      territorially in the post-World War II era.

215. JACKSON, R. H. and C. G. ROSEBERG. "Why Africa's
      Weak States Persist: The Empirical and Juridical in
      Statehood." *World Politics*, XXXV (1982), 1-25.
      The authors question why African states survived despite their
      national governments' inability to control the people's organi-
      zations and activities, but note the stability of national bound-
      aries. Discuss various conceptions of the state, noting their
      legal, institutional, philosophical and sociological dimensions.
      Explain that despite their weaknesses, all of the countries had
      remained theoretically equal members of the international soci-
      ety of states, mainly because the international and regional sys-
      tems (OAU) had provided legal protection from internal and
      external encroachments.

216. JOHNSTON, Ray Edward, ed. *The Politics of Division, Partition, and Unification.* New York: Praeger, 1976.
    A collection of essays dealing with the political phenomena of division, partition, and unification. An introductory essay points out directions that an empirical study of political partition might take, and proposes some functional requisites of an integrated political system in order to derive an empirical definition of national partition and unification. Six chapters include case studies on Northern Ireland, Berlin, the German Republics, Korea, China and Taiwan, and Bangladesh.

217. LANE, Jan-Erik. "Principles of Autonomy." *Scandinavian Political Studies,* IV, New Series (1981), 321-49.
    Claims that autonomy had two faces — individual and institutional. Political systems dealt not only with demands for individual freedom, the traditional rights of citizens to freedom of opinion, association and contract. Institutional autonomy was a pervasive property of all kinds of political systems. To international political systems and to local and regional political systems, autonomy was a basic property. Both types of systems faced the difficult task of maintaining stable relations with the nation-state, securing an amount of control for the nation-state while retaining some autonomy for themselves. The demand of various regions for independence or semi-independence within nation-states had been the dominant theme in the politics of the 1960s and 1970s. The autonomy of the nation-state was its sovereignty. International political systems presented a threat to the autonomy of the nation-state, while at the same time they might provide mechanisms by means of which other sources of infringements on autonomy could be counteracted. Autonomy was a fundamental political property. A theoretical understanding of autonomy was conducive to the explanation of those aspects of political systems that were related to stability. Such an interpretation might place autonomy in an equilibrium analysis of how demand and supply of autonomy interacted with other basic political properties, such as influence and control.

218. LAPONCE, J. A. *The Protection of Minorities.* Berkeley: University of California Press, 1960.
    Explores options that states had when dealing with minorities, including violent suppression, assimilation encourged by state action, the implementation of some form of local sociocultural autonomy, language accommodations for the minority groups,

the creation of voluntary *millet* system with virtual autonomy in religious and social matters, the use of the more rigid *mellah* confinement in Islamic North African cities for groups unwilling or unable to be assimilated, or a fairly high degree of political involvement or autonomy.

219.   LEIBOWITZ, A. H.   *Colonial Emancipation in the Pacific and the Caribbean: A Legal and Political Analysis.*   New York: Praeger, 1976.
Deals with decolonization of Caribbean and Pacific islands which, although self-governing, had retained a legal association with their former "metropoles."   Examines the Philippines, Puerto Rico, the Trust Territory of the Pacific Islands, Guam, the Cook Islands, Papua New Guinea, and the West Indies.

220.   MCRAE, Kenneth, ed.   *Consociational Democracy: Political Accommodation in Segmented Societies.*   Toronto: McClelland and Stewart, Carleton Library No. 79, 1974.
The contributors indicate how the successful accommodation of serious political cleavages in certain countries had given rise to the concept of consociational democracy.   Suggest means whereby societal conflict might be managed by using a variety of methods for permitting some degree of autonomy in order to undercut tensions that could lead to secession.

221.   PADDISON, Ronan.   "Federalism: Regional Diversity within National Union."   *The Fragmented State: The Political Geography of Power.*   Oxford (England): Basil Blackwell, 1983, pp. 97-144.
Contends that the territorial integrity of the state constituted its primary goals.   Reviews how federalism evolved and the reasons commonly considered as having contributed to the act of federalizing.   Finds no single universally important factor which explained the origins of the federal state.   Economic and political centralization and processes of "nationalization" tended to confirm the view that federalism was appropriate for a state in the early stages of its formation than it was later.   However, federalism also encouraged the maintenance of territorial differences through its spatial segregation of political processes. The salience of regional differences varied between federations, depending on such factors as population size, economic wealth, and ethnicity of constituent regions.   Despite numerous challenges to the territorial structure of various federations, they showed a remarkable resilience to reform.   Considers some of

the costs of federalism, including the degree of variation in how public services were provided.

222. PADDISON, Ronan. "Politics, Space and the State." *The Fragmented State: The Political Geography of Power.* Oxford (England): Basil Blackwell, 1983, pp. 1-26.
Introduces some basic concepts related to the fragmented state. Discusses the role of the state, the increasing role of government activity, and the meaning of power. Contrasts liberal and Marxist approaches to how local government fitted into the wider context of the state. Identifies two basic models of the state – one emphasizing integration, the other stressing competition for local power – and finds both useful in explaining the spatial division of power. Space was important to the fragmented state, because it was both a politically organizing factor and a territorial principle, binding people to localities. However, to argue for the significance of space independent from the social, economic and political processes that took place within it was a difficult position to sustain theoretically. Reviews some of the major factors underlying political centralization and decentralization within the modern industrial state.

223. PADDISON, Ronan. "Territory and Power: Some Basic Concepts." *The Fragmented State: The Political Geography of Power.* Oxford (England): Basil Blackwell, 1983, pp. 27-56.
Outlines the major types of territorial power distribution, including federal, unitary, and various forms of compound unitary states. Relates each type to specific geographical factors. Argues that fiscal measures were relevant but not exclusive indicators of local autonomy. The size of the polity, its cultural heterogeneity and political culture, and the structure of government were all important factors in explaining differences of political centralization within and between countries. Discusses various political and administrative values, and objectives underpinning the territorial distribution of power.

224. POLESE, Mario. "Economic Integration, National Policies, and the Rationality of Regional Separatism." *New Nationalisms of the Developed West.* Eds. Edward A. Tiryakian and Ronald Rogowski. Boston: Allen and Unwin, 1985, pp. 109-27.
Proposes a conceptual framework for analyzing the costs and benefits of regional separatism. Breaks down the economic as-

pects of separation into three composite dimensions: economic integration, systemwide economic policies, and interregional transfer payments. Each dimension represented an exogenous variable describing existing economic links (affecting the potential costs and benefits of separation), and an endogenous variable which might be integrated into the separatist option, thus modifying it and the associated costs and benefits. Hypothesizes that the costs of regional separatism would be minimized — or the benefits maximized — under the following conditions: (1) little trade or other economic relations between regions; or in the opposite case, the maintenance of interregional or multinational economic integration; (2) a perception that systemwide policies had either little significant effect on the underlying spatial trends of the economy, or that their effects had been clearly unfavorable, and that separation would increase or at least not diminish the region's capacity to influence those policies; and (3) evidence that interregional governmental transfer payments either had a marginal effect on the regional economy or translated into a net outflow of funds.

225. ROTHCHILD, Donald and Victor A. OLORUNSOLA. "African Public Policies on Ethnic Autonomy and State Control." *State versus Ethnic Claims: African Policy Dilemmas.* Eds. Donald Rothchild and Victor A. Olorunsola. Boulder, CO: Westview Press, 1983, pp. 233-50.
In the face of multinational African reality, it seems likely that incompatible values would at times arise regarding notions of ethnic autonomy and state control. The authors argue that policy analysis must enhance choice and the reduction of intense and destructive conflict. It accomplishes this in part by providing decision élites with detailed information on the comparative costs and benefits of various forms of interaction. Distinguish between hegemonial and bargaining models: the former sought to control conflict from the top downward, strengthening authoritative institutions at the center with some risk of system overload and low responsiveness; the latter was based upon a mutual adjustment of conflicting interests, decentralizing control and increasing autonomous participation with some cost in coordinated decision-making. Propose four general conflict regulating strategies, associated with hegemonial and bargaining approaches, followed by an array of suboptimized choice strategies. By recognizing both the high cost of destructive conflict and the broad range of available alternatives, it becomes possible to restructure conflict along more constructive

lines. At this point, the issue became largely one of determining the most important means of structuring relations in order to emphasize the area of overlapping interests.

226. ROTHCHILD, Donald and Victor A. OLORUNSOLA. "Managing Competing State and Ethnic Claims." *State versus Ethnic Claims: African Policy Dilemmas.* Eds. Donald Rothchild and Victor A. Olorunsola. Boulder, CO: Westview Press, 1983, pp. 1-24.

The authors introduce the various contributions to the volume, as well as draw on several theoretical issues. Emphasize how today's African states might be able to preserve and enhance their coherence, while at the same time accommodating the legitimate demands advanced by ethnic groups for autonomy.

227. SAID, Abdul and Luiz R. SIMMONS, eds. *Ethnicity in an International Context.* New Brunswick, NJ: Transaction Books, 1976.

Collection of essays, including examinations of autonomy and internal self-determination.

228. SMITH, Tony. "A Comparative Study of French and British Decolonization." *Comparative Studies in Society and History*, XX (1978), 70-102.

Maintains that numerous factors had conspired to terminate European overseas empires after 1945, but that Europeans could nevertheless significantly influence this process in most cases by grooming their successors. Explains that by exploiting the internal divisions of nationalist movements, the colonial powers had maintained a strong voice in the decolonization process. Outlines four major areas in which Great Britain had enjoyed advantages over France in this regard: (1) Great Britain had been prepared to meet colonial discontent with reforms leading to gradual devolution, whereas the French blindly trusted their "assimilation" policy whereby the colonies would eventually join France; (2) the British had enjoyed close links with the United States, which made them view the changing world order with guarded optimism, whereas the French had deplored their loss of world influence and had sought to re-generate France as a nation; (3) the two countries' domestic political institutions had influenced their ability to manage the decolonization process; Great Britain's stable "loyal opposition" two-party system and strong executive branch had proved advantageous in this regard; and (4) France's refusal to

collaborate with nationalist élites had sparked conflict and violence, highlighted by the revolutions in Indochina and Algeria,
whereas the British had followed a reform within order policy
designed to guarantee a continued British presence in their former colonies. The use of violence thus had been largely avoided
in British decolonization, with the exception of Egypt, where
United States and Soviet intervention had complicated matters.

229.   STEVENS, R. Michael. "Asymmetrical Federalism: The Fed-
        eral Principle and the Survival of the Small Republic."
        Publius: The Journal of Federalism, VII, 4 (1977), 177-204.
Conceives federacy as an unrecognized form of federalism
which joins separate, distinct communities of disproportionate
size in a political association designed to maintain the integrity
of the smaller community. It had developed in the wake of
World War II to accommodate the proliferation of mini-states
emerging out of the ruins of old empires, and the reawakening
of national aspirations by ethnic communities, which had
heretofore been integrated into the social and political order of
the nation-states. Rejects the traditional structural definitions
of federalism in favor of those based on the processes of
integration-differentiation. Federation involved political integration processes which extended throughout the fabric of the
entire society of the federation; in confederation, the scope of
political integration was limited to the interaction of the
constituent states. Federacy was unique, in that it was a form
of bilateral association involving some degree of integration,
but with extraordinary protection of the integrity of the smaller
state built into the terms of the association. Introduces
federacies as a class of political systems through a description
of their basic characteristics: small size, insularity, and, often,
strategic importance. Cultural characteristics, including language, religion, ethnicity, and economic activity, were also
important in distinguishing associated states from their associated powers. The asymmetry of federacy produced unique
institutional characteristics, including the right of unilateral
withdrawal, complementary patterns of power distribution, and
definitions of distinct citizenship rights for persons of the
smaller community that were not reciprocated to citizens of the
associated power. The experiences of many associated states
provided examples for the success of small territories, including
economic prosperity and security for indigenous political
development. Concludes that federacy might provide solutions

to the problems of very small states, and states with vocal ethnic or political minorities.

230.   TIRUCHELVAN, Neelan.   "Ethnicity and Resource Allocation." *From Independence to Statehood - Managing Ethnic Conflict in Five African and Asian States.* Eds. R. S. Goldmann and A. J. Wilson.   London: Frances Pinter (Publishers), 1984, pp. 185-95.
Examines the interaction between ethnic rights and economic development.   Suggests that in a plural society with limited resources, access to higher education, employment and land were indices of group advancement.   In this context the principles of allocating benefits of development were drawn into interethnic conflict and confrontation.   States that the role of perception, the competing conceptions of justice and relative deprivation, as articulated by an "achieving minority" and an ethnic majority, was critical.   These often historically-derived perceptions shaped and defined the parameters of competition, the patterns of political patronage, the process of representative democracy, and had specific implication for interethnic relations.   Concludes that resolution of these conflicts depended upon the creation of techniques for political bargaining and the institutionalization of forums for direct negotiation.

231.   VAN DEN BERGHE, Pierre L.   "Protection of Ethnic Minorities: A Critical Appraisal." *Protection of Ethnic Minorities: Comparative Perspectives.*   Ed. Robert G. Wirsing.   New York: Pergamon Press, 1981, pp. 343-56.
Argues that state-ethnic relations, and the role minority protection played in these relations, could only be understood in the broad context of means and relations of production, and of relations of power.   Since the United Nations was in fact an organization of states, the same rule applied at the international level.   Characterizes some of the main types of ethnic policy, including   nonrecognition   of   ethnicity,   assimilation, consociation,   imperialism   and   colonialism,   slavery   and genocide.   Objects to policies of affirmative action because of their paternalistic ideology and their effect of reinforcing and perpetuating group inequalities.   Protectionism was a reformist philosophy and would not end systems of ethnic and racial exploitation and oppression.   For large groups with a viable territorial base, national self-determination was a realistic option.   Recommends policies of "benign neglect" for small and/or dispersed groups.

232.   WATERMAN, Stanley. "Partition - A Problem in Political
       Geography." *Political Geography: Recent Advances and
       Future Directions.* Eds. Peter Taylor and John House.
       London: Croom Helm; New York: Barnes and Noble,
       1984, pp. 98-116.
Territorial partitioning was a solution for division when some
other means for accommodating cultural discord did not suffice,
such as the granting of autonomy, provincial or cantonal status,
or incorporation. The specific causes and effects were local, but
external forces also operated. Territorial partitioning appeared
as a process more prevalent in non-Socialist states and in the
Third World than in the Soviet bloc. To achieve understanding
of the process, the gap must be closed between abilities to
develop theories of society and international relations on the
one hand, and to develop appropriate methodologies for the
study of specific case studies, on the other.

233.   WEINER, Myron. "The Pursuit of Ethnic Equality through
       Preferential Policies: A Comparative Public Policy
       Perspective." *From Independence to Statehood - Managing
       Ethnic Conflict in Five African and Asian States.* Eds. R.
       S. Goldmann and A. J. Wilson. London: Frances Pinter
       (Publishers), 1984, pp. 63-81.
Examines the processes and consequences of policies intended
to reduce ethnic differences through preferential treatment of a
minority group.   Questions why these policies were controversial. Defines ethnicity as individuals and groups characteriz-
ing themselves on the basis of language, race, religion, place of
origin, shared culture, values, and/or history.   Suggests three
bases for ethnic equality: equality of opportunity, equality of
results, and equality of treatment. Compares the use and results
of preferential policies in the United States and India.   Uses
"political logic" to describe the creation of "political space."
Outlines eight elements of the "political logic" of preferential
policies: group preferences, types of preferences, mobilization,
backlash, institutional opposition, intragroup conflict, and social markings. Discusses the differences in the context of policy
process, of ethnic equality versus other forms of equality, especially class equality. Suggests three questions which must be
posed before a state pursued a course of preferential policies.
Was the kind of society produced by a system of ethnic preferences more just than a society that might be produced by other
kinds of policies intended to reduce ethnic differences? If a
policy of ethnic preferences occurred, was it politically possible

to place limits on who received preferences and what kind? If preferential policies were adopted, how, if at all, could they be terminated? Suggests that no democratic political system could tolerate a social order which was based on ethnic lines in education, income and occupational fields, but questions if preferential policies were the most suitable means to bridge these lines.

234. WHITAKER, Benjamin. "Minority Rights and Self-Determination." *Human Rights and American Foreign Policy.* Eds. Donald P. Kommers and Gilburt D. Loesher. Notre Dame: University of Indiana Press, 1979, pp. 63-76.

Asserts that reconciling the conflicting interests of majorities and minorities was an endemic and inescapable problem in society. Although the United Nations had been confronted with minority problems since 1947, it had been unable to agree upon any definition of the term "minority," let alone the principles that should govern minority rights. Argues that to view minority rights simply in terms of individual rights was too legalistic when for practical reasons rights were often inevitably determined for and by groups. The decision whether to integrate or assimilate must be one for the individual, but the availability of real choices was a prerequisite for any such choice. Outlines the practical problems involved in the application of secession, autonomy, and positive rights. Recommends establishing human rights machinery in the United Nations for the protection of minority rights.

235. WIRSING, Robert G., ed. *Protection of Ethnic Minorities: Comparative Perspectives.* New York: Pergamon Press, 1981.

The contributors assert that the protection of minorities had assumed a new urgency because of a widespread resurgence of ethnic conflict, sometimes tied to the concept of self-determination. Twelve papers explore the role of ethnic tensions within a variety of states or world regions, principally from the perspective of management of the tensions in order to prevent secessionist threats, although for some situations various other forms of autonomy were sought.

Separatism and Secession

236. BERAN, Harry. "A Liberal Theory of Secession." *Political Studies*, XXXII (1984), 21-31.
Considers separatism a major contemporary sociopolitical problem and a basic but neglected problem for political philosophy. Demonstrates its theoretical importance by developing a liberal normative secession theory. Liberalism allegedly required that secession be permitted if a territorially concentrated group desired it, and was morally and practically possible. Argues that the permissive principle of secession was theoretically or practically acceptable, but specifies some of the conditions which might render secession unviable.

237. BUCHHEIT, Lee. *Secession: The Legitimacy of Self-Determination.* New Haven, CT: Yale University Press, 1978.
Focuses on secessionist movements within independent states and traces the impact of their claims to self-determination at the international level, particularly under international law. Ascribes the rise of the principle of self-determination to the effects of "involuntary political association." Suggests that the doctrine's "lethal weakness" was its assumption that "nations" constituted self-evident political units desiring self-government. The use of self-determination, after World War II, within the colonial context, eventually led to the formulation of its application to "peoples." Believes that this terminological development had "incendiary" implications. Examines the "right" to secede from the perspective of natural and positive law. Examines several case studies: the Congo, the Kurds, Biafra, Somali-Kenya/Ethiopia, the Nagas and Bangladesh. Maintains that (1) secessionist activity was an irrepressible feature of contemporary international life; (2) many of the movements relied on the doctrine of self-determination for legal justification; (3) international consensus was lacking on the status of secession or its legitimacy; (4) the latter thus hampered effective action by the international community to prevent unwarranted third party intervention in such conflicts; and (5) unrestrained intervention involved the inherent danger of escalation and major power bloc confrontation.

238. BURGHARDT, Andrew F. "Canada and Secession: Some Consequences of Separatism." *Readings in Canadian*

Geography. Ed. Robert M. Irving. Third edition. Toronto: Holt, Rinehart and Winston, 1978, pp. 10-6.

Notes that every vital nationalism required a territorial base in which to anchor nationalist activity. Questions whether Québec had a right to self-determination that included secession from Canada. Examines the Austro-Hungarian parallel problem with its solution in the 1867 Compromise agreement, which, however, had failed to solve the problems of the Hapsburg Monarchy, intensified old controversies, and added a few new ones. Concludes from that example that associated states were likely to be unsuccessful. Examines Canada in terms of territorial and economic unity. Asserts that because of historic and physical factors, Canada had been settled along an east-west corridor, and that, with the exception of the Atlantic Provinces, no province could secede from Confederation short of destroying that corridor, without which Canada could not survive.

239. DALE, Edmund H. "The State-Idea: Missing Prop of the West Indies Federation." *Scottish Geographical Magazine,* LXXVIII (1962), 166-76.

Traces how the Federation of the West Indies came into being and demonstrates how the lack of a shared "state-idea" led to the collapse of the union.

240. ENLOE, Cynthia H. "Central Government's Strategies for Coping with Separatist Movements." *Collected Seminar Papers on The Politics of Separatism, no. 19.* London: University of London, Institute of Commonwealth Studies, 1979, pp. 79-84.

Cites examples of the paradox that, although separatism appeared to be more common and widespread than before, it was less successful now than it had been in the last two centuries, with Bangladesh the sole successful exception. Discusses this paradox in order to clarify some of the "analytical fuzziness" surrounding the analysis of "separatism," and to redirect attention to the impressive powers a state apparatus wielded. Explains that separatist hopes were being nourished by ethnic cohesion, density of population and resources, atrophied institutions with the potential for servicing the dissident community, and visible patterns of policy weakness, which undermined the central government's authority. Considers the conditions encouraging separatism as not being the same as those which ensured the creation of new sovereign states.

241. HOROWITZ, Donald L.   "Patterns of Ethnic Separatism."
      Comparative Studies in Society and History, XXIII (1981),
      1965-95.
      Believes that, although the ideology of self-determination and
      utilitarian theories of a "balance of advantages" might help ex-
      plain a people's inducements to choose separatism, these models
      did not identify patterns of separatism. Argues that in order to
      explain variations in the behavior of potential secessionist
      groups, variables across space rather than variables across time
      had to be first considered. Establishes models among the vari-
      eties of contemporary ethnic separatisms by distinguishing be-
      tween movements in relatively advanced and in backward
      regions, and between those based on either élite or mass dis-
      content. Defines the political claims, precipitants, calculations,
      timing and frequency of secessionist movements in differing
      group and regional positions in post-colonial situations.

242. JACOBS, Jane. *The Question of Separatism: Quebec and the
      Struggle over Sovereignty.* New York: Random House,
      1980.
      Considers the rationality of the Quebec debate impaired by the
      nationalist emotions of the separatists and their pro-Canadian
      opponents.   Compares Quebec separatism with Norway's
      secession from Sweden in 1905. Confidence and pride created
      by economic successes, reinforced by cultural attainments, had
      served to ignite Norway's independence movement, whereas
      Canadian leaders supported regressive economic colonialism.
      Urges Anglophones to accept French Quebec's theory of
      "duality," *i.e.*, the recognition that Canada consisted of two
      equal founding peoples, in order to forestall Quebec's secession.
      Fears, however, that combining the duality of English and
      French Canada with the Confederation scheme involving ten
      provinces presented an inherently insoluble situation.

243. JOURNAL OF CONTEMPORARY HISTORY, VI, 1 (1971).
      Special theme issue on "nationalism and separatism" consider-
      ing a variety of sub-state regional identities, the accom-
      modations within their respective states, and, for some, the
      threat they represented to their "host" states because of
      separatist desires and actions.

244. KAMANU, Onyeonoro.   "Secession and the Right of Self-
      Determination: An OAU Dilemma." *Journal of Modern
      African Studies*, XII (1974), 355-76.

Points out that after gaining independence, African states had agreed to accept the European boundary delineation as a guiding principle in their relations. This principle had been extended to include secessionist claims by domestic groups, whereby all such claims were to be set aside. Argues that self-determination must not be divorced from considerations of human rights and the concerns of minorities. Claims that the OAU failed to deal realistically with secessionist conflicts. Its "benign neglect" policy was an inadequate response to the explosive nature of such conflicts and the potential involvement of foreign powers.

245. MCCORD, A. and W. McCORD. "Ethnic Autonomy: A Socio-Historical Synthesis." *Ethnic Autonomy - Comparative Dynamics.* Ed. Raymond L. Hall. New York: Pergamon Press, 1979, pp. 426-36.
The authors identify a 20th-century paradox: as the world became more unitary, varied lines of commitment were being drawn based on differences in power, religion, language or race. Assert that the subjective variable of separatism was related to its mythical base. Objective factors affecting separatist movements included differential access to power, language, religion, economic divisions, culture and geography.

246. SAGARIN, Edward and James MONEYMAKER. "Language and Nationalist, Separatist, and Secessionist Movements." *Ethnic Autonomy - Comparative Dynamics.* Ed. Raymond H. Hall. New York: Pergamon Press, 1979, pp. 18-45.
The authors identify language as a major factor, and often a major issue of contention between conflictual groups. Language offered a symbol and a mechanism for the homogenization of a people, and for distinguishing such a people from others around them. Outline territorial and socioeconomic factors which influenced linguistic divisions and survival. The territorial integrity of a people identifying with one another was one of the correlates of secessionism. A linguistically-dispersed group, no matter how strong its other correlates of ethnic and national identity, was unlikely to aim at separatism. Propose bilingualism as a useful defusing of secessionism.

247. SHIELS, Frederick L. "Introduction." *Ethnic Separatism and World Politics.* Ed. Frederick L. Shiels. Lanham, MD: University Press of America, 1984, pp. 1-15.

Analyzes the nature of separatism and the transnational and foreign policy dimensions of this type of struggle, such as the unsuccessful 1967-70 Ibo-led Nigerian secession movement; the successful Bengali independence movement; the Québécois separatist movement in Canada, the Basques in Spain; and the several Yugoslav nationalist entities seeking revision of Yugoslavia's political order. Emphasizes four aspects of the case studies: (1) to address the question of how the separatist group operated in the internal or national political environment; (2) to dissect the external environment of foreign policy; (3) to investigate various action alternatives for separatist ethnics and status quo states; and (4) to identify thresholds between autonomy bids and secession attempts. Maintains that a federal system would be more flexible if confronted with an overt challenge.

248. SMITH, A. D.   "Nationalism, Ethnic Separatism, and the Intelligentsia." *National Separatism.*   Ed. Colin H. Williams.   Cardiff: University of Wales Press, 1982, pp. 17-41.
Claims that separatism represented the purest and simplest form of nationalism. Examines recent theories of ethnic separatism and nationalism and argues that they assumed too close a link between nationalism and economic development which failed to explain the peculiar character, differing intensities, and specific directions of given nationalist movements. Locates the social background of ethnic movements in the growth of modern rational-legal bureaucracies. Contends that the new strata of secular intelligentsias sought a new rationale for themselves and their community through their ethnic culture and history. The new ethnic intelligentsia consciousness became politicized as the result of ethnic competition for urban bureaucratic positions. Links the rise of autonomist and separatist forms of nationalism to periods of economic contraction and the concomitant restraint in bureaucratic mobility. Considers bureaucratic insensitivity by government élites and ethnic majorities the decisive factors tending toward separatism. Attributes the relative lack of separatist success to an unfavorable international climate; considers the support of a neighboring world power as being essential for success.

249. SMITH, A. D.   "Towards a Theory of Ethnic Separatism." *Ethnic and Racial Studies,* II (1979), 21-37.

Focuses on ethnic separatism as an important subcategory of nationalisms. Outlines recent theories of ethnic resurgence. Examines differential development, language and separatism, history and ethnicity, the rise of scientific bureaucracies and secular education, and the relationship between ethnic policies and separatism. Considers substantial politicization of the ethnic community as an essential prerequisite for nationhood. Discerns a pattern of "event-sequences" leading to separatism: the introduction of a scientific and centralized bureaucracy and the growth of rationalist critical education which undermined the traditional religious institutions; a new historical understanding (arising out of the first stage) that formed the basis for ethnic political claims; and governmental policies that determined the specific direction of political action.

250. STEINER, Jürg. "Decision Modes toward Separatist Movements: Some Conceptual and Theoretical Considerations." *New Nationalisms of the Developed West.* Eds. Edward A. Tiryakian and Ronald Rogowski. Boston: Allen and Unwin, 1985, pp. 147-56.
Presents a conceptual framework classifying the decision modes regarding separatist movements available to political authorities. Considers structural explanations of separatism as being useful on scholarly grounds, but they conveyed very little to political authorities concerning how to deal with a separatist movement. Describes four decision modes with which state authorities could confront a separatist movement: (1) a majority vote; (2) an amicable agreement; (3) repressing demands; or (4) seeking a decision by a third party. Applies the proposed conceptualization to the Swiss Jura case.

251. STERLING, Richard W. "Ethnic Separatism in the International System." *Ethnic Autonomy - Comparative Dynamics.* Ed. Raymond L. Hall. New York: Pergamon Press, 1979, pp. 413-25.
Examines separatism as a phenomenon of the world system. Explores the relationship between nationalism and separatism. Considers 19th-century Western democratic-nationalisms as majority nationalism that replaced the old barrier between élite and mass with a new barrier between ethnic majorities and minorities. Outlines several strategies available to minorities to maximize their power against the national majority: internal alliances, internal development, external alliances, and secession.

252. WHEBELL, C. F. J. "A Model of Territorial Separatism."
      Proceedings of the Association of American Geographers, V
      (1973), 295-8.
      Considers territorial separatism a process whereby territorially-
      defined formal and informal organizations attempted to achieve
      increased autonomy. The process could be observed at all
      territorial scales, and included economic and cultural compo-
      nents. Identifies five basic dimensions of territorial separatism:
      territory, scope, rationale, institutionalization and style. Pre-
      sents a schematic territorial separatism process model.

253. WOOD, John R. "Secession: A Comparative Analytic Frame-
      work." *Canadian Journal of Political Science*, XIV (1981),
      107-34.
      Reviews a wide range of social science concepts and pre-theories
      in order to establish a comparative analytical framework of
      secession. Takes a process-oriented approach based on a re-
      versal of Hass' concept of political integration. Examines the
      evolution of secessionist attempts in five sections: (1) the
      preconditions of secession; (2) the rise of secessionist move-
      ments; (3) the response of central governments; (4) the direct
      precipitants of secession; and (5) the resolution of secessionist
      crises by armed conflict. Evaluates the factors influencing the
      many results in light of the experience of failed, successful or
      current secession attempts. Advocates the development of
      specific types of comparative research on secessionism.

PART IV

WORLD REGIONAL PERSPECTIVES AND STATE CASE STUDIES

Africa

254. ADAM, Hussein M. "Language, National Consciousness and Identity - The Somali Experience." *Nationalism and Self-Determination in the Horn of Africa.* Ed. I. M. Lewis. London: Ithaca Press, 1983, pp. 31-42.

Surveys the role of the Somali language in the formulation of Somali identity and self-determination. Considers language, along with Islam, as the basis of Somali national consciousness, and since 1972 the use of written Somali as being crucial for strengthening Somali national identity and integration. Reviews Somali historical development, oral tradition and the problems involved in deciding upon the proper form for Somali script. The evolution was allegedly a continuing process that challenged the language to develop a suitable vocabulary and style to suit all aspects of life. Provides examples of adaptation, such as policies propagating written Somali through literacy campaigns, translations of folklore, school expansions, and slogans emphasizing pride in the national mother tongue. Explains that rapid communications had reduced the gap between state and public (Somali had replaced English and Italian as the language of administration) to ensure increased public participation in politics and the general raising of the Somali people's cultural, technical and political awareness. Exemplifies Somali, an African polity relying extensively on its indigenous linguistic resources, as a model for the Horn of Africa and Africa as a whole.

255.   ADEJUYIGBE, Omolade.   "Ethnic Pluralism and Political
       Stability of Nigeria." *Cultural Discord in the Modern
       World.*   Eds. L. J.   Evenden and F. F. Cunningham.
       Vancouver: Tantalus Research Ltd., 1973, pp. 83-110.
       Multinational states often solved the problem of reconciling the
       aspirations of "ethnic nations" in order to avoid separation or
       secession through federation.   In Nigeria's case the initial fed-
       eral structure had proven inadequate, and in the Biafran in-
       stance, autonomy was sought, or secession threatened, and
       actually attempted.   Contends that every "ethnic nation" in
       Nigeria might have to gain constitutional recognition to manage
       its own affairs and to participate effectively in national govern-
       mental decision-making.   This might relieve the pressures to
       seek self-determination by secession.

256.   BADAL, R. K.   "The Rise and Fall of Separatism in Southern
       Sudan." *The Politics of Separatism.   Collected Working
       Papers, no. 19.*   London: University of London, Institute
       of Commonwealth Studies, 1976, pp. 85-93.
       Examines the nature and character of the most articulate ele-
       ments of Southern Sudanese separatism as a reflection of
       North-South conflict in the Sudan.   Reviews the foundations
       of Southern separatism, noting the vast complexity of ethnic,
       cultural, and especially linguistic, compositions, social dis-
       tinctions and the importance of history.   Identifies three foci of
       vacillations in the goals of Southern separatists: (1) the
       separatist movement's leadership; (2) the amount of mass sup-
       port it could muster; (3) accidental factors such as dramatic
       events – war or revolution – that might ease secession or make
       compromise with the central government possible.   Discusses
       these variables in terms of the Southern movement's changing
       circumstances.   Evaluates the Addis Ababa Agreement of
       March 1972, concluded between the Sudan government and
       Southern leaders in terms of long-term resolution of the conflict.
       Concludes that success depended upon continued cooperation
       between northerners and the small but growing southern edu-
       cated class.

257.   BAXTER, Paul.   "The Problems of Oromo or the Problem for
       the Oromo." *Nationalism and Self-Determination in the
       Horn of Africa.*   Ed. I. M. Lewis.   London: Ithaca Press,
       1983, 129-50.
       Reviews the position of Ethiopia's Oromo, a minority compris-
       ing one-third to one-half of the state's population.   Examines

the Amhara minority's political and cultural dominance, which had given Ethiopia the appearance of possessing a unitary culture. Confirms the dominance of centralist policies, notwithstanding revolutionary slogans and pretense that "No Nationality Will Dominate Another." Depicts Ethiopian history largely as an Amhara-Oromo struggle. Notes the similarities and differences in the societal and political organization of the two tribes, discovering possibilities for unity in their common origins, shared customs and language. Examines the current Amhara policy of "civilizing" or "Amharizing" the Oromo, the role of the *Naftaanya*, or armed settlers in inter-national relations, the Oromo perception of the Amhara, the history of local resistance and rebellion, as well as the Oromo lingual awakening centered in Arussi province. Assesses Oromo nationalism since the revolution, noting that the movement's strong base in terms of growing national consciousness, large numbers, favorable geographical position and natural resources had made the Oromo indispensable to Ethiopia, and subject to official oppression. Believes the Oromo internal problem to have been exacerbated by the inertia of the OAU and by great power interests. Doubts the possibility of peaceful devolution.

258. BOATENG, E. A. *A Political Geography of Africa.* Cambridge (England): Cambridge University Press, 1978.
Traces colonial territorial expansion into Africa and examines salient political and socioeconomic problems and issues facing Africa's various regions and states in their search for political stability and economic viability. Advocates further self-determination within that frame, involving at least partial regional economic independence and, more especially, inter-state and inter-regional cooperation along the lines advocated by the OAU and the Eocnomic Commission for Africa.

259. BREYTENBACH, W. J. *Self-Determination in African Politics.* Pretoria: African Institute of South Africa, 1978.
Considers self-determination an essentially Western concept rooted in the nationalist and liberal traditions. Distinguishes between territorial and ethnolinguistic self-determination, and claims that in Third World countries the territorial principle had superseded the latter. All demands for ethnolinguistic separation and secession had been brutally suppressed owing to the territorial bias of African leaders. South African ethnonational homelands were being offered autonomy and even sovereignty if they wished to exercise either option, but were denied inter·

national recognition and acceptance because their existence allegedly violated the territorial principle.

260.   CAPLAN, Gerald L. "Barotseland: The Secessionist Challenge to Zambia." *The Journal of Modern African Studies*, VI (1968), 343-60.
Within the Barotse Province of Zambia the Lozi ruling class had reportedly demanded secession from the colonial and post-colonial state. In 1880, the Lozi king had signed the Lochner concession that placed his country under the "protection" of the British South Africa Company. The colonial administration regarded the territory as part of Northern Rhodesia. The region had obtained special status because of various pressures, some of which could have led to secession. Great Britain had told the people it could not afford to support Barotseland financially if it were divorced from Northern Rhodesia. Claims that now it was impossible to conceive of Barotseland as an entity separated from Rhodesia. Thanks to British colonial policy, the territory became "a backward, isolated, wholly undeveloped, and essentially insignificant labour reserve, comprising only one-sixth of the land mass and containing less than one-tenth of the population of Zambia." Reports secessionist rhetoric still occuring, but factors supporting a secessionist move did not exist.

261.   COLEMAN, James S. "Tradition and Nationalism in Tropical Africa." *New States in the Modern World*. Ed. Martin Kilson. Cambridge: Harvard University Press, 1975, pp. 3-36.
Examines the relationship between tradition and nationalism in Africa, especially how tradition had affected nationalism in the preindependence period. The genesis and evolution of African nationalism had been significantly affected by, and in turn had affected at least three different aspects of African tradition: traditional ethnic groupings, traditional political élites, and traditional political cultures. Territory enjoyed primacy over traditional ethnic groupings in the formation of the nation because of the opportunities it provided for modernizing élites, the integrity the artificial boundaries acquired during the colonial period, and the sheer practicalities of seeking independence within existing power units. Identifies three particularly significant variables in determining the role of ethnicity in the development of territorial nationalism: the ecology and political structure of traditional societies; the nature of colonial policies regarding traditional ethnic groupings; and the ethnic pattern

of the territory. Contends that, although the relationship between traditional élites and modernizing nationalists had tended to be marked by distrust and opposition, there had been phases and situations in the development of territorial nationalism where they had made common cause. Hypothesizes that variations in nationalistic assertiveness among ethnic groups in many cases demonstrated the differences in the political cultures of the ethnic groups concerned, especially the traditional status mobility and the scale and degree of hierarchism of the traditional political systems. Considers African territorial nationalisms as being characteristically eclectic, populist, and futurist; these commonalities could be explained by two generic traits of traditional African societies: egalitarianism and political primacy.

262. DENG, William and Joseph ODUHO. *The Problem of the Southern Sudan.* London: Oxford University Press, 1963.
The authors demonstrate the reason why the Southern Sudanese required self-determination to ensure the survival of the indigenous Africans in the Southern Sudan. Outline the area, geography, population and ethnic composition of the North and South Sudan. Explain the history leading to self-government, with reference to the Southern Administration and the politics in the Sudan and the South. Argue that as the result of North-Arab domination over the South, between independence (1953) and 1963, the Sudanese government had been aiming at destroying the African Negroid personality in the Sudan and to replace it with an Arabicized and Islamicized South. Assert that the result of government policies had been administrative, educational, economic, social and religious domination of the South by the North.

263. DOORNBOS, Marin R. "Protest Movements in Western Uganda: Some Parallels and Contrasts." *Ethnic Autonomy - Comparative Dynamics.* Ed. Raymond L. Hall. New York: Pergamon Press, 1979, pp. 263-82.
The Kumanyana movement in Ankole and the Rwenzururu movement in Toro were rooted in subordinate populations which reacted against established orders too inflexible to accommodate participation by new political groups. However, structural factors had caused them to develop along quite different lines. In Ankole, mechanisms designed to widen popular participation in decision-making had accommodated demands to a substantial degree, and were thus conducive to

political integration; in Toro, however, they were incapable of coping with the challenges they had fostered and eventually broke down.

264. DUGARD, John. *The South West Africa/Namibia Dispute.* Berkeley: University of California Press, 1973.

Analyzes the dispute over the international status of South West Africa (Namibia) through the decisions of the International Court of Justice, resolution and debates of the General Assembly and the Security Council, reports of the U.N. Committees, political addresses and academic commentary. Describes the territory and its people. Discusses the major aspects of the disputes including the approach taken under the League of Nations and the mandate under the United Nations system until South Africa refused to submit reports. Comments on political developments during the early 1960s, *e.g.*, Resolution 1514 and the creation of SWAPO and SWANU. Discusses the 1971 International Court of Justice Namibia Decision. Provides an extensive bibliography on the South West Africa (Namibia) dispute.

265. ELAIGWU, J. Isawa and Victor A. OLORUNSOLA. "Federalism and the Politics of Compromise." *State Versus Ethnic Claims: African Policy Dilemmas.* Eds. Donald Rothchild and Victor A. Olorunsola. Boulder, CO: Westview Press, 1983, pp. 281-303.

The authors consider the dilemma of ethnic self-determination and state coherence by examining the problems of federal balance in Nigeria. The 1966 military coup had tilted the delicate balance between North and South, concentrating political and economic power in the hands of Southern leaders. This imbalance had created problems for the federal system, which the 1979 Constitution tried to rectify. Maintains that attempts to defuse the North-South conflict through the creation of a new state system were hampered by demands for additional states. In addition to the imbalances in the federal structure, consider the problem of balancing state autonomy with federal control. Old fears and suspicions, stemming from the North-South dichotomy, ethnoregional political parties, minority-majority ethnic group cleavages, differential education, revenue allocation, and generational conflicts echoed throughout the new federal structure. Emphasize that some issues defied balancing; too much pressure to equalize them might destroy the system.

266. ELEASY, Uma O. "The Constitutional Structure and Development in Nigeria." *From Independence to Statehood - Managing Ethnic Conflict in Five African and Asian States.* Eds. R. S. Goldmann and A. J. Wilson. London: Frances Pinter (Publishers), 1984, pp. 17-30.

Regards ethnic tension as the greatest source of conflict in Nigeria. This conflict had caused war, but the state had remained united, at least for now. Identifies the fear of domination by one region as Nigeria's major problem. The fundamental objective and directing principles of the Nigerian constitutional structure and political development thus were equal treatment, national integration and state loyalty. These principles were reflected in the federal character of Nigeria. The basis of this promotion of national unity, combined with national loyalty, was the fundamental right of non-discriminatory treatment. Discusses specific aspects of the political system, such as the executive, political parties, the role of the armed forces and voting behavior with respect to these overarching themes. Concludes that the search for lower tension was a continuous process which demanded patience. Considers the acceptance of the idea of Nigeria's "federal character" as an encouraging step.

267. ERLICH, Haggai. "The Eritrean Autonomy 1952-1962: Its Failure and Its Contribution to Further Escalation." *Models of Autonomy.* Ed. Yoram Dinstein. New Brunswick, NJ: Transaction Books, 1981, pp. 171-82.

Examines the history of Eritrean autonomy. Regards the 1952-62 Eritrean autonomy as essentially fictitious, because absolutist Ethiopia would not tolerate an autonomous entity within its territory. The liquidation of the symbols of Eritrean autonomy coincided with the rise of Eritrean nationalism. The 1974 revolution in Ethiopia revitalized the idea of an autonomous solution in Eritrea, but because the *Derg* refused to operate through existing Eritrean organizations, it had failed to reach a compromise with Eritrean nationalists.

268. ETHIOPAWI. "The Eritrean-Ethiopian Conflict." *Ethnic Conflict and International Relations.* Eds. A. Suhrke and L. Noble. New York: Praeger, 1977, pp. 127-45.

Examines ethnic identification and linkages as the chief factors responsible for the development and escalation of the conflict between Eritrean separatists and Ethiopian government; explains how and why the conflict had become "internationalized." Characterizes Eritrea as a microcosm of Ethiopia's complex ethnic composition, its identity shaped by the region's experience vis-à-vis the central government. Examines these four external influences on Eritrean self-identification: (1) different colonial experiences; (2) the unpopular 1950 United Nations decision to return Eritrea to Ethiopia; (3) the hostile response of the Arab states to unification; and (4) Soviet support of and activities in Ethiopia, combined with the central government's harsh treatment of Eritrea.

269.   FRAENKEL, Peter.   *The Namibians of South West Africa.* London: Minority Rights Group, Report No. 19, 1974.
Contends that the dispute over Namibia, formerly the trust territory of South West Africa, provided the most straightforward contemporary challenge to international law.   The Treaty of Versailles had given the British Crown a mandate to steer the survivors of the former German colony to eventual self-determination, and the mandate was vested in South Africa for implementation.   The League of Nations had criticized the subsequent conduct of South African rule, and the U.N. Security Council and the International Court of Justice considered the occupation of Namibia illegal.   Maldistribution of economic resources   and   political   power   meant   that   "separate development" was a myth.   Namibia's black and white economies were totally dependent on each other.   Considers positive action by the British government, including disinvestment, as influential in pressing the South Africans into peaceful withdrawal.

270.   FRANCK, Thomas M.   "The Stealing of the Sahara." *American Journal of International Law*, LXX (1976), 694-721.
Contends that the United Nations had mishandled disposition of the Sahara case, namely, the settlement of the issue in favor of Morocco's claim of historic title and the denial of self-determination to the Sahrawi people.   By successfully using force to control the Western Sahara without the consent of its people, Morocco and Mauritania had strengthened the tendency of Third World states to pursue their national interest by military means rather than through law and diplomacy. Furthermore, they had frustrated the international community's insistence on respect for established boundaries.   Reviews the events involved in the unsuccessful U.N. effort to secure the Sahrawis' right to self-determination, delineating the various positions adopted by Spain, Morocco and Mauritania.   Ana-

lyzes the "wholly ineffectual" U.N. reaction and opposition to the Moroccan government's announcement of the mobilization of 350,000 "unarmed civilians," Spain's "sale" of the Sahara, and the subsequent "mopping up" exercises, as Mauritanian and Moroccan troops dispersed the remaining forces of the Algerian-supported Sahrawi liberation movement POLISARIO.

271. GIFFORD, Prosser and William Roger LOUIS, eds. *The Transfer of Power in Africa: Decolonization 1940-1960.* New Haven, CT: Yale University Press, 1982.
The volume contains nineteen chapters by various authors, including several background papers, historical case studies, chapters of a theoretical nature, as well as two historiographical essays designed for use as reference tools and bibliographic supplements.

272. GILKES, Patrick. "Centralism and the Ethiopian PMAC." *Nationalism and Self-Determination in the Horn of Africa.* Ed. I. M. Lewis. London: Ithaca Press, 1983, pp. 195-211.
Examines the positions and developments in the Ethiopian nationality issue, beginning with the lack of preparation and unity by the "vanguard of the revolution," the Provisional Military Administrative Council (PMAC) or Dergue, and by the major civilian leftist groups in 1974. Reviews the 1976 National Democratic Revolutionary Program and the official policy regarding regional autonomy and secession, especially on Eritrea. Links Ethiopian political positions to Stalinist and Leninist writings and to nationality models in Communist societies. Stresses the importance of "progressive" ideas in the formulation of positions on national issues. Believes that the PMAC had raised expectations of freedom without satisfying desires, and had frequently resorted to repression.

273. HARVEY, William B. and W. H. B. DEAN. "The Independence of Transkei - A Largely Constitutional Inquiry." *Journal of Modern African Studies*, XVI (1978), 189-220.
The authors argue that notwithstanding United Nations references to the "fictitious or sham independence" of Transkei and to its government as a "puppet authority," the rejection of Transkei's bid for membership in the international community must be explained and justified, if at all, on the basis of factors independent of the legal government structure and status of Transkei, the effectiveness of its control over its territory, or

even of its political and economic relations with South Africa, its former sovereign parent. In the face of Transkei's strong claim to self-determination, the negative international reaction could only be explained and justified by the desire to pressure South Africa to alter its internal racist policies.

274.   HEALY, Sally. "The Changing Idiom of Self-Determination in the Horn of Africa." *Nationalism and Self-Determination in the Horn of Africa.* Ed. I. M. Lewis. London: Ithaca Press, 1983, pp. 93-110.

Reviews the historical evolution of the meaning and concept of national self-determination, especially its relation to the Horn of Africa. Perceives three distinct self-determination phases: (1) Eastern European nationalism, expressed in the Versailles settlement of 1919-20; (2) post-1961 anti-colonial nationalism; and (3) the present nationalist wave. Emphasizes the importance of having had external powers recognizing self-determination cases in earlier periods, and stresses its absence in the post-colonial era, when movements had largely occurred within independent states. Illustrates the changing conceptions regarding the principle in the Horn, explaining the uniqueness of the region's self-determination problems. Recognizes a shift emphasizing cultural-national factors after 1945, to the statist approach of the 1960s. Considers the nature of Ethiopian, Somali, Eritrean, and Oromo definitions and notes their arguments for and against self-determination. Emphasizes the Marxist-Leninist influence in some of these instances, observing that linkage between self-determination and decolonization had meant that the question of "what is a nation" had been replaced by "what is a colony." Identifies obscurities remaining in the meaning of the principle of self-determination within independent states, and suggests that the criterion for permitting the right should be the measure of oppression within a state rather than ethnic or historical considerations.

275.   HELLER, J. A. "Independence or Colonial Determinism? The African Case." *International Affairs,* XXXXIV (1968), 691-700.

Argues that, like neocolonialism, decolonization involved a false sense of achievement or purpose insofar as it equated intention with purpose, clouded the issues which underlay economic and political development, and impeded the proper analysis of the limitations of the decolonization process. Examines the so-called "relic features" to determine the extent to which colonial determinism had not been mitigated by political autonomy. Outlines two geographic features, frontier and the location of capitals, in terms of the detrimental effect on economic development and national integration. Argues that the establishment of dual economics represented the political aspect of the colonial legacy finding a geographical expression. Explains that the departed colonials' determination of the economic geography of the African countries had led to aberrant development patterns, creating factors that countervailed self-determination. Suggests that size in itself was not a sufficient criterion of viability, but must also be considered with population and resource distribution. In this regard, the failure of the departing colonials to abolish the haphazard boundaries, thereby reconstituting Africa along lines more suitable to development, had caused Africa's compartmentalization, and the inability to eradicate the detrimental colonial legacy which would permit the creation of a new Africa.

276. JOHNSON, Willard R. "The Cameroon Federation: Laboratory for Pan-Africanism?" *New States in the Modern World.* Ed. Martin Kilson. Cambridge: Harvard University Press, 1975, pp.89-120.
Claims that the 1961 reunification experience of the former British and French colonies of Cameroon offered some valuable lessons for partisans of African unity. Considers the Cameroon political integration attempts to be on the whole successful despite disparities, which led to the emergence, in 1973, of the Unitary Republic of Cameroon. Maintains that the Cameroon experience demonstrated the possibility of a gradualist and functional approach to political unification, despite heterogeneity and social disintegration. The case highlighted the more troublesome aspects of any union of British and French legacies, especially in the economic and commercial spheres; unless offset by cross-cutting affiliations, these legacies in a unitary state might increase cultural and political competition rather than reduce it.

277. KNIGHT, David B. "Racism and Reaction: The Development of a Batswana 'raison d'être' for the Country." *Cultural Discord in the Modern World: Geographical Themes.* Eds. L. J. Evenden and F. F. Cunningham. Vancouver: Tantalus, 1974, pp.111-26.
Identifies the efforts by Botswana's political élites to formulate distinctive goals, as they sought and then achieved political

self-determination for their state. Demonstrates how the basic goals need not remain purely abstract, and how the élites had made their goals understandable and attainable for the populace by linking them to traditional societal values and behavior patterns. Contends that the basic goal was a vital sociopolitical union at the time of political independence. Notes the limiting impact geographical location has had on the goals, since Botswana to a large degree depended economically upon the Republic of South Africa.

278.   LAITIN, David. "The Ogaadeen Question and Changes in Somali Identity." *State versus Ethnic Claims: African Policy Dilemmas.* Eds. Donald Rothchild and Victor A. Olorunsola. Boulder, CO: Westview Press, 1983, pp. 331-49.

Provides a dialectical analysis of state coherence and national identity by examining the dynamics of multinational states, with Ethiopia in mind, and the dynamics of change in national identity, with the Somalis in mind. Argues that the OAU failed to solve the Ogaadeen problem because its charter favored the Ethiopian definition of the issue, and it lacked coercive authority and organizational expertise. Considers the thesis that the Ethiopian empire was on the verge of collapse. Finds that Ethiopia's Amharic center had the capacity and desire for ruthless and purposeful action. Believes that the Ogaadeen Somalis would remain a subject population to an increasingly coherent Ethiopian state. Examines the dynamics of Somali cultural identification and offers three examples of national redefinition: (1) that of Somalis seeing themselves as Arabs; (2) that of Oromos seeing themselves alternately as Oromos, as Somalis, and as Amharas; and (3) that of Somalis seeing themselves primarily in terms of clan affiliation.

279.   LEMARCHAND, Rene. "The Limits of Self-Determination: The Case of the Katanga Secession." *The American Political Science Review,* LVI (1962), 404-16.

Observes that in the Katanga secession, the United Nations had been in the paradoxical position of denying the right of self-determination explicitly recognized by its Charter. Suggests that this reflected the ambiguity of the concept of self-determination, which referred to the right of a people to determine its own political destiny. Outlines the following problems: (1) no legal criteria existed to determine which groups might legitimately claim this right; (2) no accepted universal standard had been developed to measure the freedom a group lacked that presumably must exist before the principle could be exercised; (3) no consensus existed regarding the feasibility of the principle itself; and (4) the concept could not be stated in terms applicable to any context, resulting in the fact that self-determination had been both a cohesive and centrifugal factor, dependent on the circumstances. Examines two underlying factors of disunity as they bore on the exercise of self-determination: (1) differences in economic development and how they influenced the political options of the Katanga leaders; and (2) disparities in the numerical importance and economic status of the settler populations. Cites important economic and political limitations to the right to self-determination that would depend on the context and circumstances of the question.

280. LEWIS, I. M., ed. *Nationalism and Self-Determination in the Horn of Africa.* London: Ithaca Press, 1983.
The contributors explore the ambiguous relation between state and nation. The eleven essays examine the competing movements for autonomy and centralization and the various elements of linguistic and structural division. Examine implications within regional as well as Pan-African and international contexts.

281. MAYALL, James. "Self-Determination and the OAU." *Nationalism and Self-Determination in the Horn of Africa.* Ed. I. M. Lewis. London: Ithaca Press, 1983, pp. 77-92.
Examines and explains the apparent paradox of the OAU as an organization claiming to support self-determination of all African peoples, but which was committed to the existing state order by charter, convention, and the Cairo Resolution. Observes two trends: (1) the growing importance of national self-determination as the principle of international legitimacy, more recently linked with decolonization; and (2) the inability of African leaders to agree on integration or boundary alterations which had played a central role in the formulation of the Pan-African ideology. This had caused the "domesticization" of the movement and the creation of an institutional framework based on state supremacy. Discusses the impact of this result on the OAU's problematic policy toward South Africa.

282. MERCER, John. *The Sahrawis of Western Sahara.* London: Minority Rights Group, Report No. 40, 1979.

A people with a sense of their own distinctiveness, the Sahrawis had come into being over the past century under Spanish colonialism. Outlines the internal and external problems of Morocco and Mauritania which had influenced their decision to claim the Western Sahara. The United Nations had denied in 1975 that either country had demonstrated past sovereignty over the Western Sahara, and recommended that the Sahrawis be allowed self-determination. The Tripartite Agreement had divided the "decolonized" territory between Morocco and Mauritania, but underestimated the power of the Sahrawis to resist foreign control. The resulting war had weakened both Mauritania and Morocco, and brought France and Algeria into the conflict. The U.N. and OAU had been ineffective in asserting self-determination for the Sahrawis. By 1979, the SADR was leading a social revolution in Sahrawi territory, but Sahrawis in occupied territories and refugee camps were suffering from severe repression.

283. MERCER, John. *Spanish Sahara*. London: George Allen and Unwin, 1976.
Investigates the geology, landscape and history of the area in order to demonstrate two divided cultural streams: African and European. Analyzes Sahrawi nomadic society as well as the influence of Europe as the contexts for the conflict and attendant difficulties of independence development. Describes the sequence of internal political development and the organization of participants in the Spanish Sahara. Explains Sahrawi three-way fragmentation: (1) those preferring material culture and continued Spanish presence; (2) those demanding independence; and (3) those requesting association with Morocco. Analyzes the various claims by France, Morocco, Mauritania and Algeria. Believes that Mauritania had the most valid case based on traditional grounds. Observes that with the evolution of the POLISARIO as a genuine independence movement, as opposed to the Spanish-instigated PUNS, the Spanish options to make withdrawal from Africa as graceful as possible were being reduced.

284. MERON, Theodor and Anna Mamalakis PAPPAS. "The Eritrean Autonomy: A Case Study of a Failure." *Models of Autonomy*. Ed. Yoram Dinstein. New Brunswick, NJ: Transaction Books, 1981, pp. 183-213.
The authors claim that the Eritrean people had not exercised the principle of self-determination when the federal-autonomy

project was initially adopted and implemented, nor when it was dissolved. Although the wishes of the Eritrean people received much lip service, as were considerations of the peace and security of the region, the U.N. General Assembly was ultimately motivated by geopolitical considerations to choose a federal solution. Resolution 390(v) had not created a "real" federation, because Eritrea became a subordinate unit within Ethiopia. Consider the dissolution of the Federation by the Eritrean Assembly illegal without the consent of the General Assembly and the Eritrean people.

285. MOJEKWU, Christopher C. "Self-Determination: The African Perspective." *Self-Determination: National, Regional, and Global Dimensions.* Eds. Yonah Alexander and Robert A. Friedlander. Boulder, CO: Westview Press, 1980, pp. 221-39.
Identifies human rights as a basic concept prevalent in precolonial African society; but whereas 18th- and 19th-century European liberals had emphasized individual rights, concepts of the nation-state, ideas of sovereignty and impersonal authority structures, African societies had stressed communal rights, and grouped themselves into kinship communities governed through familial chiefs and elders with shared authority. Western European contacts had transformed African societies into replicas of Western nation-states. The United Nations' interpretation of self-determination had forced Africans to accept colonial boundaries. The incorporation of the principle of territorial integrity into the Charter of the Organization of African Unity had preserved Africa's traditional division based on foreign commercial interests. The United Nations principle, recently transformed into universal individual human rights, discriminated against the African concept of rights, and threatened to destroy the basis of African family structure and culture. Considers the slogan "Africa for the Africans" a myth.

286. MORRISON, G. *The Southern Sudan and Eritrea: Aspects of Wider African Problems.* Revised edition. London: Minority Rights Group, Report No. 5, 1973.
Reviews the internal ethnic conflicts in the Sudan and Eritrea, within the context of Africa, and internationally. Summarizes the geographic, ethnic and historical situation in the Sudan, emphasizing the events leading up to independence and their effect on north-south cooperation within the Sudanese state. Discusses the political situation in the years leading up to armed

conflict and then to peace, noting the importance of the role of safeguards for the south if unity was to be maintained. Similarly analyzes the situation in Eritrea, highlighting the opposing historical interpretations of the province as independent or as a natural part of Ethiopia. Considers the federation period and the radicalization of the separatist movement. Analyzes the roles of the USSR, the USA, China, Israel, Uganda, Congo-Kinshasa, and the host states.

287.   NIXON, Charles R. "Self-Determination: The Nigeria/Biafra Case." *World Politics*, XXIV (1972), 473-97.
        Questions whether or not the concept of self-determination could have any meaning in post-colonial Africa by examining the political aspects of the Biafran claim and the Nigerian government's challenge to that claim for self-determination. Suggests that the Biafran and Nigerian claims were both sound, the latter to the extent that it drew on a new conception of Nigeria that was "real" and required the defeat of Biafra. Explains that the emergence of this new conception of Nigeria fundamentally challenged how the Biafran issues were posed, thereby somewhat altering the Biafran claims. Mentions three problems arising from this: (1) the problem of a new context in which claims to self-determination may arise; (2) the problem of the multilateral character of such claims; and (3) the problem of international responsibility generated by such claims. Argues that the concept of self-determination must be understood not as a principle for unilateral implementation, but as a principle guiding the adjustment of competing claims for national recognition in the system of international order. Contends that the principle of self-determination generated international responsibility, because such claims succeeded or failed on the basis of international recognition. Sees a need for further exploration of the international community's responsibilities for a viable settlement and the need to recognize the variety of competing claims involved in the advocacy of self-determination.

288.   NNOLI, Okwudiba. "The Creation of States: Theoretical and Practical Problems." *Regional Development at the National Level.* Eds. Timothy M. Shaw and Yash Tandon. Lanham, MD: University Press of America, 1985, I, 67-94.
        Addresses two questions: (1) how was the popular movement for the creation of new states in Nigeria to be understood scientifically? (2) what should be the attitude of progressive forces

to these popular demands? Identifies two contradictory streams in the movement for the creation of states: (1) domination of the petty-bourgeois and comprador classes, which were unable to play a creative role in production but rather thrived on the exclusion of one another; and (3) the mass political line, embodying a genuine desire to surmount conflicts among communal groups as quickly as possible. Sees the tension between human rights and communal rights evident in the contradictory provisions of the Nigerian Constitution and Federation. Asserts that the movement for the creation of new states was not a national movement. Identifies nationalism as a historically specific movement associated with the rise of a national bourgeoisie. The movement for the creation of states in Nigeria was ethnic in character. Deems the resulting internal fragmentation antithetical to the progressive development of capitalism. Concludes that mass action in support of "ethnic liberation" could not be ignored, but must be transformed into a revolutionary attack on capitalism and imperialism.

289.   OYOVBARIE, Sam Egyte. "Structural Change and the Problems of National Cohesion." *From Independence to Statehood - Managing Ethnic Conflict in Five African and Asian States.* Eds. Robert S. Goldmann and A. J. Wilson. London: Frances Pinter (Publishers), 1984, pp. 1-16.

Examines the basis of recent changes in Nigeria in terms of their contributions and limitations to the enhancement of national cohesion. Considers national cohesion a more useful term to evaluate the direction of government policy than national integration; the latter reflected theory but not the practice of national development. Sees national integration as a contradiction in terms, because national development did not bridge economic and class interests. Reviews national cohesion in three ways: (1) not as an end in itself, but as conceptually valuable, as it related to building authority and community in Nigeria; (2) as a point of comparison between contemporary communal structures and precolonial and colonial origins; and (3) as a means for evaluating the structural designs of the Constitution of the Second Republic. Describes the three dominant structural characteristics of this state as the plurality of subcultures or communal groups, an élitist or class conscious political concept, recruitment and organization, and the existence of class-dominated political cleavages, which revolved around Nigeria's multiple subcultures. Reviews Nigerian constitutional history and the work and results of the Constitution Drafting Committee. Concludes that the 1979 Constitution was designed consciously to respond to problems generated by the complexity of the society and the factor of class interests by adopting liberal democracy as a "cushion" for the political structure. The Nigerian political system had thus adjusted to the structural imperatives.

290.   PANTER BRICK, S. K. "Biafra." *The Politics of Separatism. Collected Working Papers, no. 19.* London: University of London, Institute of Commonwealth Studies, 1976, pp. 31-6.

Discusses the events relating to the Biafran secession between July 1966 and May 1967. Enumerates Nigerian precedents for deciding on a separation policy. Cites three occasions when the "embryonic Federation" had been in danger of being rejected, emphasizing regional and electoral politics. Considers it more useful to label the events separation than secession, because the situation reflected a general break-up rather than the desertion of one part. Labels the period under discussion as one of negotiations to decide upon the logistics of separation, because most Nigerians had taken the break-up for granted. Concludes that "Gowan's coup," which had proclaimed a State of Emergency and issued a decree dividing Nigeria into twelve states, had resulted from the impatience with the negotiation process.

291.   POOL, David. "Eritrean Nationalism." *Nationalism and Self-Determination in the Horn of Africa.* Ed. I. M. Lewis. London: Ithaca Press, 1983, pp. 175-93.

Examines five processes in the evolution of Eritrean nationalism linked with the patterns of external domination and internal social and economic changes: (1) colonial Eritrea's transformation; (2) Eritrean nationalistic policies in the 1940s; (3) the establishment of the Eritrean Liberation Front (ELF); (4) the crisis that had brought about the formation of the Eritrean People's Liberation Front (EPLF); and (5) the consequences of this development. Identifies the uneven effects of the social and economic transformation begun by Italian colonial rule as the basis of Eritrean nationalism. Emphasizes the gulf separating those transformed and those untouched by the transition to precapitalistic forms of production rather than ethnic or religious differences as the cause of the split in the nationalist movement. Believes that despite differences in the programs and actions of the ELF and the ELPF, and notwithstanding

Soviet influence, neither group would act unilaterally to resolve Eritrean self-determination.

292. REISMAN, Michael. "Somali Self-Determination in the Horn: Legal Perspectives and Implications for Social and Political Engineering." *Nationalism and Self-Determination in the Horn of Africa.* Ed. I. M. Lewis. London: Ithaca Press, 1983, pp. 151-73.
Examines the legal perspectives as well as ecological and historical features of the dispute over Western Somaliland and the possible bases for solution. Identifies four reasons for the Somalis' valid claim to self-determination: (1) only a provisional administrative line demarcated the region; (2) recent legal developments, particularly the opinion of the International Court of Justice on the question of Western Sahara, might be interpreted as upholding self-determination claims even if they challenged existing state structures, provided that the will of the people could be determined; (3) states must justify their rule by the will of the people – the existing regime lacked popular support; and (4) pursuant to the OAU's Cairo Resolution, the Western Somali dispute must be resolved on the basis of social and political stability, the principle of ecological integrity, the principle of rationalization of boundaries, and the identification of relevant groups in the disputed area. Reviews possible models for a solution based on independence, association or integration, subject to popular support and self-determination.

293. SHAKED, Haim. "Anatomy of an Autonomy: The Case of Southern Sudan." *Models of Autonomy.* Ed. Yoram Dinstein. New Brunswick, NJ: Transaction Books, 1981, pp. 151-70.
Dwells on five major points: the agreement of 1972; the basic tenets of the Southern problem; the conditions that made an agreement possible in 1972; the problematic aftermath of the agreement; and some general conclusions which might have implications for other Middle Eastern situations. North-South tension within Sudanese society evolved out of geographical and historical factors, enhanced and accelerated by the late 1940s' and early 1950s' independence process. The 1972 Agreement was made possible by the emergence of a common interest in the termination of the war in the South. The problems that nourished the North-South conflict remained, but the Agreement had proven workable and capable of withstanding pressure. Concludes that the 1972 Agreement had come into being

under particular circumstances and had remained workable due to specific conditions. In the last analysis, neither the model nor the process could be transplanted into another environment.

294.   TOUVAL, Saadia. "Africa's Frontiers: Reactions to a Colonial Legacy." *International Affairs*, XXXXII (1966), 641-54.
Concentrates on the African border problem. Agrees that borders in Africa were artificial, but argues that this did not differ from international borders elsewhere, for example Hungary and Yugoslavia, or the United States and Canada. Argues that European ideas concerning the "Nation State" were not equally cherished in Africa, and had little or no basis in African social or cultural conditions. For example, numerous African tribes and ethnic groups had been divided by borders, yet irredentist movements had been few. Views African attitudes toward frontiers as ambivalent, because they condemned the boundaries as imperialist impositions, yet accorded them legitimacy. Explains that all African states felt vulnerable to possible frontier claims. Lists factors which determined the nature of the frontier dispute as being the size of the territory and the issues at stake as perceived by the rival claimants. The African position was to respect boundaries as they had existed at independence. Concludes that, except in a few cases, boundaries in Africa had not been challenged, but the possibility of this occurring could not be ruled out.

295.   TOUVAL, Saadia. *Somali Nationalism.* Cambridge: Harvard University Press, 1963.
Outlines the African problem of political units not comprising communities which could be easily recognized as nations. Argues the need for shifting existing boundaries. As an example, focuses on the Somali nation divided into five political units: Italian Somaliland, French Somaliland, British Somaliland, Ethiopia and Kenya. Describes history, ancestry and the Somalis' nomadic nature, and the factors contributing to the rise of nationalist feeling. Points out that Somali nationalism constituted a challenge to the territorial integrity of Kenya and Ethiopia. Contends that the conflict between Somali nationalism and the interests of the neighboring peoples endangered the peace in the Horn of Africa.

296.   TRIULZT, Allesandro. "Competing Views of National Identity in Ethiopia." *Nationalism and Self-Determination in the*

Horn of Africa. Ed. I. M. Lewis. London: Ithaca Press, 1983, pp. 111-27.

Discusses the nature of the Ethiopian polity, including a list of possible reasons for the prolonged survival of the culturally united "Greater Ethiopia" myth, and the linkage of regionalist questions with the problem of the feudalistic character of the state. Considers the role of socialist ideas within the debate and evolution of revolutionary movement factions. Examines the discrepancies between those who had recognized oppressed nationalities in terms of whether or not self-determination should be carried out gradually or immediately, or whether the existence of the right had necessarily meant the need to exercise the principle. Interconnected factors involved in policy formulation and implementation had included questions as to the nature of Ethiopian feudalism, the extent of Ethiopian "colonial" rule over the southern provinces, and "Amhara domination" over the subject peoples.

297. WAI, Dunstan M. "Geoethnicity and the Margin of Autonomy in the Sudan." *State Versus Ethnic Claims: African Policy Dilemmas.* Eds. Donald Rothchild and Victor A. Olorunsola. Boulder, CO: Westview Press, 1983, pp. 304-31.

Examines the North-South conflict in the Sudan, and the margin of regional autonomy the South achieved following the successful 1972 Addis Ababa peace talks. Argues that the right to self-determination had not functioned within Sudan. Applies the concept of "geoethnicity" to the Sudan, and finds that North-South differences were not as fundamental as the schism between them. The Sudanese state had reflected the identity of the Arab Northern Sudanese since independence; its legitimacy suffered in the view of Southerners because it had failed to recognize their values. With the locus of power in the north, Southern material and security needs were neglected. Attempts by Northern bureaucrats and politicians to subvert the agreement, including threats to subdivide the South into powerless provincial units, were being strongly resisted by the Southerners.

298. WASSERMAN, Gary. "The Politics of Consensual Decolonization." *The African Review.* V (1974), 1-16.

Argues that African decolonization was being shaped by an adaptive reaction of colonial political and economic interests to the political ascendancy of a nationalist élite and to the threat of disruption by the masses. The theses of adaption, cooption and preemption aimed at altering political authority in order to preserve the essential features of the colonial political economy. Rather than a disjuncture, the result of consensual decolonization was the integration of an indigenous leadership into colonial political, social and economic patterns.

299.   WEINSTEIN, Brian. "The Western Sahara." *Current History*, LXXVIII, 455 (1980), 110-4 and 136-7.
Claims that economic considerations, a long-simmering competition between Morocco and Algeria, competing ideologies, and geopolitical considerations had fueled the conflict in the Western Sahara. Points out four broad issues involved in the conflict: (1) despite the OAU's recognition of colonial frontiers as a framework for nation-building, the Western Sahara illustrated how some Africans based their demands for independence on ethnic affinities, history and geography; (2) the majority nomad issue in the Sahara; nomad lifestyle posed serious problems for any ruler; (3) the struggle for control of the Western Sahara was a purely intra-African affair, in which European, Asian and United States interests were not directly involved, although one or another of the participants might try to encourage outside intervention; and (4) the issue of self-determination and the limits of its application in small states. Views the Western Sahara as a battleground for clashing nationalisms: the Moroccans sought to reconstitute their perceived frayed national unity; the Sahrawis sought to assert their distinctive character. Examines the clashing policies of Spain, Morocco, Algeria, and Mauritania in the Western Sahara. Believes that United States military involvement would spawn negative consequences without resolving the local African conflict.

300.   YOUNG, Crawford. "Comparative Claims to Political Sovereignty: Biafra, Katanga, Eritrea." *State Versus Ethnic Claims: African Policy Dilemmas.* Eds. Donald Rothchild and Victor A. Olorunsola. Boulder, CO: Westview Press, 1983, pp. 199-232.
Considers three instances in which particular groups in different ways challenged the OAU principle of territorial integrity, claiming to override it with a higher principle: self-determination. Outlines the Biafra, Katanga and Eritrea cases. Owing to the difficulties in articulating a culturally defined claim to political sovereignty in these instances, the U.N. asserted the right to self-determination for territorial units.

301. YOUNG, Crawford. "Nationalism and Separatism in Africa."
    New States in the Modern World. Ed. Martin Kilson.
    Cambridge: Harvard University Press, 1975, pp. 57-75.
    Considers nationalism a paradoxical phenomenon. On one
    hand, the mass political mobilization associated with
    nationalism was necessary to confer legitimacy on the new
    African states; on the other, it might generate contrary forces
    and result in fragmentation. Outlines the primary factors en-
    couraging emergence of nationalism in Africa. Considers
    ethnicity the most frequent source of fragmentation; it might be
    related to traditional political and cultural groupings, differ-
    ential acculturation, social stratification, or electoral compe-
    tition. Regionalisms might develop in countries with wide
    disparities between center and periphery, or those having two
    competing centers. Linguistic or religious pluralism also had
    major fragmentation potential in Africa. Also identifies certain
    specific types of situations which seem to catalyze separatist
    potential. The separatist option was more easily available in
    areas distant from the center and having minimal political re-
    sources to confidently envisage an independent future. The
    most successful form of separation involved the negotiated dis-
    mantling of the colonial entity in cooperation with the colonial
    power; post-colonial secession was a more difficult undertaking.
    Separatist tactics had ranged from complete severance of poli-
    tical ties with the former territory to the mere invocation of the
    separatist alternative as a negotiating lever to obtain certain
    advantages within the existing framework. Concludes that, al-
    though separatism had thus far been kept in check by the
    consensus among African leaders, colonial boundaries were to
    be respected.

Americas

302. CAMERON, David. *Nationalism, Self-Determination, and the
    Quebec Question.* Toronto: Macmillan of Canada, 1974.
    Links the historical development of nationalism with the in-
    creasing bureaucratization and depersonalization of social
    functions in modern society, and the concomitant threat to cul-
    tural identity. Examines the extension of the liberal notion of
    individualism to the nationalist doctrine of the self-
    transforming, self-constituting potentialities of nations. Con-

siders nationalism a political doctrine distinct from but not
implacably hostile to liberal democracy. Urges English Canada
to permit Quebec to pursue its own destiny for the sake of a
possible new equilibrium, in view of the structural tensions currently besetting the Canadian federal system, as well as the
changed dynamics currently operating in Quebec society. Denies the existence of Quebec's right to self-determination for
four reasons: (1) Canadian law did not permit confederation
members to secede; (2) natural law applied only to individuals,
not to aggregates of individuals; (3) the status of self-
determination in international law was uncertain, although, in
practice, it currently applied only to colonial or dependent
territories; and (4) even if French Canadians had a moral right
to preserve themselves in any way, the rest of Canada had no
duty to respect their action. Maintains, however, that Canadians' civil values precluded the application of force to stop a
secessionist movement.

303. DOFNY, Jacques. "Ethnic Cleavages, Labor Aristocracy, and
      Nationalism in Quebec." *New Nationalisms of the Devel-
      oped West*. Eds. Edward A. Tiryakian and Ronald
      Rogowski. Boston: Allen and Unwin, 1985, pp. 353-73.
Examines the question of an ethnically stratified Quebec working class by considering the influence of Quebec's colonial situation upon the structure and orientations of labor during early
industrialization. Maintains that historically the British had
been the skilled and most prosperous workers in Quebec industry, and the dominant union group. English-speakers had
comprised an "aristocracy of labour," because of their highly
skilled training, union membership and rejection of nonskilled
workers. Urges reconsideration of the theory of a labor
aristocracy; recommends its linkage with ethnic cleavages and
the national question. Attributes the lack of a Quebec
working-class party to the tacit alliance between the Roman
Catholic Church and the politically and economically dominant
British ruling class.

304. DUNNETT, Denzil. "Self-Determination and the Falklands."
      International Affairs, LIX (1983), 405-28.
Examines the validity of Margaret Thatcher's appeal to self-
determination at the height of the Falklands crisis and finds it
wanting, especially regarding the following assumptions: (1)
that self-determination was a universally approved imperative
in United Nations documents and declarations; (2) that self-

determination meant "let the people decide their destiny;" and (3) that "people" meant inhabitants. The lack of definition for terms such as "people," "nation," and "the right to self-determination," as well as the problem of territorial integrity, had obscured the Falklands case. Argues that the concept involved people *and* territory, and denies the absolute importance of either one *or* the other.

305.   ERFAT, Edgar S. "Self-Determination: Canadian Perspectives." *Self-Determination: National, Regional, and Global Dimensions.* Eds. Yonah Alexander and Robert A. Friedlander. Boulder, CO: Westview Press, 1980, pp. 21-42.
Outlines two basic issues regarding self-determination in Canada: (1) Francophone pressure for the preservation of a distinct French identity against the Anglophone majority; and (2) the assertion of a national Canadian identity vis-à-vis increasing cultural, economic and political pressure exerted by the United States. Lists a number of disintegrative factors resulting from the translation of British constitutional principles to the Canadian federal system. Considers the federation held together by Canadians' fears of the alternatives. Canada's external self-determination was being curtailed by economic and military dependence on the United States. Believes Canadian foreign policy to be largely a product of two factors: the physical proximity of the country to the United States, and its traditional attachment to Great Britain. However, Canada's emerging identity had bred an increasingly independent foreign policy.

306.   FORMAN, James R. *Self-Determination and the African-American People.* Seattle, WA: Open Hand Publishing, 1981.
Considers that the African-American people in the Black Belt region of the American South were an oppressed nation. Advocates immediate self-determination, first through autonomy, and later through sovereignty.

307.   GLAZER, Nathan. "Federalism and Ethnicity: The Experience of the United States." *Publius: The Journal of Federalism,* VII, 4 (1977), 71-88.
Considers the general pattern in the United States one of "new world ethnic diversity." Identifies three important exceptions to this general pattern: (1) the Spanish-speaking population of the Southwest which preceded the formation of the United

States; (2) the Blacks concentrated in the Southern states; and (3) the American Indians.   Believes ethnicity in the United States to be largely a symbolic matter that lacked corporate self-consciousness or opportunity for political self-expression. Delineates three phases in the relationship between American ethnicity and federalism: (1) the dominance of white British-origin settlers; (2) the political ascendancy of non-British ethnic groups; and (3) the creation of federal standards for the protection of minority group and ethnic group rights.

308.   HAMILTON, Richard and Maurice PINARD.   "The Quebec Independence Movement." *National Separatism.*   Ed. Colin H. Williams.   Cardiff: University of Wales Press, 1982, pp. 203-33.

The authors maintain that French cultural erosion, reaching crisis proportions in recent years, had boosted nationalist urgency long dormant within Quebec society.   Argue that support for the Parti Québécois had not meant championing independence; its electoral success had been based on its ability to attract non-separatist voters moved by nationalistic considerations.   Considers the thesis that independence was inevitable due to demographic shifts flawed, because it assumed sentiment in favor of independence to be highly committed or permanent among young voters.   In fact, however, the intelligentsia comprised the strongest and most influential core of support for the Parti Québécois and independence.   The P.Q.'s provincial referendum, which had sought a mandate to negotiate sovereignty-association instead of full independence, had hoped to gain the uncommitted public's support.   Consider the economic factor the principal consideration barring the way to a simple translation of ethnic grievances and loyalties into support for independence.

309.   HECTOR, B. J.   "Puerto Rico: Colony or Commonwealth." *New York University Journal of International Law and Politics,* VI (1973), 115-37.

Analyzes the impact of the Puerto Rican controversy on the United Nations by outlining the history and procedure of the Special Committee established under General Assembly Resolution 1514 to investigate whether Puerto Rico was a colony of the United States.   Perceives no major dissatisfaction in Puerto Rican relations with the United States.   Describes the legal relationship binding the United States and Puerto Rico, and the self-determination criteria suggested by previous United Nations cases. Discusses possible alterations in the U.S.-Puerto Rican bond in conformity with the criteria for self-determination and the political motivations underlying the Puerto Rican controversy.

310. KNIGHT, David B. "Canada in Crisis: The Power of Regionalisms." *Tension Areas of the World.* Ed. D. G. Bennett. Champaign, IL: Park Press, 1982, pp. 254-79.
Traces the historical development of Canada and its various regionalisms, particularly the continued distinctiveness of French-Canadian society in Quebec. Identifies the variety of centrifugal forces operating within, and against, the Canadian state.

311. KNIGHT, David B. "Regionalisms, Nationalisms, and the Canadian State." *Journal of Geography,* LXXXIII (1984), 212-20.
Identifies the Quebec (nationalist) separatist movement, rooted in a vibrant Quebec regionalism as not the only centrifugal force threatening the Canadian state. Notes other strong regionalisms and considerable tensions between the provincial and central federal governments. Discusses centrality versus regionalisms, the Québécois separatist movement, recent constitutional reform attempts that involved various interregional alliances, and patriation of the British North America Act. Investigates Canada's indigenous peoples and notes the dilemma of contrasting interpretations of "self-determination." Believes that the process of territorial and administrative fission had not yet ended in Canada, and that the issue of how best to accommodate territorial identities would always remain.

312. LERNER, Natan. "Puerto Rico: Autonomy, Statehood, Independence?" *Models of Autonomy.* Ed. Yoram Dinstein. New Brunswick, NJ: Transaction Books, 1981, pp. 125-34.
Notes that, despite having a distinct cultural and political identity, Puerto Rico was one of the few Latin American territories not to have achieved independence. It had, however, gained a status equivalent to "autonomy," including advanced self-government. Identifies the meaning and degree of autonomy as the central ingredient in the debate on the future of Puerto Rico. Summarizes the positive and negative aspects of the present situation. Proposes a realistic alternative for the near future: the continuation, with some improvements, of the present ambiguous autonomy status, or full statehood.

313. LERNER, Natan. "Self-Determination: The Latin American
      Perspective." *Self-Determination: National, Regional, and
      Global Dimensions.* Eds. Yonah Alexander and Robert A.
      Friedlander.   Boulder, CO: Westview Press, 1980, pp.
      63-78.
      Maintains that self-determination, the equivalent of a people's
      right to determine its political status freely, did not directly and
      immediately concern the peoples of Latin America and the
      Caribbean.   Minority groups in Latin America were not
      irredentist, and self-determination was not one of their prob-
      lems. Although continental legal instruments did not refer to
      the principle of self-determination by name, the Charter of the
      Organization of American States had enshrined it.   Latin
      American writers and governments had generally agreed with
      the outcry against all forms of colonization, and had endorsed
      the Third World's view of the concept of self-determination.
      Puerto Rico exemplified the fact that self-determination and
      political independence represented dissimilar principles. Asserts
      that in Belize, self-determination must be considered along with
      British and Guatemalan territorial claims, whereas in the
      Falklands-Malvinas, self-determination for the tiny population
      clashed with historical titles.

314. LEVESQUE, René. *La Passion du Québec.* Montréal: Editions
      Québec/Amérique, 1978.
      The political leader of the P.Q., a separatist political party,
      establishes the basis for Quebec being granted "sovereignty-
      association" apart from but still linked to Canada. Establishes
      fundamental qualities of Québécois separateness, the key point
      being that "self-determination is an absolute necessity for the
      growth to maturity of a society which has its own identity."

315. MARTINEZ, Rubén Berríos. "Independence for Puerto Rico:
      The Only Solution." *Foreign Affairs*, LV (1977), 561-83.
      Demonstrates that the convolutions of Puerto Rican political
      history could be understood only as a prolonged and vain at-
      tempt to circumvent independence as the self-evident right of
      Puerto Ricans. Considers American occupation to be signif-
      icant in the analysis of present-day Puerto Rico. The estab-
      lishment of a Commonwealth in 1952 had given Puerto Rico no
      additional powers, and was used to create the myth that Puerto
      Ricans had exercised the right to self-determination. Puerto
      Rico would continue to be a political and economic anach-
      ronism under the Commonwealth. Examines the choices of

commonwealth, independence and statehood as possible solutions to Puerto Rico's problems. Favors an independent Republic of Puerto Rico; it would (1) protect the rights and interests of the people of Puerto Rico; (2) free the American taxpayer of the increased burden of maintaining an unworkable economic system; and (3) would make U.S. policies conform to the principles on which the Union was founded, as well as principles of international law.

316. PAINCHAUD, Paul. "Territorialization and Internationalism: The Case of Quebec." *Publius: The Journal of Federalism*, VII, 4 (1977), 161-76.
Suggests the development of a new type of federalism between Canada and Quebec, a "diplomatic federalism," whereby both parties would simultaneously share internal and external sovereignty. Emphasizes two essential points: (1) because the Canadian Confederation favored a true division of sovereignty, it had allowed the growth of a Quebec territorial nationalism opposed to the territorial nationalism for all of Canada; (2) since the majority of Quebec's population formed a singular cultural group that was distinct from other French communities in Europe and North America, the province had already become a nation-state. Considers Quebec's participation in the international system an integral part of the modernization process occurring in the 1960s' political and social spheres; it had allowed Quebec to push territorialism to its limits, but without breaking with Canada. Suggests that this kind of diplomatic federalism, if applied elsewhere, could permit the continuation of strong ties between parts, while promoting territoriality for cultural nations.

317. ROMERO-BARCELO, C. "Puerto Rico, USA: The Case for Statehood." *Foreign Affairs*, LIX (1980), 60-81.
Argues in favor of statehood for Puerto Rico on the grounds that the "commonwealth" arrangement with the United States was essentially cosmetic and politically inadequate. Suggests that few Puerto Ricans favored independence. Describes the benefits of statehood, with the ultimate goal of political equality.

318. SABOURIN, L. "The Socio-Cultural Bases of Quebec Separatism: A Design for Collective Equality." *Collected Seminar Papers on the Politics of Separatism, no. 19.*

London: University of London, Institute of Commonwealth Studies, 1975, pp. 49-56.
Discusses the social bases of Québécois separatism by analyzing
the radical changes that had swept Québec in the last few decades. Believes that a mixture of long-term phenomena, such as
urbanization and industrialization, and short-term progressive
elements (such as the Faculty of Social Sciences at Laval
University and the writers for *Le Devoir* and *Cité libre*) had
caused changes in "a new psychological climate." The impact
of these changes included reform of the educational system, the
rise of new élites and proliferation of television and *la culture
québécoise*, the assertion of "l'Etat du Québec," decline of
Roman Catholic Church influence, and a diminished birth rate.
Highlights the concept of sovereignty as opposed to separatism
as the goal of Québec self-assertion. Summarizes the components of Québécois separatism: (1) a democratic movement; (2)
an ideological movement; (3) an urban-based movement; (4) an
idealistic movement; (5) a combined young and old movement;
(6) a "middle-of-the-road" movement; and (7) a solidly-based
movement. Comments that Québécois separatists funda-
mentally searched to discover a collective equality design.

319. SANCHEZ, M. A. "Self-Determination and the Falklands Is-
      lands Dispute." *Columbia Journal of Transnational Law*,
      XXI (1983), 557-84.
      Discerns no clear solution under international law to the com-
      peting claims of Argentine sovereignty and Falklanders' right
      to self-determination. Suggests that the population's origin and
      size ought not to be a factor in the claim to self-determination.
      Points out that the U.N. General Assembly had assigned prior-
      ity to the sovereignty issue, but required that the interests of the
      inhabitants would be considered in the determination of terri-
      torial status.

320. SAYWELL, John. *The Rise of the Parti Québécois 1967-76.*
      Toronto: University of Toronto Press, 1977.
      Narrates the history of the Parti Québécois and its context in
      Quebec politics and society. Credits René Leveque's efforts
      with having been the catalyst that turned the idea of independ-
      ence into a political party in 1967. Separatism had become a
      major political force in Québec and Canada with the alliance of
      the P.Q. with nationalist groups in 1968. The central issues of
      the 1970 and 1974 provincial elections revolved around
      questions of the constitution and independence. The P.Q.'s

policy of "separatism by stages" and the sacrifice of certain principles, combined with the incumbent Liberal Party's unpopularity, enabled Levesque to win the 1976 provincial election. For the first time, independence was regarded as one of the rational and legitimate options open to Québeckers.

321. WILLIAMS, Colin H. "Identity through Autonomy: Ethnic Separatism in Quebec." *Political Studies from Spatial Perspectives.* Eds. A. D. Burnett and P. J. Taylor. Chichester: John Wiley and Sons, Ltd., 1981, pp. 389-418. Considers separatism an expression of ethnic identity which challenged the inevitability of assimilation, and an ideology capable of providing a path to political power and privilege. Evaluates Hechter's "internal colonialism" and Smith's work on the role of the ethnic intelligentsia, and applies both in an examination of ethnic separatism in Quebec. Identifies ethnicity and territory as the distinct components of separateness. The process of nationality formation and politicization enabled objective differences between peoples to acquire subjective and symbolic significance, become transformed into group consciousness, and the basis for political demands. Demonstrates that the uneven spatial impact of modernization, coupled with the cultural division of labor, were important structural determinants of ethnic relations in Quebec.

Asia and the Pacific

322. CLARK, R. S. "The Decolonization of East Timor and the United Nations Norms on Self-Determination and Aggression." *Yale Journal of World Public Order*, VII, 2 (1980), 2-44. Analyzes Indonesia's actions in the invasion and annexation of East Timor. Maintains that Indonesia had violated two fundamental norms of international law: it deprived East Timor of the right to self-determination, and it perpetrated a military act of aggression, forbidden by the U.N. Charter and customary law. Examines and dismisses Indonesia's claims that integration with Indonesia obeyed the will of the East Timorese people and therefore constituted self-determination; that the historical, ethnic, geographical and cultural ties between the two countries established East Timor as an integral part of the Indonesian

archipelago; and that East Timor was not economically viable and required direction and assistance from an economically stable country to survive. Notes the "legal" bases of Indonesia's claim resembled the Western Sahara Opinion. Further criticizes and dispenses with Indonesia's attempts to justify the use of force against East Timor on grounds of self-defense, invitation by the East Timorese, Indonesia's and Southeast Asia's future stability, and humanitarian purposes.

323.   CLARK, R. S. "Self-Determination and Free Association - Should the United Nations Terminate the Pacific Islands Trust?" *Harvard International Law Journal*, XXI (1980), 1-86.

Examines proposed arrangements between Micronesia and the United States on whether the U.N. trusteeship should be terminated. Reviews the historical events and factors surrounding the creation of the trusteeship and analyzes the respective interests and positions of the United States, Micronesia, and the United Nations. Outlines the proposed arrangements for the establishment of a Marianas Commonwealth, as well as the 1980 United States-Marshall Islands Compact, identifying and evaluating the proposals regarding government, the economy, security and defense relations. Believes that the United Nations' willingness to end the trust would depend on the extent to which the Micronesians had achieved the appropriate measure of self-government. Discusses the evolution of the concept of "free association," with particular reference to Puerto Rico, the Kingdom of the Netherlands, Resolutions 1514 and 1541, the Cook Islands and Niue, the West Indies Associated States, and the Declaration on Principles Concerning Friendly Relations. Assesses the "appropriateness" of terminating the Trust. Concludes that the prospects for a Security Council Resolution terminating the Trust were not particularly good.

324.   DEMPSEY, Guy. "Self-Determination and Security in the Pacific: A Study of the Covenant Between the United States and the Northern Mariana Islands." *New York University Journal of International Law and Politics*, IX (1976-77), 302-77.

Discusses the dilemma of the United States since World War II regarding Micronesia: its desire to control the area for defense reasons, versus its responsibility to recognize the right of the region's people to determine their own future. Analyzes the 1976 Covenant, essentially a commonwealth plan, signed by Presi-

dent Ford. Ventures that, as commonwealth states did not fit
into any political status categories approved by the United Nations, it would likely draw negative international reaction.
Discusses possibilities for an international review of the
Covenant.

325. DE SILVA, Chandra Richard. "Sinhala-Tamil Ethnic Rivalry:
      The Background." *From Independence to Statehood -
      Managing Ethnic Conflict in Five African and Asian States.*
      Eds. R. S. Goldmann and A. J. Wilson. London: Frances
      Pinter (Publishers), 1984, pp. 111-24.
Examines the ethnic composition and pre-1948 history of Sri
Lanka, rooting the Sinhala-Tamil conflict in the two groups'
negative attitudes. The majority Sinhala community had enjoyed political power but lacked full economic opportunity.
The minority Tamil community had feared its economic
advantages would be eroded by the majority's political power.
Explains why the independence period had not bred struggles
and armed conflict. Leaders had achieved political compro-
mises, including the adoption of a secular state with equitable
religious and linguistic policies. Considers these structural
changes as necessary but insufficient conditions for the easing
of ethnic tensions.

326. DREYER, June T. "The Kazakhs in China." *Ethnic Conflict in
      International Relations.* Eds. A. Suhrke and L. Noble.
      New York: Praeger, 1979, pp. 146-77.
Examines the role of the Kazakhs, a Turkic Muslim people, as
one of the several minorities divided by the artificial boundary
of the Sino-Soviet frontier in Central Asia. The Kazakhs
constituted a minority in their host states and within the
Kazakhstan and Sinkiang provinces. Regards the nationality
policies of the Soviet Union and China as failures, because neither state could be certain of the loyalties of its minorities.
Discusses the benefits this competition offered the Kazakhs, but
suggests that minorities enjoyed meager opportunities for
manipulating their governments.

327. ERDMAN, Howard L. "Autonomy Movements in India."
      Ethnic Autonomy - Comparative Dynamics. Ed. Raymond
      L. Hall. New York: Pergamon Press, 1979, pp. 394-412.
Maintains that, although India had been confronted by numerous autonomist movements, the Union was not in jeopardy,
because partition had removed the large and troublesome

Muslim population. India's federal democracy had functioned effectively because of the central government's accommodating approach to minorities. Numerous factors would affect India's ability to maintain unity, including the extent of group interaction, external factors and geopolitical considerations, and the scope of autonomist challenges.

328.   JORGENSEN-DAHL, A. "Forces of Fragmentation in the International System: The Case of Ethnonationalism." *Orbis*, XIX (1975), 652-74.
Identifies ethnonationalism as a fragmenting force with specific reference to Southeast Asia. Argues that ethnic separatism differed completely from other types of liberation movements. In ethnonationalism, citizens owed their primary loyalty to the ethnic group rather than to their country. In ethnic separatism this sentiment became translated into a desire for separate statehood. In Southeast Asia, ethnic counsciousness responded to the degree and nature of interethnic contact. Explains that ethnic awareness had yet to crystallize into demands for secession in this region, because separate statehood could be achieved only with external assistance. Examines the likelihood of having minority grievances exploited by such external groups, particularly Communists. Explains why ethnonational movements desiring secession aided by foreign states and international institutions had thus far lacked support, with the sole exception of Bangladesh. Maintains that in view of the strength of the social forces involved in ethnonationalism, the "choice may be between an international system with a membership many times larger than today's or the application of a much higher level of violence and suppression to prevent this from happening."

329.   KNIGHT, David B. "Changing Orientations: Elements of New Zealand's Political Geography." *Geographical Bulletin*, I (1970), 21-30.
Traces the slow development of the idea that New Zealanders should distance themselves from Great Britain. Identifies the growth of a distinctive sense of nationhood and discusses New Zealanders' actions that could be construed as attempts to institute self-determination.

330.   LEIFER, Michael. "Decolonization and International Status: The Experience of Brunei." *International Affairs*, LIV (1978), 240-52.

Examines the international status of Brunei in light of Great
Britain's request for the Sultanate's self-determination and independence. Argues that the concept of decolonization, which
had been used as a standard for analyzing Brunei's international
status, was inapplicable to the small territory, because of
Brunei's determination to retain a bilateral association with
Great Britain as long as possible. Discusses Brunei in terms of
decolonization and international status. Maintains that the
British connection had sustained an anachronistic political system that denied self-determination and independence.

331. LYON, Peter. "Separation and Secession in the Malaysian
   Realm." *The Politics of Separation. Collected Seminar
   Papers, no. 19.* London: University of London, Institute
   of Commonwealth Studies, 1976, pp. 69-78.
   Rejects separatism discussions that gravitated toward zero-sum
   analyses. Suggests that sophisticated analysis required a set of
   differentiated and consistent concepts geared to the subtleties
   of the subject. For example, it was useful to differentiate
   separatism, a movement seeking to resist further incorporation;
   subordination of a small unit within the larger political authority; and secession, a movement seeking to separate from the
   principal political authority. Maintains that explanations of
   these movements stemmed from decolonization terminology
   and an understanding of the transformative role of nation-
   building. Reviews the history of Malaysian "separatism without separation" (1948-57) to illustrate anti-federation protest
   movements. Labels the secession of Singapore as an
   "eviction." Summarizes four preconditions for a successful
   movement: (1) a deep sense of separate identity; (2) a legitimate
   political organization and leadership; (3) a strong determination
   to assert political independence; and (4) a favorable
   constellation of external forces. Comments on the persistence
   of colonial territorial arrangements, whether challenged by ethnic or states' rights confrontations.

332. MACDONALD, Barrie. "Secession in the Defence of Identity:
   The Making of Tuvalu." *Pacific Viewpoint,* XVI (1975),
   26-44.
   Examines the secession of the Ellice Islands from the Gilbert
   and Ellice Islands Colony. Traces the origins of racial dishar-
   mony to educational inequalities which had fostered the
   development of an Ellice élite. The Gilbertese had resented
   Ellice domination of the civil service, claiming perpetuation

through favoritism. The Gilbertese National Party had aimed at securing a greater proportion of government jobs at the expense of Ellice Islanders; fearful of being submerged by the Gilbertese majority in the Colony, the Ellice Islanders perceived a separate identity for themselves. The overwhelming support for the Ellice Islanders' separation demonstrated the strength of the sense of national identity which had existed for generations, but which had not found distinct political expression. Considers the Ellice Islanders' movement for secession a product of British colonial policy: the two groups, each with a distinctive culture and language, had been combined in a single administration without any serious attempt to foster integration; as well, centralization policies had been vigorously pursued on the grounds of cost and efficiency, whereas decentralization might have fostered national unity and dispelled perceived prejudices.

333.   MAXWELL, Neville. *India and the Nagas.* London: Minority Rights Group, Report No. 17, 1972.
Examines the fate of the Nagas, a hill people attached to India by "historical accident." The Nagas claimed the right, and attempted the fact, of gaining independence upon British departure in 1947. Since then, the Nagas had remained unreconciled to their inclusion within India, which had used a variety of methods to stop the Nagas' resistance movement. Discusses Naga identity and its implications prior to India's independence. Recounts the history of the Naga independence movement, the Naga National Council, and the Indian government's response. Surveys the developments in the post-1947 period, highlighting Nehru's denouncement of Naga independence in 1952, the use of force beginning in 1955, and the allegations of atrocities from 1955 to 1960. Studies the implementation of autonomy for Nagaland and the formation of the Peace Commission in 1964. This mediation effort had broken down and confrontations resumed. Contrasts the Nagaland case with that of the Mizo who had attempted to secede from Assam province.

334.   MCVEY, R. "Language, Religion, and National Identity in Southern Thailand." *The Politics of Separatism: Collected Seminar Papers, no. 19.* London: University of London, Institute of Commonwealth Studies, 1976, pp. 94-9.
Examines the sources and limitations of Thailand's Pattani separatist movement in terms of élite and mass orientations to

separatism and to questions of national integration and socioeconomic change. Explains that the Muslim Malay-speaking Pattani had more in common with neighboring Malaysians than with the Buddhist Thais. Old definitions of community had been destroyed by secularization, education, expansion of communications and economic development, but new definitions had failed to accommodate nonconforming groups such as the Pattani. Argues that the Pattani autonomist movement was limited by the nature of Pattani élites, in that both religious and secular leaders had much to gain by cooperating with the Thai state and something to lose with separation. The real energy of the movement allegedly lay with the peasant unrest, because recent government activity had subjected peasants to new demands without any corresponding increase in benefits.

335. MISRA, K. P. *The Role of the United Nations in the Indo-Pakistani Conflict, 1971.* Delhi: Vikas Publishing, 1973.
Notes two sharply divergent views expressed during the December 1971 Security Council and General Assembly debates concerning the conflict in East Bengal. First, that the conflict was a liberation movement by a group of people who merited the right to self-determination. Second, that it was essentially a secessionist movement. Considers the conflict a case of Pakistani aggression against India. Perceives the East Bengal situation as a liberation struggle, not a secessionist effort.

336. NANDA, Ved P. "Self-Determination Outside the Colonial Context: The Birth of Bangladesh in Retrospect." *Self-Determination: National, Regional, and Global Dimensions.* Eds. Yonah Alexander and Robert A. Friedlander. Boulder, CO: Westview Press, 1980, pp. 193-220.
Investigates the validity of the claim that East Pakistan's secession was justified under the principle of self-determination. Explains that under international law self-determination enjoyed priority over territorial integrity, if the state failed to represent the whole people. Establishes two criteria for evaluating the merit of territorial separation: (1) whether the group constituted a separate, identifiable people; and (2) whether the nature and extent of this group's human rights deprivation justified a valid claim for secession. Asserts that the East Pakistani territorial separation claim was justified by racial, cultural, geographic, and linguistic differences between East and West Pakistan, the political and economic disparities suffered

by East Pakistan, and the repressive measures the West
Pakistani military forces employed to crush the East Pakistanis.
Moreover, Pakistan's government did not represent the whole
people. Recommends the establishment of international guidelines to gather and evaluate claims for territorial separation.

337.   NAYAR, M. G. K. "Self-Determination Beyond the Colonial
         Control: Biafra in Retrospect." *Texas International Law
         Journal*, X (1975), 321-45.
       Examines the contemporary international law on self-
       determination. Defines self-determination as the inherent right
       of peoples to dispose of their own destinies and asserts that
       self-determination could be implemented through an independ-
       ent state, a free association, or any other status freely deter-
       mined by a people. Examines the Biafran episode from the
       standpoint of the right to self-determination; identifies its legal
       aspects and explains how regional and international organi-
       zations had responded to the incident. Identifies the problems
       leading to the strife: Nigeria's borders had been drawn by out-
       siders with little regard to ethnic and religious differences or the
       impact of Western civilization. Fearing a chain reaction of
       separations, the OAU had ordered Biafra to restore peace and
       unity in Nigeria. The U.N., which favored non-intervention in
       domestic affairs and territorial integrity versus self-
       determination, had concurred with this view. Believes that the
       principle of self-determination should have flexible guidelines
       rather than rigid rules, and that certain basic norms should be
       observed.

338.   NAYAR, M. G. K. "Self-Determination: The Bangladesh
         Experience." *Revue des droits de l'homme/Human Rights
         Journal*, VII (1974), 231-71.
       Examines whether the emergence of Bangladesh had con-
       tributed to international legal self-determination norms. U.N.
       practice considered all colonialism as illegitimate. Self-
       determination was revolutionary and complex, and required
       norms and guidelines, not rigid rules. Suggests five norms: (1)
       states had a duty to respect and promote a legal right to self-
       determination; (2) the right belonged to *all* colonial and non-
       colonial peoples; (3) internal colonialism must be recognized; (4)
       the right was continuous; and (5) a people could freely deter-
       mine to implement any political status. Concludes that, al-
       though Bangladesh satisfied all of the standards and criteria for

the exercise of self-determination, the U.N. could not ensure its realization.

339. PREMDAS, Ralph R. "Ethnonationalism, Copper, and Secession in Bougainville." *Canadian Review of Studies in Nationalism*, IV (1977), 247-65.
Considers Bougainville secessionism an ethnonationalist movement determined to gain liberty from external Australian control, and from the internal ethnic colonialism of the Papua New Guinea government. Distinguishes between the primordial basis of Bougainville self-determination, including race and cultural values, and the non-primordial basis of economic neglect and exploitation. Contends that the Bougainville secessionist movement threatened the Papua New Guinea government because of the possible loss of the copper mine, and because one successful breakaway movement might undermine the central government's authority. Independence prospects for Bougainville were significantly diminished by external geopolitical factors: it threatened to cripple or destroy Papua New Guinea's economic viability; and its anti-capitalist philosophy posed a potential menace to regional stability.

340. PYE, Lucian W. "Ethnic Minorities in China." *Ethnicity: Theory and Experience*. Eds. Nathan Glazer and Daniel P. Moynihan. Cambridge: Harvard University Press, 1975, pp. 488-512.
Asserts that the Chinese Communists had expected national minorities to adopt Chinese nationalism. Notes that the concentration of minorities in border territories linked them to national security issues. The Chinese Communists had moved from espousing the right to self-determination to tolerating only surface cultural differences. Outlines various means used for controlling the national minorities, including the use of military force. Expects China's national minority problems to become more acute with industrialization.

341. RAHMAN, Mizanur. "Bangladesh." *The Politics of Separatism. Collected Working Papers, no. 19*. London: University of London, Institute of Commonwealth Studies, 1976, pp. 37-48.
Examines the historical context of Bengal separatism in Pakistan that had resulted in the birth of the sovereign Bangladesh state in 1971. Roots this movement in the pre-1947 stress and strain of regional Hindu-Muslim politics and the

1947-48 autonomist movement. Emphasizes the role of various classes in the political development of East Pakistan in the 1950s and 1960s. Reviews events culminating in the national liberation war, especially the waning of religion in favor of ethnicity as the basis of politics, and the region's economic grievances. Suggests that East Bengal's separation might be viewed in Hegelian-Marxian terms: Pakistan in general and the Ayub system in particular had created their own contradiction. The Pakistani regime's failure might be seen as inevitable, or as the result of the leaders' lack of understanding regarding the fuctionings of social engineering in nation-creation.

342.   SCHWARTZ, W. *The Tamils of Sri Lanka*. London: Minority
         Rights Group, Report No. 25, 1975.
         Outlines the position of the Tamils in Sri Lanka as a "classic minority problem." Discusses the roots of the conflict, national Tamil and Sinhalese myths, the colonial history of separate development until 1815, and the importation of Indian Tamils as laborers under British rule. Reviews the process that had led to political independence for the island state, notes the move toward a "Sinhala only" policy, and outlines the role of languages pertaining to the present conflict. Describes the Indian Tamil community and its relations with the Sri Lankan Tamils. Surveys recent developments in education, employment, the government's "internal colonization" policies, and the boundary delimitation of constituencies. Urges compromise and moderation by Tamils and Sinhalese in language and education if violence was to be avoided.

343.   SUTER, Keith. *East Timor and West Irian*. Revised edition.
         London: Minority Rights Group, Report No. 42, 1982.
         Explains that Indonesia's 1963 West Irian takeover and the violent 1975 East Timor invasion had placed the inhabitants of these territories in the position of becoming Indonesian regional "minorities." The people had consistently resisted Indonesian control, with little assistance from the international community to Indonesia's human rights abuses. Indonesia faced problems in developing and maintaining Indonesian national unity after having incorporated the territories. The situation in the two territories had raised questions concerning the world community's commitment to international protection of human rights, and to the issue of whether or not self-determination constituted a universal right.

344.   TALALLA, Rohini.   "Ethnodevelopment and the Orang Asli
       of Malaysia: A Case Study of the Betau Settlement for
       Semai-Senoi." *Antipode*, XVI, 2 (1984), 27-32.
       Explains that ethnodevelopment had been designed to make
       indigenous minorities less vulnerable to surrounding dominant
       societies through culture-sensitive programs and economic, so-
       cial and political autonomy.   Considers the Orang Asli under-
       developed due to interference by the government, Islamic
       missionaries and educators, and the market economy, although
       the Betau Resettlement project appeared to have encouraged
       more culture-sensitive and self-reliant development.   Argues
       that jungle security policy issues and Orang Asli integration into
       the mainstream of Malaysian society had often conflicted with
       the goals of ethnodevelopment.

345.   TINKER, H.   "Burma: Separatism as a Way of Life." *The
       Politics of Separatism. Collected Working Papers, no. 19.*
       London: University of London, Institute of Common-
       wealth Studies, 1976, pp. 57-68.
       Examines the numerous Burmese groups demanding autonomy,
       despite minimal chance of success.   Describes this situation
       which, for many separatists, had been "not so much a pro-
       gramme, more a way of life."   Explains the "impasse" in terms
       of the peculiar demographic structure in which between two-
       thirds and three-quarters of the population had regarded itself
       as one people with a living culture and national tradition,
       whereas the remainder had lacked a sense of identity with the
       Burmese but considered Burma as its homeland, with the
       exception of the Shans.   Describes the characteristics of the
       larger groups, and the patterns of interethnic relations prior to
       independence in 1947.   Reviews governmental and adminis-
       trative policies used to deal with the ethnic "impasse" since in-
       dependence.   Suggests that more emphasis on a single ideology
       might have made the unity policy viable.   Hints at the danger
       of the "balance of instability," in which separatism could suc-
       ceed only with strong external support.

346.   TIRUCHELVAN, Neelan.   "The Politics of Decentralization
       and Devolution: Competing Conceptions of District
       Development Councils in Sri Lanka." *From Independence
       to Statehood - Managing Ethnic Conflict in Five African and
       Asian States.*   Eds. R. S. Goldmann and A. J. Wilson.
       London: Frances Pinter (Publishers), 1984, pp. 196-209.

Evaluates the establishment of district development councils as a structural arrangement designed to ease ethnic tensions in Sri Lanka. This move had been a highly controversial response to the need for Tamil regional autonomy in the north and east. Highlights the conceptual transformation in the character of Tamil aspirations, the various interest groups involved in and/or accommodated in the decision-making process and the institutional and legal arrangements. Reviews the forces that might seek to thwart implementation of this policy, and particularly the differing and conflicting conceptions regarding decentralization. Describes the character and functions of the councils and the district ministers, emphasizing the conciliatory role of the council executives. Believes in concerted action at all government levels to resolve the developmental and ethnic rivalry crises. Suggests that the institutionalization of the development councils could prove to be a bold experiment in participatory democracy that might redress some of the Tamil grievances.

347. VAN WALT VAN PRAAG, M. C. "Tibet and the Right to Self-Determination." *Wayne Law Review*, XXVI (1979), 279-305.

Outlines the Tibetan revolt of 1959 by examining the status of the principle or right to self-determination under International Law and its application to the Tibetan people. Discusses Wilson's Fourteen Points, and the support of Lenin and the USSR for self-determination. Believes that the language of General Assembly Resolution 1514 and 2625, the United Nations impact on self-determination (particularly regarding decolonization), and the Human Rights Covenants had converted self-determination into an enforceable right in international law, as confirmed in the Western Sahara and Namibia cases as well as by state practice. Discusses the definition of "people," and concludes that the Tibetan people met these criteria. Lists the determining factors considered crucial in resolving claims to self-determination, and discusses these factors vis-à-vis the Tibetan people. Accuses the People's Republic of China of denying the Tibetans the exercise of their right to self-determination.

348. WHEBELL, C. F. J. "Non-National Separatism: With Special Reference to Australian Cases Past and Present." *Collected Seminar Papers on the Politics of Separatism, no. 19.*

London: University of London, Institute of Commonwealth Studies, 1976, pp. 19-30.
Proposes a general model to explain non-national separatism in
states where the territorial system's unity rested on economic
gain. Explains the operations of modern political systems based
on layers of spatial units, each of which had a small area or
specific location as a core, the site of which established the spatial conditions of political authority and dependency for the
respective unit at each level in the territorial hierarchy. Applies
this model to the history of administrative integration in
Australia, and examines the various separatist attempts in the
19th and 20th centuries. Believes that, although core-periphery
disparity was common, it did not necessarily spur separatism.
Separate status would be appropriate only where a peripheral
section had a socio-economic identity. Even so, widespread
popular support, effective leadership and financial viability
were prerequisites for separatism to form. Points out a paradox: the most viable peripheral sections were those the state
wished to retain. Speculates on the possible tactical adoption
of separatist scenarios to lessen disparity and attain effective
decentralization.

349. WHITAKER, Ben. *The Biharis in Bangladesh.* London:
Minority Rights Group, Report No. 11, 1972.
Examines the past, present and future aspects of the Bihari
community's predicament in Bangladesh, caught between India
and Pakistan. Reviews the social, political and linguistic roots
of this group's treatment since 1947 and the partition to the
1970s and Bangladesh independence. Analyzes the situation in
demographic and geographic terms and recounts the living
conditions. Discusses the potential role of the United Nations,
the Pakistani prisoners-of-war trials, and the reconstruction and
expansion of the Bangladesh economy. Concludes that an
honest solution would come with security for the Biharis, integration of Biharis willing to become Bangladeshi citizens, and
acceptance of those not wishing to stay by Pakistan and India.

350. WIRSING, R. G. *The Baluchis and Pathans.* London: Minority
Rights Group, Report No. 48, 1981.
Reviews the situation of two tribal groups situated in the "arc
of crisis," the region adjacent to the Arabian Sea that extends
from the Indian sub-continent in the east to the horn of Africa
in the west. Political turmoil had brought this region, with its
large concentration of tribal peoples, to the forefront of inter-

national conflict. Discusses the internal importance of these peoples (in terms of their vast numbers and historical importance) and their external significance (based on their geopolitical placement astride the boundaries of Pakistan, Afghanistan, and Iran). Analyzes the internal tribal problems, intertribal relationships, and developments within and among the three states they inhabit. Examines their future in light of the international strategic importance of the region. Concludes that the interrelated layers of interests make the difficult situation nearly impossible to resolve according to tribal needs. Finds the threatened territorial integrity and political independence of the host states as being the primary factors which worked against the satisfaction of tribal demands, even as the tribes attempted to address various new economic and technological forces. Sees the Baluchis and Pathans as potentially the most explosive tribal issues of the 1980s.

351. WRIGHT, T. P., Jr. "South Asian Separatist Movements." *Collected Seminar Papers on the Politics of Separatism, no. 19.* London: University of London, Institute of Commonwealth Studies, 1976, pp. 5-18.

Identifies separatism as the desire of articulate portions of a population in a section (usually a province) of a sovereign state to loosen or sunder the political and legal bonds which tied the part to the whole. If the aim was only to loosen this tie, then it was termed a quest for autonomy. Owing to the coalescence of "nation" and "state" in modern political thought and organization, separatism was tantamount to a denial by the separatist movement of integration with a nation, or at least the assertion of a regional, subnational identity. Notes South Asia's proneness to the emergence of separatist movements, mainly due to the characteristics of the region's nation-states: they were huge, religiously, linguistically and regionally diverse, and therefore fragile. This vulnerability had prompted states to deny requests for national self-determination. Suggests the following eight categories as a fruitful approach to achieving a fair level of generalization in the study of separatism: (1) origin, and the connection between the province and the possessing state; (2) the population's size and characteristics relative to the whole; (3) the province's location within the country relative to neighbors; (4) the separatist movement's various and changing goals; (5) support for and opposition to the movement; (6) the movement's and the government's methods; (7) leadership goals and values, if separable from the followers' aspirations; and (8) the international context. Applies the first six points to South Asian separatist movements. Establishes a typology that classifies the Kashmir, Tamilnad and Nagaland movements in India, and the Bangladesh, Pushtunistan and Baluchistan movements in Pakistan according to the elements of the categories most relevant to each region.

Middle East

352. ALEXANDER, Yonah. "The Jewish Struggle for Self-Determination: The Birth of Israel." *Self-Determination: National, Regional and Global Dimensions.* Eds. Yonah Alexander and Robert A. Friedlander. Boulder, CO: Westview Press, 1980, pp. 259-303.
Traces the Jewish experience in Palestine from the emergence of Zionism in the 1880s to the creation of the state of Israel in 1948, and establishes the continuity of Jewish life in Palestine for the past 4,000 years. Parallels the emergence of Zionism with the rise of contemporary Arab nationalism, manifested in religious and ethnic assertiveness. Focuses on anti-Jewish Arab violence and sporadic terrorism from 1920 onward, and notes the Jewish countermeasures through the efforts of the Yishuv. Portrays the British as sometime victims of Arab violence, and as occasional perpetrators; as sometime proponents of the Zionist cause, and as occasional opponents of a Jewish homeland.

353. BENJAMIN, C. "The Kurdish Nonstate Nation." *Nonstate Nations in International Politics: Comparative Systems Analysis.* Ed. J. S. Bertelsen. New York: Praeger, 1977, pp. 69-97.
Outlines the historical and political developments of Kurdish attempts in Iraq to gain autonomy. Argues that the Kurds' strategy for obtaining autonomy since 1958 included domestic military action against Iraq and securing international support.

354. BERTELSEN, J. S. "The Palestinian Arabs." *Nonstate Nations in International Politics: A Comparative Analysis.* Ed. J. S. Bertelsen. New York: Praeger, 1977, pp. 6-35.
Argues that, although Palestinian Arabs had no nation-state, they played a critical role in the resolution of the Israeli-Arab

conflict. Outlines the strategies and goals of the Palestinian Arabs and traces their impact on the international community.

355.   BOYLE, F. A. "International Law and Organizations as an Approach to Conflict Resolution in the Middle East." *Contemporary Issues in International Law.* Ed. T. Buergenthal. Strasbourg: N. P. Engel, 1984, pp. 515-40.
Doubts the possibility for Middle East peace until the Palestinian people were allowed to exercise their right to self-determination. Asserts that the Reagan administration had unilaterally foreclosed the option of a Palestinian sovereign state.

356.   BRAWER, Moshe. "Dissimilarities in the Evolution of Frontier Characteristics Along Boundaries of Differing Political and Cultural Regions." *Pluralism and Political Geography: People, Territory and State.* Eds. Nurit Kliot and Stanley Waterman. London: Croom Helm; New York: St. Martin's Press, 1983, pp. 159-72.
Examines population distribution patterns and socioeconomic differences over the past thirty-five years due to boundary changes in Israel and the Israeli-occupied territories.

357.   BRUNN, Stanley D. and Gerald L. INGALLS. "Identifying Regional Alliances and Blocs in the United Nations Voting - Some Preliminary Results of Votes Affecting Israel." *Pluralism and Political Geography: People, Territory and State.* Eds. Nurit Kliot and Stanley Waterman. London: Croom Helm; New York: St. Martin's Press, 1983, pp. 270-83.
The authors explore U.N. voting patterns, including an examination of the May 1949 vote on the admission of Israel.

358.   CHANG, King-Yuh. "The United Nations and Decolonization: The Case of Southern Yemen." *International Organization*, XXVI (1972), 37-61.
Describes United Nations' involvement in the decolonization of the Republic of Southern Yemen, political problems in the area, and the position of various independence groups in South Yemen in 1963-64. Assesses the involvement of the U.N. Special Committee regarding the implementation of the Declaration of the Granting of Independence to Colonial Countries and Peoples. The Special Committee had sympathized with the independence groups and had their support, but considers the

Committee unsuccessful because it had failed to call an election before or after independence, and had been unable to conciliate the diverse independence groups to ensure a peaceful power transfer. Believes that U.N. decolonization effectiveness depended on a territory's domestic situation and the policy of external powers. Where (1) independence groups were unified, and (2) where cordial relationships governed such groups and the administering power, the United Nations machinery would be effective. Such had not been the case in Southern Yemen.

359. COBBAN, Helena. *The Palestinian Liberation Organization: People, Power and Politics.* New York: Cambridge University Press, 1984.
Details the multi-factioned PLO vis-à-vis the Middle East and the world community.

360. DINSTEIN, Yoram. "Autonomy." *Models of Autonomy.* Ed. Yoram Dinstein. New Brunswick, NJ: Transaction Books, 1981, pp. 291-303.
Relates the lessons of autonomy to aspects of negotiations between Israel and Egypt concerning self-government for the inhabitants of the West Bank and Gaza. Considers the spirit of togetherness that unites the two countries despite their differences an indispensable condition for viable autonomy. Since the Palestinian people had not joined the negotiations, their autonomy would have to be imposed by Israel and could not be viewed as an expression of self-determination. The text of the document which ordained autonomy was important but could not, by itself, settle all outstanding issues. Whereas Israel viewed autonomy as a conduit to drain Palestinian nationalism, Egypt saw it as a channel to ultimate statehood.

361. DINSTEIN, Yoram. "Self-Determination and the Middle East Conflict." *Self-Determination: National, Regional and Global Dimensions.* Eds. Yonah Alexander and Robert A. Friedlander. Boulder, CO: Westview Press, 1980, pp. 243-57.
Considers self-determination to be a collective human right. Defines a "people" by (1) the objective element, grounded in a strong ethnic-historical link; and (2) the subjective element, based on the will of the people. Explains that every people enjoyed the right to self-determination, but that self-government implied a seceding people's location in a well-defined territory in which it formed the majority. Believes the thrust of self-

determination to be that a people – if it so willed – was entitled
to independence from foreign domination. Palestinian Jews and
Arabs had the right to self-determination in the same land.
Partition of Palestine was the only solution, but the Arabs had
yielded to an all-or-nothing impulse and had attempted to
thwart the exercise of the Jewish right to self-determination by
force. Suggests that the Palestinian problem be solved through
compromise, leading to peaceful Arab-Jewish coexistence.

362.   DRYSDALE, Alasdair and Gerald H. BLAKE. *The Middle
        East and North Africa: A Political Geography.*   Oxford
        (England): Oxford University Press, 1985.
Trace and critically examine the geographic roots of many of
Middle East and North African political problems.   Discuss
state creation and the problem of nonstate peoples who desired
to achieve self-determination.

363.   ELAZAR, Daniel J., ed. *Self-Rule/Shared Rule: Federal Sol-
        utions to the Middle East Conflict.*   Ramat Gan (Israel):
        Turtledove Publishing, 1979.
Collection of papers which explore cultural, social, economic
and political aspects of federalism, drawing from examples in
many states, and then explore the ways, means and forms for the
application of a federal solution of the Israeli-Arab conflict.

364.   GABAY, Mayer. "Legal Aspects of the Camp David Frame-
        work for Peace in Relation to the Autonomy Proposal."
        Models of Autonomy.   Ed. Yoram Dinstein.   New
        Brunswick, NJ: Transaction Books, 1981, pp. 255-60.
Outlines the problematic issues of interpretation found in various articles of the Camp David Accords. Maintains that despite
the apparently irreconcilable differences with respect to the details of the solution, the mere fact that the accords were reached,
indicated that a peace agreement could be reached.

365.   GERSON, Allan. *Israel, The West Bank and International
        Law.* London: Frank Cass, 1978.
Contends that despite the U.N. Charter's limitation of the use
of force to instances of self-defence, however defined, the thesis
had been advanced that even where no threat to the security of
the intervening state existed, foreign intervention might be
justified if for the purpose of aiding self-determination movements. Observes that the U.N.'s Special Committee on the Definition of Aggression in 1974 had been ambiguous over the

claimed right to use force in aid of self-determination struggles. Concludes that notwithstanding the infusion of rhetoric and ambiguity, the traditional rule of international law and limiting recourse to force to instances of self-defense had apparently prevailed or at least had not been clearly deposed.

366. GOTLIEB, Yosef. *Self-Determination in the Middle East.* New York: Praeger, 1982.
Defines self-determination as the right of groups and individuals to govern their socioeconomic, political and cultural affairs without extended encumbrances. Considers the view of the Middle East that stressed the Arab-Israeli conflict as misinformed. Contends that the Middle East conflict had its base in the right of all Middle East peoples to self-determination. Discusses the problems of the Rinds, the Sudan, the Berbers and the Armenians, none of which had achieved emancipation in the post-colonial era, so that domination of the peoples had shifted from foreign imperialists to indigenous totalitarian élites. Believes that the only solution to the Middle East problems was to realign states with the region's cultural, linguistic and ethnic diversities.

367. HARKABI, Y. "The Position of the Palestinians in the Israeli-Arab Conflict and Their National Covenant (1968)." *New York University Journal of International Law and Politics,* III (1970), 209-44.
Discusses the issue of whether Palestinians were a people or a nation. Describes the position of the Palestinians on the West Bank and the Gaza strip. Reproduces the *Palestinian National Covenant* and stresses certain points: identifying Palestinians; claiming the entire country for Arab Palestinians; declaring that any solution short of total liberation was illegal; and that total liberation must be achieved militarily. Considers warfare against Israel legal.

368. HARRIS, G. S. "The Kurdish Conflict in Iraq." *Ethnic Conflict and International Relations.* Eds. A. Suhrke and L. Noble. New York: Praeger, 1977, pp. 68-92.
Examines how and why Iraq's Kurdish movement had lost its independence and came to be manipulated by political forces from abroad. Cites the Kurds as a good example of an ethnic group fragmented among several sovereign states, in which the interaction of geography, political legitimacy and leadership have had a critical impact upon the fate of an ethnic movement.

Traces the origins of the Kurdish revolt to domestic grievances
attributed to Iraqi policies. Analyzes the independent phase of
the conflict from 1961-63 to 1963-65, when foreign support had
become important.   Suggests that deteriorating Iraqi and
Iranian relations had prompted Iran to supply heavy weaponry
to the Kurdish separatists. The changing "constellation of foreign factors," including superpowers, had increasingly shaped
the internal ethnic conflict. In 1970, these factors had strengthened the Kurdish position and prompted the signing of the
March Accord as a platform for the negotiation of Kurdish
rights.   In March 1975, Iraqi and Iranian rapprochement had
sounded the separatist movement's death knell. Believes that
the revolt had lasted long because it had been confined to Iraq.
Had it spread to Turkey, Syria and Iran, these states might have
collaborated to eradicate Kurdish separatism.

369.   HARRIS, William W. *Taking Root: Israeli Settlement in the
         West Bank, the Golan and Gaza-Sinai, 1967-1980.* New
         York: John Wiley and Sons, 1980.
A critical analysis of Israel's settlement policies and their application in the captured territories.

370.   KASSIS, H. "Religious Ethnicity in the World of Islam - The
         Case of Lebanon." *International Political Science Review*,
         VI (1985), 216-29.
Examines the ideological, ethnic and religious confrontation
between Lebanon's Muslims and non-Muslims.   Reviews the
Arab terminology on ethnicity, and describes the ethno-
geographic and historical factors in the Lebanese conflict. Explains that the communities in Lebanon's disparate regions had
developed along regional-sectarian lines; neither solely verti-
cally, in terms of economic stratification, nor horizontally,
along sectarian lines.   Explains that Lebanon remained a
conglomeration of "primitive" [sic] groups which had rarely defined Lebanon in terms beyond their immediate regional and
ethnic interests.

371.   KLIOT, Nurit. "Dualism and Landscape Transformation in
         Northern Sinai: Some Outcomes of the Egypt-Israel Peace
         Treaty." *Pluralism and Political Geography: People, Terri-
         tory and State.* Eds. Nurit Kliot and Stanley Waterman.
         London: Croom Helm; New York: St. Martin's Press,
         1983, pp. 173-86.

Establishes the significance of attachments to place as part of a group's identity. Indicates how such ties, and place creation, could emerge in newly captured territories, and identifies some issues related to the loss of those territories and to the deprivation of a sense of place.

372. KÖCHLER, Hans, ed. *The Legal Aspects of the Palestinian Problem.* Wien: Wilhelm Braumüller, 1981.
Includes discussions of the Palestinians' right to self-determination.

373. LAND, D. M. and C. WALKER. *The Armenians.* London: Minority Rights Group, Report No. 32, n.d.
The authors place the Armenian minority problems in perspective in the light of recent historical and archeological research. Outline the geographic, linguistic and historical origins of the Armenians.

374. LAVIE, Samdar and William C. YOUNG. "Bedouin in Limbo: Egyptian and Israeli Development Policies in the Southern Sinai." *Antipode*, XVI, 2 (1984), 33-44.
The authors document and interpret the effects of Israeli and Egyptian development policies on the Sinai Bedouin. Argue that these policies had collided with the ecological and social realities of the peninsula. Fear that the fragile ecological balance of the peninsula would be disrupted, and the Bedouin would become marginal migrant laborers in their own lands.

375. LILIENTHAL, Alfred M. "The Right of Self Determination: Why Not the Palestinians?" *The Legal Aspects of the Palestinian Problem.* Ed. Hans Köchler. Wien: Wilhelm Braumüller, 1981.
Considers self-determination the most precious contemporary right. Claims that the creation of the State of Israel had deprived 1.3 million Arab Palestinians of the right to live in possession of their land. Acknowledges that Palestine had never enjoyed a separate or independent existence. Reviews the creation of Israel, and emphasizes anti-Zionist interpretatons of and attitudes toward the Balfour Declaraion.

376. MCDOWALL, David. *Lebanon: A Conflict of Minorities.* London: Minority Rights Group, Report No. 61, 1983.
Views Lebanon as "deeply and intrinsically composed of minorities;" a country in which each resident belonged to a

minority group. Analyzes the two primary Middle East loyalty bonds: kinship and religion. Considers loyalty bonds in the immigrant communities. Discusses the impact of the West, emphasizing modernization and nationalism, and the French role in the protection of Christian Lebanon. Examines the interests of independent Lebanon, the components of the "Lebanese consensus," and political life from 1943-75. Points to the socioeconomic impact of economic development and its effect on the conflicts. Juxtaposes these internal traditions and changes with outside pressures and influences – the Palestinian presence, the 1975-77 Civil War, the Syrian intervention, Israel's invasion and occupation, and the present status of "outsiders."

377. MEO, Leila. "The War in Lebanon." *Ethnic Conflict in International Relations.* Eds. A. Suhrke and L. Noble. New York: Praeger, 1979, pp. 93-126.
Explains how Lebanon, an apparently stable, balanced and enlightened democracy, could be wracked by a vicious and lengthy civil war. Examines the war's origins, expansion and sudden end. Suggests four factors as conflictual causes: (1) the interaction between ethnic-socioeconomic forces and political structures and processes in Lebanon; (2) the Palestinian community's role in Lebanese exile; (3) the impact of the Palestinian question on Lebanon's internal politics and external relationships; and (4) the motivation behind Syrian diplomacy in Lebanon, and roles by other Arab states, Israel, and the United States. Concludes that the nature of the internal conflict, although not strictly ethnic in nature, had influenced external interventions.

378. MESA, Roberto. "Les fondements historique et juridiques du droit à l'auto-détermination du Peuple Palestinien" (The Historical and Juridical Foundation of the Palestinian People's Right to Self-Determination). *The Legal Aspects of the Palestinian Problem.* Ed. Hans Köchler. Wien: Wilhelm Braumüller, 1981, pp. 67-93.
Reviews U.N. decisions that Palestinians could use to lay a claim to self-determination under international law.

379. MEZVINSKY, Norton. "The Palestinian People and the Right to Self-Determination." *The Legal Aspects of the Palestinian Problem.* Ed. Hans Köchler. Wien: Wilhelm Braumüller, 1981, pp. 34-49.
Traces Palestinian nationalism to the end of the nineteenth century, but notes that no distinctive Palestinian people or entity

had existed before the British Mandate after World War I. A distinctive Palestinian consciousness had emerged as a twin-response to the 1920 British Mandate and to Jewish nationalism in Palestine. Early expressions of Palestinian nationalism had stressed the overthrow of British controls and European influences. Traces the history of Palestinian nationalism from the British Mandate until the late 1970s.

380. NACHMIAS, D. and R. ROCKAWAY, "From a Nonstate Nation to a Nation-State: The Zionist Movement, 1897-1947." *Nonstate Nations in International Politics: Comparative System Analysis.* Ed. J. S. Bertelsen. New York: Praeger, 1977, pp. 36-68.
The authors examine the rise of Zionism and trace its development to the establishment of the State of Israel. Argue that nonstate nations must be creative in the use of formal and informal mechanisms to establish their claims. Assert that Zionists had employed both violent and nonviolent means to influence world opinion, and that violence had catalyzed the process of forcing states to articulate unambiguous policy positions. Conclude that humanitarian and political reasons had played equal roles in the support which Zionists ultimately secured for their cause.

381. NIJIM, Basheer K. and Bishara MUAMMAR. *Toward the De-Arabization of Palestine/Israel, 1945-1977.* Dubuque, IA: Kendall/Hunt Publishing Co. for The Jerusalem Fund for Education and Community Development, 1984.
The authors examine the impact of the creation of the State of Israel and that country's control of neighboring territories. Trace the changing patterns underlying Palestinian claims to self-determination.

382. RABINOVICH, Itamar. "The Autonomy Plan and Negotiations for the West Bank and the Gaza Strip in Their Political Context." *Models of Autonomy.* Ed. Yoram Dinstein. New Brunswick, NJ: Transaction Books, 1981, pp. 261-82.
Places the Palestinian issue in the context of attempts to settle the Arab-Israeli conflict. Highlights the political aspects of the issue in a discussion of the Camp David agreements, the signing of the peace treaty, and the autonomy negotiations. Notes that the latter had failed to produce any tangible results as the respective positions of Egypt, the United States, and Israel

hardened, and other developments had made the autonomy negotiations seem remote and irrelevant. Contends, nevertheless, that this failure had not led to a serious crisis in Egyptian-Israeli relations.

383.   SAID, Edward W. *The Question of Palestine.* New York: Time Books, 1979.
Deplores the plight of the four-million scattered Muslim and Christian Arabs known as Palestinians, who had been disenfranchised and deprived of their homeland, now under Israeli control. Develops the case for Palestinian self-determination.

384.   SHAPIRA, Amos. "Reflection on Autonomy: The Camp David Accords and the Obligation to Negotiate in Good Faith." *Models of Autonomy.* Ed. Yoram Dinstein. New Brunswick, NJ: Transaction Books, 1981, pp. 283-89.
Argues that the deliberate linguistic vagueness of the Camp David Accords had permitted Israel and Egypt to discover support for contradictory concepts within the agreements. The Israelis had regarded the autonomy regime as a means of preserving the essence of the existing political-strategic state of affairs in the West Bank and Gaza. The Egyptians had aspired to a comprehensive political-territorial Palestinian sovereignty.

385.   SMITH, Colin. *The Palestinians.* Fourth edition. London: Minority Rights Group, Report No. 24, 1982.
Traces the recent history of the Palestinians and recounts their feelings about recent political and diplomatic actions. Outlines the history of Palestine and the birth of Israel, relating to the exodus of Palestinians from their homeland. Surveys recent political and diplomatic events in two periods: until the mid-1970s and 1975-82. Describes the dispersal of Palestinians, identifies Palestinian political factions, and outlines Middle East peace plans, 1979-82. Illustrates Palestinian perceptions and objectives through selections from 1975 interviews. Summarizes the situation in the West Bank and Gaza and the aftermath of the 1982 Lebanese-Israeli war.

386.   STONE, Julius. *Israel and Palestine: Assault on the Law of Nations.* Baltimore and London: Johns Hopkins University Press, 1981.
Examines, *inter alia*, Jewish and Arab claims to self-determination, the status of U.N. General Assembly resolutions

under international law, territorial rights in Palestine under international law, and the role of the General Assembly with regard to the issue. Claims that a series of studies on the Arab-Israeli conflict carried out under U.N. auspices in 1978 and 1979 (attributed to the Committee on the Exercise of Inalienable Rights of the Palestinian People) were consistently anti-Israel. Suggests that this raised a serious question about the adequacy of the U.N. vis-à-vis international law. Argues that certain basic theses contained in the studies were erroneous, and that Israel had actual or potential sovereign rights in East Jerusalem, the West Bank and Gaza under international law.

387. THABIT, Robert W. "The Right of Self-Determination for the Palestinians." *The Legal Aspects of the Palestinian Problem.* Ed. Hans Köchler. Wien: Wilhelm Braumüller, 1981, pp. 94-7.

Contends that several U.N. General Assembly resolutions supported the right of Palestinians to self-determination but that this right had been denied to them. Maintains that the 1978 Camp David (Peace) Accords had denied the principle of self-determination. Suggests that Palestinians be permitted to express their views freely whether they desired local autonomy under the State of Israel, federation with the Hashemite Kingdom of Jordan, or an independent state of their own.

388. United Nations, Committee on the Exercise of the Inalienable Rights of the Palestinian People. *The Right of Self-Determination of the Palestinian People.* New York: United Nations, ST/SG/SER.F/3, 1979.

Examines the right of self-determination under international law generally, and focuses specifically on its application to Palestinians. Considers the right to self-determination a crucial element in international life, regardless of whether it was deemed a "principle" or a "right." Outlines the development of the concept through international instruments, together with juridical and academic options. Cites Hocking, Sureda, Brownlie, Higgins, Cobban, Gross, Emerson, and Judges Tanaka, Jessup and Lachs. Examines Palestinian self-determination within the context of the Peace Conference, the Mandate period, and the U.N. Points out that in recent years the U.N. had consistently and repeatedly reasserted the Palestinian peoples' right to self-determination.

U.S.S.R. and Eastern Europe

389.   ARMSTRONG, John A. "Federalism in the U.S.S.R.: Ethnic
       and Territorial Aspects." *Publius: The Journal of
       Federalism*, VII, 4 (1977), 89-106.
       Examines Soviet federalism from the conceptual perspective of
       center-periphery relations. Claims that Marx and his early fol-
       lowers had adamantly opposed any form of federalism and had
       favored democratic centralism. Lenin had broken with basic
       doctrinal considerations and advocated federalism for tactical
       reasons, including the need to utilize the Russian Empire's
       minorities as wedges for the expanding revolution, and to
       counter the factionalism inherent in cultural autonomy formu-
       lations. Traces the pros and cons of federalism in the USSR.
       Contends that it had become increasingly difficult to maintain
       Russian dominance within the federalist façade, in view of
       changing political, economic and demographic realities.

390.   BRACHT, Hans Werner, *et al. Das Selbstbestimmungsrecht der
       Völker in Osteuropa und China* (The East European and
       Chinese People's Right to Self-Determination).   Köln:
       Wissenschaft und Politik, 1968.
       Essays on the interpretation and application of the concept of
       self-determination in the U.S.S.R., Poland, Czechoslovakia,
       Hungary, Romania, Yugoslavia, Bulgaria, the G.D.R. and
       China.

391.   BURG, Steven L. "Ethnic Conflict and the Federalization of
       Socialist Yugoslavia: The Serbo-Croat Conflict." *Publius:
       The Journal of Federalism*, VII, 4 (1977), 119-43.
       The conflict between the Serbian and Croatian ethnic commu-
       nities in Yugoslavia had incorporated disputes over the organi-
       zation of the state and the distribution of political power, and
       among competing religions, cultures and languages. Traces
       Yugoslav federalism from the Party policy of encouraging con-
       tact and cooperation among republics and ethnic communities
       in the 1950s to de facto confederation in the late 1960s. Claims
       that as the Party leadership abandoned centralization and
       authoritarianism to guide economic and political organization,
       and implemented the principle of self-management, the need,
       ability and tendency of republican leaderships to represent the
       interests of their republics had vigorously increased. The
       federation had proved flexible when faced with republican de-

mands, but the Party leadership would not tolerate overt nationalism by the nationalities. Suggests two broad considerations for the Yugoslav political decision-making process to function: (1) the Party as a whole, and each of its republican and provincial organizations in particular, must be internally disciplined; and (2) the Party must be able to enforce certain limitations on the actions of social institutions.

392. DENITCH, Bogdan. "The Evolution of Yugoslav Federalism." *Publius: The Journal of Federalism*, VII, 4 (1977), 107-18.
Traces the development of federalism in Yugoslavia from the formation of the Yugoslav national state onward. The new state was bedeviled with numerous integration problems stemming from diverse and sometimes hostile populations, isolated and underdeveloped regions, and divergent political traditions. The Yugoslav Communist Party had stressed the need for federal autonomy in this early period to counteract Serb dominance in the central apparatus. Claims that Yugoslav federalism in the post-World War II era had been ambivalent: on one hand, traditional local demands were held in high regard; on the other, the Communist Party had been centralizing and was committed to a planned economy with little promise of providing a genuine basis for autonomy. Outlines the movement toward decentralization during the 1960s, with increasing reliance on a market economy, increasing emphasis on decentralization to the republics, and increasing stress on the prerogatives of the communes. Indicates, nevertheless, that supra-republic bonds, such as the army, a shared market, and political élite unified the country. Considers the Yugoslav federation a success.

393. KRISTOF, Erich. *Die Lehre von Selbstbestimmungsrecht in der Völkerrechtsdoktrin der DDR* (The Theory of Self-Determination in the GDR's Doctrine of International Law). Frankfurt am Main: Athenäum Verlag, 1973.
Explores how the Marxist-Leninist theory of self-determination had found expression in the GDR, as the East German nation and state developed.

394. LEVKOV, Ilya. "Self-Determination in Soviet Politics." *Self-Determination: National, Regional and Global Dimensions.* Eds. Yonah Alexander and Robert A. Friedlander. Boulder, CO: Westview Press, 1980, pp. 133-90.

Argues that the potentially disintegrative concept of self-determination had become an element of territorial consolidation and expansion in the Soviet Union. Attributes this radical change in the function of self-determination largely to the Soviet Union's redefinition of the concept of sovereignty by establishing the concept of double-sovereignty for each republic, thus creating a unique Soviet federalism. Following the October Revolution, the Soviet Union had radically redefined Lenin's conception of the right to self-determination as a centripetal force in order to meet tactical exigencies. The period of contractual federation had served to incorporate the republics into the Union. The Soviet Union had viewed constitutional change as a battleground of the central authority's colliding interests against the demands of the republics, and considered the concepts of state, nation, language and culture to be the moving forces of self-determination in the Soviet Union. Recently the Soviet state became more centralized and strengthened through the formation of a new and unique "Soviet nation." Considers Soviet theorists unable to perceive European integrative policies beyond their economic and military implications. In principle, the Soviet Union supported national liberation movements, but recent policies indicated the dominance of *Realpolitik*.

395. RAKOWSKA-HARMSTONE, Teresa. "Ethnic Autonomy in the Soviet Union." *Ethnicity in an International Context.* Eds. Abdul Said and Luiz R. Simmons. New Brunswick, NJ: Transaction Books, 1976.
Argues that notwithstanding the Soviet Union's image as a homogeneous state that had attempted to forge a "New Soviet Man," ethnic consciousness had grown increasingly divisive in recent years. Examines the key variables involved in the problem of ethnicity and the state in the Soviet Union: the demographic and political base, characteristics and roles of the Great Russians, other ethnic groups, and demographic and economic trends and requirements. Party policy had augmented assimilationist tendencies with political education campaigns, and merged smaller republics into broader entities, thereby removing the institutional territorial base as a focus of national identity for some ethnic groups. Ethnic dissatisfactions had coalesced around three major grievance areas: (1) desires for broader political autonomy; (2) recognition of republican needs in resource allocation; and (3) the demand for complete cultural

autonomy. Reviews several policy alternatives available to the leadership for solution of the ethnic problem.

396. RAKOWSKA-HARMSTONE, Teresa. "Integration and Ethnic Nationalism in the Soviet Union: Aspects, Trends, and Problems." *Nationalities and Nationalism in the U.S.S.R.: A Soviet Dilemma.* Eds. Carl A. Linden and Dimitrik Simes. Washington, DC: The Center for Strategic and International Studies, Georgetown University, 1976, pp. 31-9.

Pinpoints the dilemma of national integration in the Soviet Union: while its ideological and institutional matrix lent legitimacy to ethnic claims, the exercise of ethnic rights and autonomy was being effectively denied in view of political centralization and the Russian nation's hegemony. Identifies three main catalysts that had stimulated the growth of ethnicity in the Soviet Union: (1) the federal compromise of 1924, which had established the administrative-territorial state structure based on ethnic regions, had provided key ethnic communities with a base and instrument for the articulation of ethnic interest; (2) the impact of modernization had generated the formation of new ethnic élites and differentiated social mobilization along ethnic lines; and (3) the Russians' historically dominant role. Identifies three hindrances to Soviet national integration: (1) the basic asymmetry in the Soviet functional division of labor between the Russian core and backward borderlands; (2) linguistic and cultural differences; and (3) the non-Russian ethnic communities' political and economic dependence on the Russians. Asserts that the Soviet leadership had expected nationalism to be submerged by the class principle as the community grew, but that historical experience and current trends and realities indicated otherwise.

397. REMINGTON, R. "Ideology as a Resource: A Communist Case Study." *Nonstate Nations in International Politics - A Comparative Systems Analysis.* Ed. J. S. Bertelsen. New York: Praeger, 1979, pp. 193-222.

Examines the Croatian situation as a complex example of a nonstate nation in an international context. Suggests that the difficulty of attracting attention without provoking a repressive reaction was compounded by the number of separate groups operating essentially independently and with somewhat different goals. Notes the dilemma of utilizing socialist ideology to achieve constitutional change without appearing to forsake national goals.   The failure to achieve this balance and the Yugoslav state's repressive response had triggered Croatian terrorism.   States that violent alternatives had failed to create an autonomous or independent Croatia, but that this aggressiveness had undermined Yugoslav unity, increased psychological pressure on the government, and damaged Yugoslavia's foreign relations.

398.   SCHÖPFLIN, George.   *The Hungarians of Romania.*   London: Minority Rights Group, Report No. 37, 1978.
Investigates the status of the Hungarians (Magyars) in Transylvania, a minority, the largest in Europe, created in 1918-20 by the redrawing of the boundaries following the dissolution of the Austro-Hungarian Empire.   Describes the region's geography, population, history and religion.   Reviews the political aspects of the Szeklers, an ethnographically distinct part of the Hungarian minority in Romania.   Surveys the nationality policy in communist states and its application in Romania.   Outlines the main grievances of the minority in connection with education, cultural provisions, economics, employment, politics and administration.   Considers the international ramifications, emphasizing Romania's security fears, cultural links with Hungary and tourism.   Weighs the minority's desire to live a "Hungarian life" with the government's fears of the incompatibility of this desire with communist policy.

399.   SHEEHY, Ann.   *The Crimean Tatars, Volga Germans, and Meskhetians: Soviet   Treatment   of   Some   National Minorities.*   Revised edition.   London: Minority Rights Group, Report No. 6, 1973.
Examines the recent history and present situation of three national minorities.   Considers these groups distinguishable from other national groups in the USSR because of the grave injustices they had suffered.   Contrasts them with other minorities, such as the Ukrainians and Lithuanians, who enjoyed essentially the same rights as the Russians.   Describes the mass deportations of the groups during World War II from the eastern USSR to Siberia and Central Asia.   Depicts the three groups' current situation, emphasizing that the early Crimean Tatar and Volga German national autonomy had not been reinstated.   Notes the lack of official information and the West's reliance on samizdat documents.   These indicated that the Crimean Tatars and Muskhetians had been conducting mass campaigns since 1956-57 for the restoration of their rights.

Concludes that these despairing national minorities saw emigration as the only solution to their problems.

400. SHEVTSOV, Victor. *National Sovereignty and the Soviet State.* Moscow: Progress Publishers, 1974.
Considers national sovereignty a nation's or nationality's independence in the political, territorial, cultural and linguistic fields. However, national sovereignty was not inherent in a nation but a "democratic principle unconditionally applying to all nations and nationalities." The recognition of a nation's right to self-determination was an expression of "maximum democracy and minimum nationalism," with this right being an organic component of national sovereignty. Socialism "creates new and superior forms of human society," in which the needs and aspirations of the working masses of each nationality would be met through international unity. The Soviet federation thus was a step toward the unification of various nationalities into a single democratic and centralized Soviet state. The federation was a transitional form of government to complete unity; the federation would become redundant in the fully developed communist society where complete national unity would prevail.

401. SHEVTSOV, Victor. *The State and Nations in the USSR.* Moscow: Progress Publishers, 1982.
Presents the Marxist-Leninist conception of the integral federal multinational state, and shows how Lenin and the CPCU creatively developed the doctrine of Soviet socialist federation. Proposes a conception of the nation stressing the influence of historical and socioeconomic factors on the shapers of national distinctiveness. Outlines three significant points in the history of the formation of the USSR, including the principle of socialist federalism, the exercise of free self-determination of nations, and the association of equal Soviet Republics into an integral state. Maintains that only within the framework of a great federal state could each of the Soviet republics attain unprecedented economic, social and cultural development.

402. SMITH, G. E. "Ethnic Nationalism in the Soviet Union: Territory, Cleavage, and Control." *Environment and Planning C: Government and Policy*, III (1985), 49-73.
Challenges the widely-held Western view that ethnic nationalism necessarily threatened the Soviet state. Argues that the cross-patterned reticulation model of social and ethnic

stratification demonstrated why the politicization of national identities could not be automatic or uniform. Explores how the states controlled the politicization of ethnoterritorial cleavages: by focusing on the internal passport system, the federal structure, and language planning. Explains the problems a nationalistically sympathetic cultural intelligentsia faced in mobilizing support around ethnoterritorial cleavages. Identifies the socioeconomic and political changes likely to fuel the engines for political action where easily identifiable ethnoterritorial cleavages and a sympathetic regional political leadership made this possible.

403. YAVETZ, Zvi. "Autonomous Arrangements in the Balkan States." *Models of Autonomy.* Ed. Yoram Dinstein. New Brunswick, NJ: Transaction Books, 1981, pp. 85-96.
Proposes that autonomy might only be a transitional stage and could not last where national or international tensions prevailed. Uses Romania, which had moved from an autonomous principality to an independent state between 1857 and 1877, to illustrate this view. Although the Romanian case was unique, it had some general relevance to the present.

Western Europe: Comparative Studies

404. ALLARDT, Erik. "Implications of the Ethnic Revival in Modern Industrial Society. A Comparative Study of the Linguistic Minorities in Western Europe." *Commentationes scientiarum socialum 12* Helsinki: Societas scientiarum fennica, 1979.
Identifies a new substate phenomenon, a minority ethnic group with territorial basis and a distinct language. Discusses the social categorization and self-categorization processes through which minorities, like nations, were socially constituted and maintained. Reviews the general patterns of minority needs, requests and responses, and traces the common elements in Western Europe's present ethnic activity. Frames this discussion within an overall understanding of ethnicity and modern changes in the nature and social significance of ethnicity. Considers the interaction between modes of categorization and the cultural division of labor. Statistically analyzes linguistic minorities in this region. Discerns a general pattern

of attempts at managing ethnic conflict, partly because in modern society, ethnicity provided a social bond where old ascriptive structures had been eroded.

405. ARNAUD, Nicole and Jacques DOFNEY. *Nationalism and the National Question.* Montreal: Black Rose Books, 1977.
The authors discuss nationalism and the national question as applied to Québec and the French region of Occitanie. Regard the French central state oppressive, and favor the application of autonomy based on a decentralized form of socialism. Discuss the role of language and culture in Québec, and link this to national aspirations and social justice. Declare that in France, as in Canada, "minorities" which insisted on their own autonomous or separate existence, constituted a genuine threat for established constitutional and economic arrangements.

406. BEN-AMI, Shlomo. "The Catalan and Basque Movements for Autonomy." *Models of Autonomy.* Ed. Yoram Dinstein. New Brunswick, NJ: Transaction Books, 1981, pp. 67-84.
Highlights the socioeconomic dimensions of autonomy in the Catalan and Basque cases. As well as a reflection of national affinities, autonomism in both regions was a social protest fostered by a sense of superiority toward the "moribund" center. Francoist repression might eliminate the external manifestations of Basqueism and Catalanism; it could never uproot nationalist movements. The new Spanish government's concession of autonomous status to the Basques and Catalans had succeeded in isolating the extremists and substituting for dictatorial coercion a democratically approved constitutional consensus upon which autonomy and Spain's historic unity could coexist.

407. BRAND, Jack A. "Nationalism and the Noncolonial Periphery: A Discussion of Scotland and Catalonia." *New Nationalisms of the Developed West.* Eds. Edward A. Tiryakian and Ronald Rogowski. Boston: Allen and Unwin, 1985, pp. 277-93.
Considers Michael Hechter's model of internal colonialism marred by serious theory and measurement problems, as evidenced in the two areas of "relative overdevelopment" that did not fit the model, Scotland and Catalonia. Suggests another way of explaining the rise of nationalism was inexplicable in terms of one rule or law, but rather different conditions might produce the same result. Claims that national sentiment was

only the most recent form of a primeval emotion of community.
Wonders under which conditions this cleavage could be made
salient over the others. Points to two central features charac-
terizing Scotland and Catalonia: an independent popular culture, including the symbol of past independence; and the
country's world position, plus the extent to which the society
could develop and build a consciousness of its own interests.

408. CATUDAL, Honore M., Jr. *The Exclave Problem of Western
      Europe.* Tuscaloosa: University of Alabama Press, 1979.
      Analyzes the problems exclaves posed for international relations
      as they formed a geopolitical challenge to the nation-state.
      Defines an exclave as the existence of a part of a state in the
      territory of another state. Reviews some situations in Europe,
      Africa, the Middle East, and Asia. Discusses exclaves in re-
      lation to their different appearances, varying origins, and con-
      tinued survival, where the process of disenclavement had been
      unsuccessful. Examines the modern European exclaves in terms
      of accessibility, mainly expressed in administrative and eco-
      nomic relations with the home state. In the past, exclaves could
      opt for close ties with the home state, provided the latter was
      cooperative; they could assimilate with the "host state," or they
      could strive to be more or less independent. Currently, they
      followed a somewhat autonomous course differing mostly with
      the home state, while remedying disadvantages.

409. CONNOR, Walker. "Ethnonationalism in the First World:
      The Present in Historical Perspective." *Ethnic Conflict in
      the Western World.* Ed. Milton J. Esman. Ithaca, NY:
      Cornell University Press, 1977, pp. 19-45.
      Views recent ethnonational developments within Western
      Europe as a sequential, evolutionary step in the extension of the
      force field of nationalism. Outlines two pillars of scholarship
      characterizing the study of Western ethnonationalism: (1) the
      belief that nationalism was obsolete in Western Europe; and (2)
      the belief that Western Europe was composed of nation-states.
      Attributes the growth of ethnonationalism in Western Europe
      to modernization and more effective communications, which
      had resulted in increased ethnic self-awareness and the demon-
      stration effect of diverse claims to national self-determination.
      Recommends historical and comparative approaches to the
      study of nationalism. Suggests four pitfalls in the study of
      nationalism, with particular application to the Western
      European experience: (1) confusing terminology tending not to

recognize ethnonationalism for what it was; (2) the tendency to discern national strife as predicated principally upon language, religion, customs, economic inequity, or some other tangible element; (3) an unwarranted exaggeration of the influence of materialism on human affairs; and (4) the tendency to interpret the absence of ethnic strife as evidence of the presence of a single nation.

410. GOUREVITCH, Peter Alexis. "The Reemergence of 'Peripheral Nationalism': Some Comparative Speculations on the Spatial Distribution of Political Leadership and Economic Growth." *Comparative Studies in Society and History*, XXI (1979), 303-22.
Identifies political leadership, economic growth and development, and ethnic potential as the combination of interests that make a region an effective unit for political mobilization. Examines the experiences of the United Kingdom, Spain, France, Italy, Germany, Belgium, Yugoslavia, and Canada, concluding that geographical noncongruence between political and economic functions in the core and periphery would tend to reinforce rather than submerge regionalisms, and regions with significant ethnic potentials would produce peripheral nationalisms.

411. GRAHL-MADSEN, Atle. "The Evolution of the Nordic Autonomies." *Nordisk Tidsskrift For International Ret*, LIV (1985), 4-9.
Discusses the three autonomous territories in the north: Åland, Foroyar, and Kalaallit Nunaat (Greenland), together with Samiland. Describes the political structures of the territories. Points out that although Samiland had not yet achieved an autonomous status, the Sami were recognized as a people in their own right. Suggests that models for autonomy might be found in other jurisdictions, *e.g.*, Canada. Describes the Nordic Council and suggests that one day the Sami people would have their own representation in the Council.

412. KREJČÍ, Jaroslav and Vítězslav VELÍMSKÝ. *Ethnic and Political Nations in Europe*. London: Croom Helm, 1981.
The authors examine the perception of ethnic issues by politicians and statesmen, journalists, scholars, and the general public. Outline the political and cultural dimensions of the concept of "nation." Explain that in French- and English-speaking countries the concept of nation had followed geographical and

institutional guidelines, whereas in central and eastern Europe nations were exclusively linguistically and culturally oriented. Construct a multidimensional taxonomy of nationhood in which territory, political status, history, culture, language, and national consciousness interacted. Outline four contemporary ethnic problems: (1) ethnic groups lacking self-government; (2) ethnic groups dissatisfied with their current types of self-government; (3) artificially severed ethnic groups; and (4) recent ethnic problems created by the large-scale migration of individuals and their subsequent resettlement in alien countries. Offer a country-by-country arrangement of individual European countries according to their attitudes on political problems involving multi-ethnicity. Examine the economic causes of ethnic tensions, and caution against pushing ethnic issues onto the economic plane. Demonstrate certain dynamic aspects of ethnicity by considering scenarios involving ethnic self-preservation.

413.   LINDHOLM, Goran. "The Right of Autonomous Regions to Participate in Nordic Co-operation." *Nordisk Tidsskrift For International Ret*, LIV (1985), 79-85.
Discusses the findings of the Petri Committee establishing the position of the Nordic autonomies in Nordic Co-operation. Suggests that the Committee's recommendations followed traditional principles of public international law. Analyzes entities possessing international legal competence: states; political entities resembling states; condominiums; internationalized territories; international organizations; state agencies; organization agencies and others. Examines the legal status of Nordic autonomies under current international legal doctrines. Suggests that juridically, the position of the Faroes, Greenland, and Åland had been established and corresponded better to their status under public international law.

414.   MACIVER, D. N. "Conclusion. Ethnic Identity and the Modern State." *National Separatism.* Ed. Colin H. Williams. Cardiff: University of Wales Press, 1982, pp. 299-307.
Maintains that the nation-state's major integrative properties included coercive, instrumental, and identity factors, and that the existence of disaffected or separatist groups indicated some failure of integration. Suggests that the extent and effectiveness of political integration in advanced societies had been possibly overestimated, and that the traditional centralist state might not

be able to respond adequately to the challenge of ethnoterritorial disaffection and national separatism. Identifies social, environmental, and integrative factors as conditions which initiated and determined the development of the national separatism process. The failure of integration, especially of identity and instrumental capabilities, and the internationalization of integrative assets in sub-units, presented a potentially serious threat to the state. Discerns a contradiction between providing more effective government by enhancing regional autonomy and the marshalling of resources and coordinating powers of centralism. Most ethnic demands were not necessarily for political independence, but for recognition, together with administrative and economic support to preserve their cultural identity. Argues that consociational and federal arrangements offered more hope than regional devolution.

415. MAYO, Patricia Elton. *The Roots of Identity: Three National Movements in Contemporary European Politics.* London: Allen Lane, 1974.
Contends that modern industrial society tended to be uniformist and rootless, with the citizens being remote from those who controlled their destiny. Suggests that the revolt against centralist governments throughout Western Europe was really a fight to retain identity. Supports this thesis by examining nations in Brittany, Wales, and the Basque country, which had recently heightened their struggles against centralist bureaucracies and the proponents of social uniformity.

416. MENY, Yves and Vincent WRIGHT, eds. *Centre-Periphery Relations in Western Europe.* London: George Allen and Unwin, 1985.
Ten authors explore intergovernmental relations and the interaction between national governments – the center – and subnational minorities located in the periphery. Individual chapters investigate regional variations in the United Kingdom, France, the Federal Republic of Germany, Spain and Italy. Observe that recent evidence suggested increasing central reluctance or resistance to granting new rights to the periphery.

417. NEVITTE, Neil. "The Religious Factor in Contemporary Nationalist Movements: An Analysis of Quebec, Wales, and Scotland." *New Nationalisms of the Developed West.* Eds. Edward A. Tiryakian and Ronald Rogowski. Boston: Allen and Unwin, 1985, pp. 337-52.

Contends that "the religious factor," although certainly not the
most important variable, had contributed to nationalism,
particularly during the early phases of its life-cycles. Moreover,
religion continued to interact with contemporary nationalism in
less direct but nonetheless significant ways. A historical
summary of the relationship between religion and nationalism
in Québec, Wales and Scotland revealed the general conditions
under which the religious factor contributed to nationalism: (1)
where the national minority was distinguished by religion from
the state's dominant culture; (2) where the national church had
the institutional capacity to speak for the nation; and (3) where
religious values were a significant part of the national culture in
question. An analysis of survey data from contemporary
Québec showed that (1) the secular values associated with the
"Quiet Revolution" had not percolated throughout Québec
society; (2) over one-half of the culturally religious in Québec
identified themselves equally with the Canadian state and the
Québec nation; and (3) cultural religiosity interacted with
nationalism to depress the inclination that nationalists would
favor independence.

418. PETERSEN, William. "On the Subnations of Western
      Europe." *Ethnicity: Theory and Experience.* Eds. Nathan
      Glazer and Daniel P. Moynihan. Cambridge: Harvard
      University Press, 1975, pp. 177-208.
      Explores the application and utility of defining groups within
      European states, including nation, minority group, ethnic
      group, and community, before focusing on trends in European
      nationalism. Examines subnations, and raises questions about
      optimum size. Outlines the revival of nationalist sentiment in
      some of Europe's problem areas. Explores the situations in
      Switzerland and Belgium.

419. ROKKAN, Stein and Derek W. URWIN. *The Politics of
      Territorial Identity: Studies in European Regionalism.*
      London: Sage Publications, 1982.
      The authors identify most if not all states in Western Europe as
      multiethnic polities possessing several identity layers. Some of
      the states had metamorphosed from sub-state regional social
      distinctivenesses to political expressions of such distinc-
      tivenesses. Acknowledge four parallel change processes that
      had influenced Western European groups since 1945: (1) con-
      tinuing internationalization of territorial economies and
      persistent erosion of interstate boundaries; (2) increased de-

mands on and expectations of the resources and manpower of the machineries in each state; (3) multiplication of efforts to mobilize peripheries, regions and localities against the national centers; and (4) assertion (or reassertion) of minority claims to cultural autonomy and for separate powers regarding territorial decision-making. Identify two essential bases of political mobilization in the politicization and activation of group differences: territory and "group" identity. Any territorially non-concentrated group would offer a difficult mobilization target for any movement with political ambitions. Where the target population was geographically dispersed, politicization efforts could be easily frustrated by the state.

420. SCHREUER, Christoph. "Autonomy in South Tyrol." *Models of Autonomy*. Ed. Yoram Dinstein. New Brunswick, NJ: Transaction Books, 1981, pp. 53-66.
Discusses the background and arrangements of Italy's New Autonomy Statute for South Tyrol. Through certain constitutional, legislative and administrative measures, the statute sought to provide a framework to enable the province's German-speaking majority to pursue its interests more effectively. Although the autonomy model applied in South Tyrol could not be transposed to other situations, its moderate success provided some inspiration and ideas for autonomy negotiations elsewhere.

421. SETON-WATSON, Hugh. "Reflections on Europe's Experience of Separatism." *Collected Seminar Papers on the Politics of Separatism, no. 19*. London: University of London, Institute of Commonwealth Studies, 1975, pp. 1-4.
Considers separatism an extremely old phenomenon. Discusses the European experience, citing many examples, including a typology of aims, motives and conditions. Identifies separatism as a political movement based on the overwhelming desire to remove the community in question from subjection to, or association with, another community or communities. The aim might, but need not, be the creation of an independent state. Enumerates three motives inspiring separatism: (1) persistent traditions of independent statehood; (2) myths based on dim memories of statehood in the distant past; and (3) religious or linguistic cleavages. Separatist sentiment might be especially strong when differences between communities coincided with visible distinctions involving wealth, class and language. The two necessary, but not sufficient, conditions for separatism were

strong mass support (based on widespread socioeconomic discontent) and a leadership specifically aiming at separation.

422.   SETON-WATSON, Hugh. "Unsatisfied Nationalisms." *Journal of Contemporary History* (special issue on "Nationalism and Separatism"), VII (1971), 3-15.
Explains the essential characteristic of national movements: their members were "unsatisfied" with their condition for one or a combination of reasons; their claims had been refused; their consciousness was still in the process of formation; their spokesmen were themselves uncertain of their identity. Categorizes the national movements discussed into three types: (1) old nations left behind in the race for independence (Scots, Catalans, perhaps Welsh and Basques); (2) nations in formation (Kurds and southern Sudanese); and (3) communities with ambivalent identity (Northern Irish and Lebanese). Considers Canada a special case: whereas French-Canadians formed a distinct nation, a Canadian or English-Canadian nation did not exist. Suggests that without Québec, Canada would probably not survive as a state. Concludes that, despite widespread nationalist fanaticism, nationalism and the nation-state were probably preferable alternatives.

423.   TIRYAKIAN, Edward A. "Quebec, Wales, and Scotland: Three Nations in Search of a State." *International Journal of Comparative Sociology*, XXI (1980), 1-13.
Asserts that contemporary nationalist movements need not be qualified as "ethnic" or "minority;" like their predecessors, their essence had been firstly the endeavor to develop a national consciousness among all those inhabiting the same territory, and secondly, to mobilize this consciousness into action on behalf of establishing the collectivity's autonomy or self-determination from alien rule. Attributes part of the nationalist movement's rise in Scotland, Wales and Québec to the identity loss related to the significance and appeal to the young in the periphery of adherence and identification with the polity, society and culture of the nation-state. In Great Britain, this had been linked to the rapid decline of the country as a great power; in Québec, the movement had reflected dynamic modernization and had served as an outlet of effective protest against the establishment. Believes that if the new nationalist movements were to develop, they must overcome the psychological complexes, including inferiority, associated with being Scottish, Welsh or Québécois in relation to the pace-setting dominant

national groups. Maintains that the resurgence of nationalist movements was appropriate for comparative sociological study. Finds the movements in Québec, Wales and Scotland especially interesting, because they had emerged simultaneously within established democratic nation-states.

424. TIRYAKIAN, Edward A. and Ronald ROGOWSKI, eds. *New Nationalisms of the Developed West.* Boston: Allen and Unwin, 1985.
Sixteen papers analyze modern nationalist movements that had challenged the sovereignty of Western nation-states because they were "nations against states." Theoretical chapters are followed by regional case studies.

425. TUDJMAN, Franjo. *Nationalism in Contemporary Europe.* New York: Columbia University Press, East European Monographs, 1981.
Traces the national question from the Congress of Vienna (1815) to the Yalta Conference (1945). Examines nationalist questions involving Northern Ireland, Scotland, Wales, Brittany, Corsica, Alsace, the Basque provinces, Catalonia, Galicia (Spain), the Azores, Italy, Belgium, Friesland, the Faroes, Lapland, The Juras, Cyprus, Germany, Yugoslavia, and eastern Europe. Argues that nationalism had become the most important historical determinant. Believes that the capacity of a nation for survival was too immense for effective countermeasures. Insists that self-determination and integration in Europe were not antagonistic but rather complementary forces; only a free and sovereign nation could contribute to the world fully. The Soviet Union's experience demonstrated that new nations could not be created artificially from existing ones, because nations evolved naturally from a complex historical process. Revolutionary communist movements had been successful primarily where they had assumed responsibility for realizing national self-determination objectives.

426. WILLIAMS, Colin, H. "Ethnic Separatism in Western Europe." *Tijdschrift voor Economische en Sociale Geografie*, LXXI (1980), 142-58.
Examines ethnic separatism with three broad aims: (1) to review the process of state integration and development from a political-geographic perspective; (2) to illustrate the value of emphasizing regional variations in separatist support to meas-

ure their representativeness in minority areas; and (3) to discuss the inadequacy of existing explanations of ethnic separatism in Western European states. Recommends that the common factors in nationalist conflicts be isolated in order to construct a theory of separatism exceeding core-periphery theorizing, and increased emphasis on the class structure of the new ethnic intelligentsia.

427.   WILLIAMS, Colin H. "When Nationalists Challenge: When Nationalists Rule." *Environment and Planning C: Government and Policy*, III (1985), 27-48.
Examines procedures through which minorities in Québec and Wales had used language as a political grievance factor within nationalist-inspired group mobilization. Although the minorities had reaped tangible benefits from nationalist mobilization, they had also evoked disquiet among the majority peoples regarding the primacy ascribed to language-related policies and the future prospect of extending the legitimacy of minority tongues from public to private domains. In this respect, Québec offered a more integrative pattern than Wales, where language intrusion had engendered conflict within the Welsh-speaking minority and had bred new sources of class-based friction. Recommends that the language promotion issue be viewed not only in terms of cultural reproduction, but also as a struggle for political and economic control that might maximize access to natural resources and occupational mobility in bicultural societies.

Western Europe: Case Studies

428.   AAREBROT, Frank H. "Norway: Center and Periphery in a Peripheral State." *The Politics of Territorial Identity*. Eds. Stein Rokkan and Derek W. Urwin. London, Beverley Hills and New Delhi: Sage Publications, 1982, pp. 75-112.
Contends that regional differences in Norway had not prevented a reconfirmation of the unitary state. Reviews the origins of the Norwegian state and traces regional economic differences. Examines elements of a regional counter-culture in the west, including a strong Lutheran orthodoxy, teetotalism, and usage of the "nynorsk" written form. The Norwegian state had traditionally catered to peripheral interests by allowing electoral

overrepresentation in rural areas and permitting a relatively high degree of local autonomy. Offers three reasons for the lack of serious regional political problems in Norway: (1) in the Norwegian political system regions had very little institutional infrastructure; (2) cultural identities and aims were not tied to specific regions; and (3) the basis for Norwegian economic development had emphasized local industries rather than regional ones, at least until recently.

429. AGNEW, John A. "Place and Political Behaviour: The Case of Scottish Nationalism." *Political Geography Quarterly*, III (1984), 191-206.
Notes two dominant perspectives governing the growing support for regionalist and separatist movements in Western Europe: (1) uneven structural development; and (2) individualistic electoral approaches. Proposes a third perspective focusing on the concepts of place, social context, and territorial-cultural setting in the emergence of distinctive political identities. Utilizes Scotland as an example to demonstrate the importance of spatial variation in the formation of nationalist movements. Analyzes the nature of regional patterns of support for the Scottish National Party through this model, emphasizing geography as the dominant variable in explaining political behavior. Elaborates the basic principle underlying the argument that political action might ultimately result from individual acts, but it was best explained by the social context in which individuals functioned.

430. AGNEW, John A. "Political Regionalism and Scottish Nationalism in Gaelic Scotland." *Canadian Review of Studies in Nationalism*, VIII (1981), 115-29.
Considers two questions prompted by recent research into the rise of separatist politics in the so-called British "Celtic fringe": (1) was the rise of political regionalism an ethnically-based response to domination by English political and economic institutions? (2) Can political regionalism be treated as a "Celtic" rather than an Irish, Welsh and Scottish phenomenon? Replies negatively to both questions, and argues that political regionalism must be understood in all its "situational contexts" rather than as it emerged as something-in-itself from the ethnic mobilization model.

431. BENNETT, R. J. "Regional Movements in Britain: A Review of Aims and Status." *Environment and Planning C: Government and Policy*, III (1985), 75-96.
Analyzes the activities of regional and nationalist movements in Great Britain with respect to five hypotheses: (1) the degree and form of representation, including the role of élites; (2) the extent of participation in regional identity; (3) the form of existing and desired forms of decentralization; (4) the extent of specificity of regional issues; and (5) the extent of central economic and political dominance.   Analyzes seven major areas: Shetland, Orkney, Western Isles, Cornwall, Wessex, the North, and North Devon, with some consideration of Scotland and Wales. Demonstrates the existence of considerable regional identity in some regions, and remarkable success of regional movements in Shetland, Orkney and North Devon.   Finds participation in other regions "dormant."

432. BLACK, N. "The Cyprus Conflict." *Ethnic Conflict and International Relations*.   Eds. A. Suhrke and L. Noble.   New York: Praeger, 1977, pp. 43-67.
Examines the Cyprus conflict in terms of the difficulty of involved parties in ascertaining its essence as an ethnic conflict. Explains why observers frequently regarded Cyprus as a colonial question: the island "looks like a self-contained political entity when it is really a combination of fragments of Greece and Turkey."   Explains that the conflict had become internationalized in 1954 when Greece suggested the adoption of "enosis" to the United Nations.   "Enosis" symbolized Greek desires to reunite all former Byzantine territory still inhabited by Greek-speaking and Greek Orthodox peoples.   Suggests that the island's strategic position and the need for NATO unity had overridden the dispute's ethnic nature.   Illustrates how minimally the ethnic factor had influenced the actions of the United Nations, Muslim powers, Great Britain, and the United States.

433. BOYCE, D. G. "Separatism and the Irish Nationalist Tradition." *National Separatism*.   Ed. Colin H. Williams. Cardiff: University of Wales Press, 1982, pp. 75-104.
Traces the development of the Irish separatist ideal, arguing that, although the 1169 Norman invasion would profoundly influence the nature of national identity and the expression of political rights in Ireland, it had not immediately resulted in the birth of separatism.   Early Irish rebellions had not been motivated by the separatist ideal, but by the need to accommodate

the Crown. Religion had not been a unifying force for the Irish until the Protestant Elizabethan conquest; Cromwellianism had deepened the gulf between Catholics and their English rulers. Ireland's separatist claim had assumed firm and coherent expression with the conversion of Wolfe Tone and the United Irishmen to the ideas of French republicanism. The revival of separatist aspirations under the Fenians, and the rise of Parnellism in the 1880s, in practice had resulted in a reformist and devolutionary spirit in Anglo-Irish relations. The Ulster revolt against home rule in 1912-14, the 1916 Easter uprising, the executions which followed it, and the conscription crisis of 1918, had given the separatist ideal new strength and inspiration.

434. CAMPBELL, David B. "Nationalism, Religion and the Social Bases of Conflict in the Swiss Jura." *The Politics of Territorial Identity.* Eds. Stein Rokkan and Derek W. Urwin. London, Beverley Hills and New Delhi: Sage Publications, 1982, pp. 279-308.
Examines the secession of the French-speaking Jura from the German-speaking canton of Bern. Traces the present situation to two historical events: (1) the "Kulturkampf," which curtailed Roman Catholic practice from 1864 until 1935; and (2) the tension of World War I, which had been exacerbated by linguistic differences: whereas the German-Swiss sympathized with the Kaiser, the French-speakers supported the Allied cause. Finds that objective factors, such as language and religion, did not serve as adequate bases for defining nationalist support; rather, subjective factors, including a sense of "Jurassianness," were crucial. Support for Jurassian nationalism was strongest among lower-income, less well-educated segments of society, and included a disproportionate number of independent businessmen and workers — groups that bore the brunt of Jurassian economic decline. Names two factors that accounted for the success of separatists in the Jura; (1) the Jurassian territorial basis had permitted the possibility of independence; and (2) the Swiss federal system had allowed the Jura to become independent, while remaining an integral part of Switzerland.

435. CARROLL, Terrence G. "Northern Ireland." *Ethnic Conflict in International Relations.* Eds. A. Suhrke and L. Noble. New York: Praeger, 1979, pp. 21-42.
Discusses the roots and development of the conflict in Northern Ireland. Examines the historical, religious and national factors

which caused the gulf between the Protestant and Catholic communities. Suggests that analytically, "ethnic identification would seem to be a function of the existence of issues dividing the groups," but that this was not the participants' perception. Finds that representatives of the Catholic community were more difficult to classify within an internal/external dichotomy, because they frequently denied the legitimacy of this division. Postulates four considerations which might lead to other international forces getting involved in the conflict: (1) convenient rationalization for an attack on an enemy state already caught up in the confict; (2) the possibility of establishing a beneficial relationship with the eventual victor; (3) the desire to receive credit for settling a dispute or avoiding undesirable consequences of its continuation; and (4) effective ties with one of the internal parties.

436. CLARK, R. C. *The Basque Insurgents: 1952 to 1982.* Madison: University of Wisconsin Press, 1984.
      Examines contemporary Basque ideology and traces the spatial variations of violence and political support among the Basque people.

437. CORRADO, R. "The Welsh as a Nonstate Nation." *Nonstate Nations in International Politics — A Comparative System Analysis.* Ed. J. S. Bertelsen. New York: Praeger, 1979, pp. 131-92.
      Reviews the history of the Welsh nation since independence in the 13th century, through its conquest and Anglicization to the present resurgence of national assertiveness. Discusses the relative success of Welsh nationalism in the recent past in terms of British party and EEC politics. Considers Plaid Cymru a well-organized and multi-issue local and nationally visible political party that eschewed violence. Views the political and social organizations in Wales and the European Community as the bases for further strengthening this pacific position, and possibly allowing the Welsh national movement to achieve the "complex status of intermediate sovereignty involving national recognition and participation within the European Community but autonomy short of full independence from Britain."

438. CURRAN, Joseph. "Separatism in Northern Ireland." *Ethnic Autonomy - Comparative Dynamics.* Ed. R. L. Hall. New York: Pergamon Press, 1979, pp. 145-51.

Considers religion as the source of conflict in Northern Ireland only insofar as it was a cultural force and a badge of ethnic identity. In view of the failure of separatism and structural reform, the only possible solution to the Ulster problem appeared to be repartition and population transfers.

439. DA SILVA, M. "The Basques as a Non-State Nation." *Nonstate Nations in International Politics: Comparative System Analysis.* Ed. J. S. Bertelsen. New York: Praeger, 1977, pp. 98-130.
Focuses on the Basque struggle for recognition within Spain. Outlines the historical and political context of the problem. Concludes that the leaders' impact on the international context had been insignificant.

440. DIAZ LOPEZ, César E. "The Politicization of Galician Cleavages." *The Politics of Territorial Identity.* Eds. Stein Rokkan and Derek W. Unwin. London, Beverley Hills and New Delhi: Sage Publications, 1982, pp. 389-424.
Asserts that Spanish Galicia was geographically, linguistically, culturally, economically and politically a periphery. The future of Galicia as a differentiated community depended on the future of its language, fought on two complementary fronts: (1) the cultural, which advocated standardization of the language; and (2) the political, which aimed at the normalization of Galician for formal functions previously reserved for Castilian.

441. DRUCKER, H. M. and Gordon BROWN. *The Politics of Nationalism and Devolution.* London: Longman, 1980.
The authors explore the development of nationalist expressions in Scotland and Wales and plans for power devolution within the U.K.

442. FROGNIER, Andre P., Michel QUEVIT and Marie STENBOCK. "Regional Imbalances and Center-Periphery Relationships in Belgium." *The Politics of Territorial Identity.* Eds. Stein Rokkan and Derek W. Urwin. London, Beverley Hills and New Delhi: Sage Publications, 1982, pp. 251-78.
Present a chronological overview of factors that had structured the linguistic, economic, social and denominational issues in the relationships among Flanders, Wallonia and Brussels. Believes center-periphery relationships to be characterized largely by the territorial distribution of material and human resources. In

Belgium these relationships, and hence their territorial consequences, had been modified since 1830, when the center had
been politically and economically as well as culturally French.
Culturally, Flanders had acquired considerable autonomy;
Flemish had become an official language, and the Flemish region was constitutionally regarded as being unilaterally Dutch-
speaking. A problem had remained in finding for Brussels and
surrounding communes a status that would make the city an
acceptable capital for the Flemings, while not endangering
employment or language of the city's French-speaking majority.
Believe that social and economic change in culturally disparate
systems could produce a hardening of existing differences. The
French-speaking Belgians' reactions were of two kinds: (1)
linguistic protest in Brussels resulted from what most people
considered linguistic persecution; and (2) in Wallonia, the protest movements were based more on the need to counter social
and economic decline.

443.   GLASS, Harold E. "Ethnic Diversity, Elite Accommodation
       and Federalism in Switzerland." *Publius: The Journal of
       Federalism*, VII, 4 (1977), 31-48.
       Drawing on recent survey data, the author addresses the role of
       federalism in understanding postwar Swiss ethnic harmony.
       Contends that linguistic differences were not in themselves
       automatic determinants of conflict, but were a precondition for
       other factors, such as political dissatisfaction and relative de-
       privation. Traces the historical development of Swiss
       federalism, while emphasizing its role in minority accom-
       modation within and without the constitution. Affirms the level
       of politics in understanding the appearance of conflict in
       polities.

444.   GULEKE, Adrian. "International Legitimacy, Self-
       Determination, and Northern Ireland." *Review of Interna-
       tional Studies*, II (1985), 37-52.
       Applies international norms to the Northern Ireland conflict.
       Argues that Northern Ireland differed from other similarly di-
       vided societies, because it lacked international legitimacy. Ex-
       plains the existence of internal and international legitimacy.
       Points out that the principle of self-determination expressed in
       international law rejected the right of secessionists to form an
       independent state, with Bangladesh as the obvious exception.
       Outlines four perspectives: (1) the integrationist perspective that
       declared Northern Ireland to be an integral part of the United

Kingdom; (2) the British Isles perspective that viewed the entire area as a whole; (3) the independent Northern Ireland perspective, based on the international community's rejection of the notion that overseas territory could be regarded as an integral part of the colonial state's national territory; and (4) the nationalist perspective supported by the principle of territorial integrity, especially relating to islands and to the notion that islands were seldom divided into two sovereign entities.

445. HEIBERG, Marianne. "External and Internal Nationalism: The Case of the Spanish Basques." *Ethnic Autonomy - Comparative Dynamics.* Ed. R. L. Hall. New York: Pergamon Press, 1979, pp. 180-200.
Views Basque nationalism as a struggle for political power vis-à-vis Madrid — external nationalism — and a struggle for precedence within the Basque country — internal nationalism. Considers Basque nationalism a political response to two powerful centralizing forces: (1) state centralization, enforcing political conformity from Madrid; and (2) industrialization, which had economically integrated the Basque country from within.

446. HEIBERG, Marianne. "Urban Politics and Rural Culture: Basque Nationalism." *The Politics of Territorial Identity.* Eds. Stein Rokkan and Derek W. Urwin. London, Beverley Hills and New Delhi: Sage Publications, 1982, pp. 355-89.
Points out that 19th-century liberalism could not overcome fragmented Spanish society. A cohesive nationalism had failed to emerge in Spain because of the absence of a strong national bourgeoisie and the persistence of precapitalist agrarian structures. Considers the Basque country exceptional, because a culturally and economically developed bourgeoisie had emerged.

447. IRVING, E. R. M. *The Flemings and Walloons of Belgium.* London: Minority Rights Group, Report no. 46, 1980.
Traces the relationship between Belgium's Flemings and Walloons, and describes the evolution of Flanders and the Flemish movement and that of Wallonia, Brussels and the Francophone movements. Discusses the community problems relating to constitutional change and the political party system. Reviews the obstacles to change which had led to confrontation and deadlock. Examines the 1977-78 *Pacte Communautaire*

which had led to accommodation and eased the stalemate, but left the thorny problem of Brussels unresolved. Evaluates the prospects for a long-term solution in the context of the complexities of the communal relationship and of Belgian history.

448. KHLEIF, Bud B. "Issues of Theory and Methodology in the Study of Ethnolinguistic Movements: The Case of Frisian Nationalism in the Netherlands." *New Nationalisms of the Developed West.* Eds. Edward A. Tiryakian and Ronald Rogowski. Boston: Allen and Unwin, 1985, pp. 176-202.

Constructs a theoretical framework for viewing ethnolinguistic movements, and discusses the Frisians in the Netherlands. Rejects the "rationality model of individual actors" in favor of Touraine's social activism model. Explains that the ultimate context of social movements could be found (1) in the world-system perspective; and (2) in the internal colonialism metaphor. Finds several hypotheses useful in analyzing Friesland, including the quest for community; the corollaries of the expansion of the post-1945 welfare state; and the inhabitants' feelings of linguistic inferiority or cultural suppression resembling a colonial situation. The Frisian ethnolinguistic movement had certain socially constructed characteristics created by an intelligentsia suffering from status reduction and rising expectations cum relative deprivation. These characteristics included the quest for a respectable genealogy, the cultivation of a "providential mission" to assert the group's unique traits, and the invention of slogans as nourishment for identity.

449. KOFMAN, E. "Regional Autonomy and the One and Indivisible French Republic." *Environment and Planning C: Government and Policy*, III (1985), 11-25.

Reports that since the 1960s, regional movements in France had proposed new territorial divisions and regional autonomy. Since coming to power in 1981, the Socialists had introduced decentralization on all administrative levels. However, at the regional level, the existing *établissement public régional* had only been extended, and thus had not satisfied autonomist and separatist aspirations and demands. Examines the tensions between national and regionalist views of decentralization in relation to Corsica, the only region to be granted a *statut particulier*.

450. LAZER, Harry. "Devolution, Ethnic Nationalism, and Populism in the United Kingdom." *Publius: The Journal of Federalism*, VII, 4 (1977), 49-70.
Analyzes home rule demands in Scotland and Wales, and the constitutional and political presures upon the government in attempting to meet autonomy demands. Devolutionary politics required a finely drawn compromise balancing on one hand, the demands for self-government in Scotland and Wales and the resistance, on the other, of those opposed to any tampering with the existing unitary structure. Connects the timing of the nationalist discontent with changing perceptions of Great Britain's global political and economic position and the general worldwide rise of autonomist movements. Suggests that nationalism might be most fruitfully analyzed when subsumed under the general category of populism, which might account for the widespread belief in Great Britain that the people's will had been checked by an élitist minority.

451. LOIZOS, P., *et al. Cyprus.* London: Minority Rights Group, Report no. 30, 1976.
The authors analyze the negotiations and military interventions leading to the partition of Cyprus, emphasizing the mistakes of both communities. Present an alternative analysis of the Cyprus problem on four levels of social reality and power relations: (1) the ordinary Greek and Turkish Cypriot communities; (2) formal and informal relations among the two communities' political leaders; (3) the foreign policy-makers of Great Britain, Greece and Turkey; and (4) the U.N., NATO, Warsaw Pact and general superpower rivalry in the eastern Mediterranean. Suggest that "solution" meant agreement at some or all of these levels, satisfying a large number of interested parties and ensuring that no one had a strong interest in keeping the problem open. Outlines four key problems for future resolution: the refugees, the territorial issue, the constitutional form of the state, and the question of guarantees. Discuss three options: continued status quo; double *enosis* (each area becomes part of its "homeland"), and negotiated settlement.

452. MACARTNEY, Allan. "Autonomy in the British Isles." *Nordisk Tidsskrift For International Ret*, LIV (1985), 10-17.
Argues that Scotland, Wales and Ireland constituted "small nations," as did the Channel Islands, Shetland, Orkney and the Outer Hebrides. Defines "autonomy" in the sense of territories aspiring to or having their own laws. Describes the institutional

development of autonomy within the British Isles. Criticizes the inability of the English to distinguish between "English" and "British" identities. Suggests that the concept of "British," a significant element in Celtic acquiescence to union, was virtually meaningless to people in England.

453. MACIVER, D. N. "The Paradox of Nationalism in Scotland."
      National Separatism. Ed. Colin H. Williams. Cardiff:
      University of Wales Press, 1982, pp. 105-44.
      The separate Scottish experience had produced a unique national culture and the social institutions to maintain and transmit it. Argues that after nearly three centuries of the Act of Union, Scottish national identity and nationalism had become ambiguous in outlook and allegiance: on the one hand, Scots had participated in a multinational state and great world empire; on the other, they belonged to a self-contained, conservative and introspective civil society. Ascribes the Scottish National Party's mid-1970s electoral success to traditional Scottish grievances, Scottish suspicion of the London-based government, the demand for Scottish self-government, and hopes for a better economic future based on Scottish resources, especially North Sea oil. Maintains that Scottish desires for self-government had not been triggered by English domination, but by the determination to restore the effectiveness of the union partnership.

454. MCLEAN, Iain.   "The Politics of Nationalism and
      Devolution." *Political Studies*, XXV (1977), 425-30.
      Reviews recent writings on the politics of nationalism and devolution in the United Kingdom. Maintains that the center-periphery cleavage in British politics was as old as the familiar class orientation. Considers Welsh nationalism politically divisive, and Scottish nationalism integrative and reinforced by protest voting. The conflict over North Sea oil rights formed an important economic aspect of Scottish nationalism. Concludes that writers on democracy had overlooked constitutional theories of nationalism.

455. MEDHURST, Ken. "Basques and Basque Nationalism." *National Separatism*. Ed. Colin H. Williams. Cardiff:
      University of Wales Press, 1982, pp.235-61.
      Argues that monocausal theories of nationalism could not sufficiently explain Basque nationalism; an adequate account of the movement must examine the interactions of ethnicity,

industrialism and repression.   Traces the origins of Basque
nationalism to the 19th-century Carlist Wars, in which the rural
Basques sought to defend their traditional institutions and
communal interests against increasingly centralized state
authority.   The emergence of modern Basque nationalism had
coincided with the region's dramatic industrialization, which
might be a defensive reaction of traditionally significant groups
in Basque society whose status, interests and values seemed
threatened.   Intensive repression of the nationalists during the
Franco era had radically politicized significant sections of
previously apolitical or moderate Basques.   The left-wing character of Basque nationalism could be explained by the collective
experience of repression and rapid industrialization.   Asserts
that Basque awareness of belonging to an ethnically distinct yet
culturally beleaguered minority gave the nationalism its
characteristically intransigent quality.

456.   PATRICK, Richard A.   *Political Geography and the Cyprus
       Conflict: 1963-1971.*   Waterloo (Ontario):   University of
       Waterloo, Department of Geography Publication Series,
       No. 4, 1976.
Applies a general systems theory analysis to the Cyprus situation, and provides six short papers on geopolitical approaches
to understanding conflict and conflict resolution.

457.   PAYNE, S. G. *Basque Nationalism.*   Reno: University of
       Nevada Press, 1975.
Traces the political and historical aspects of the Basque nation-
alist movement by concentrating on basic principles held by the
Basques, and links them to feelings of national identity.

458.   PI-SUNYER, Oriol.   "Catalan Nationalism: Some Theoretical
       and Historical Considerations."   *New Nationalisms of the
       Developed West.*   Eds. Edward A. Tiryakian and Ronald
       Rogowski.   Boston: Allen and Unwin, 1985, pp. 254-76.
Sheds light on theoretical issues through a historical examination of Catalonia and Catalan nationalism.   Claims that all
nationalisms shared a common political dimension of systematic action and a cultural dimension of group membership unit-
ing the collectivity.   Identifies two factors as having been crucial
in the emergence or maintenance of nationalism: (1) the presence of institutions and structures, developed over time, that
strengthen group identity and aid mobilization; and (2) the
establishment or definition of goals to which mobilization might

be directed. Reviews certain aspects of Catalan cultural and
institutional history relevant to group solidarity and organizational potential. Concludes that economic and political
forces in themselves could not create nationalism, because they
would be altered by specific changing cultures and societies.

459. RAWKINS, Phillip. "Living in the House of Power: Welsh
      Nationalism and the Dilemma of Antisystem Politics."
      New Nationalisms of the Developed West. Eds. Edward A.
      Tiryakian and Ronald Rogowski. Boston: Allen and Un-
      win, 1985, pp. 294-314.

Explains that Plaid Cymru's electoral performance depended to
a large extent on the political opportunities that others created.
The search for respectability had pushed the party toward
"electoralism," and a willingness to compete for political spoils
on terms set by the dominant parties. The complex dilemma
facing Plaid Cymru was whether to reach a broad populace, and
risk destroying the internal solidarity generated by past adherence to the symbols and emotional trappings of nationalism,
language and cultural identity, or to emphasize these latter
points and risk reinforcing its image as the party of the privi-
leged Welsh-speaking minority.

460. RUDOLPH, Joseph R., Jr. "Belgium: Controlling Separatist
      Tendencies in a Multinational State." *National
      Separatism.* Ed. Colin H. Williams. Cardiff University of
      Wales Press, 1982, pp. 263-97.

Claims that complete separation demands had become rare in
Belgium because its political system had been able to accommodate and institutionalize ethnoregional cleavages. Until
recently, Belgium had managed the ethnoregional cleavage
through consociational politics; the Francophone élites had
been able to accommodate Flemish demands while preserving
the balance of power within the state; also, the systemwide nature of political parties and the cross-communal essence of the
religious and economic cleavages they institutionalized had kept
the potentially disruptive linguistic issues in the background.
Argues that with the depoliticization of religious issues and the
regionalization of economic ones in postwar Belgium,
consociational politics had yielded to ethnoregional politics.
Attributes the emergence of Flemish nationalist activity to the
shift in economic power from the Walloon south to the more
populous north, thus producing a strong sense of Flemish self-
awareness, frustration and resentment that Flemish-speaking

Belgians were still not being employed by the state commensurate with their demography and economic status. Reports that Francophone organizations had countered Flemish nationalism by publicizing Wallonia's declining political and economic influence. These developments had drawn strong reactions in Brussels, where regionalism had meant a reduction of the center's influence, and in German-speaking parts of Belgium. Maintains that demands for political separatism in Belgium had been reduced by the willingness of political leaders to accommodate ethnoregional demands, the desire of ethnoregional spokesmen to join the country's decision-making cartel, the unattractiveness of integration into a neighboring state, and for the Flemish, the possibility of someday controlling the central government.

461. STEPHENSON, Glenn V. "Cultural Regionalism and the Unitary State Idea in Belgium." *Geographical Review*, LXII (1972), 501-23.
Identifies and evaluates the forces that had exacerbated regional differences in Belgium, and examines the government's attempts to deal with requests for regional autonomy within the framework of a highly centralized bureaucracy. Maintains that the hardening of the linguistic divide in Belgium in recent years had been accompanied by government moves toward decentralization in the cultural and economic spheres. The increasingly dichotomous nature of the country had weakened the concept of a strong unitary administration, and was contributing to the growth of regional identity among the French-speaking majority in Brussels. Describes the position of those who wished to see decentralization of political power to the nine provinces while retaining the unitary state, and those who desired political restructuring which would harden Belgium's *de facto* ethnic federation into a *de jure* one. Contends that instead of attempting a major modification of the unitary state system or placing priority on the question of national cohesion, the government had tried to compromise with palliatives.

462. TOURAINE, Alain. "Sociological Intervention and the Internal Dynamics of the Occitanist Movement." *New Nationalisms of the Developed West*. Eds. Edward A. Tiryakian and Ronald Rogowski. Boston: Allen and Unwin, 1985, pp. 157-75.
Relates the Occitanist nationalist movement to the broader class of social protest movements. Utilizes a new methodology of

"sociological intervention" in order to study the internal dynamics of the movement. Considers the Occitanist movement multidirectional and lacking unity. Claims that the Occitanist struggle had grown out of three divergent forces: cultural, national, and economic, and that the movement had bred two opposing tendencies: traditionally-oriented national affirmation, and the modernizing struggle against regional and economic underdevelopment. They had merged in the name of cultural specificity in order to oppose the centralizing, capitalist, and bureaucratic French state and the increasing duality of French society. Relates the Occitanist movement to broader questions of class and national struggle, and claims that although they might be intermingled, they could not be unified.

463. URWIN, Derek W.   "Territorial Structures and Political Developments in the United Kingdom." *The Politics of Territorial Identity.*   Eds. Stein Rokkan and Derek W. Urwin.   London, Beverley Hills and New Delhi: Sage Publications, 1982, pp. 19-74.
Considers the British state positive and flexible in responding to the demands of a multicultural society; it sought gradual change and accommodation within prevailing structures. Distinguishes four British levels of domination from center to periphery, each corresponding to varied territorial expansion phases: (1) a central core consisting of London and the immediate environs of the south-east; (2) an outer center comprising Wessex, East Anglia and the Midlands; (3) an inner periphery embracing Cornwall, the northern English shires and Wales; and (4) an outer periphery composed of Scotland and Ireland. Explains that in the 20th century regional policy had provided flexible and differential treatment of peripheral areas, allowing considerable institutional accommodation of territorial variation.

464. WILLIAMS, Colin H.   "Separatism and the Mobilization of Welsh National Identity." *National Separatism.*   Ed. Colin H. Williams.   Cardiff: University of Wales Press, 1982, pp. 145-202.
Asserts that the preservation of Welsh culture had become synonymous with the desire for Welsh political independence, for which nationalism had become the chief vehicle; the main effect of separatism had been to redefine social class and regional economic problems as Welsh "national" problems. Since its inception, Plaid Cymru had been primarily a nationalist pressure group to counteract the cultural encroachment of

Anglicization, especially in terms of language and religion. Claims that by stressing English-Welsh cultural differences, Plaid Cymru had, by implication, also emphasized the internal cultural language differentiation within Wales. Explains the spatial pattern of nationalist support in Wales in terms of socioeconomic correlates of franchise. In order for separatism to become the central political issue in Wales, nationalists would have to mobilize broad popular support. Identifies Welsh nationalism as a reaction against English territorial and ethnic encroachment. Believes that theories of internal colonialism had been neglecting the ethnolinguistic basis of nationalism.

465. WILLIAMS, Glyn. "The Political Economy of Contemporary Nationalism in Wales." *New Nationalisms of the Developed West.* Eds. Edward A. Tiryakian and Ronald Rogowski. Boston: Allen and Unwin, 1985, pp. 337-52.
Contends that ethnicity was not an abstract self-definition, but represented the only form of expression for some peoples. In Wales, economic and sociostructural processes had generated contradictory group formations. Shows that changes in the Welsh economy had not been spatially uniform as a consequence of state capitalism. Developments in metropolitan centers and the industrial enclaves had marginalized and fragmented regional populations. Traces changes in the Welsh class configuration, and the opposition of alien and non-alien bourgeoisie.

PART V

THE FOURTH WORLD: INDIGENOUS PEOPLES

Indigenous Peoples: General and Comparative Perspectives

466. ALFREDSSON, Gudmundur. "Greenland and the Law of
      Political Decolonization." *German Yearbook of Interna-
      tional Law*, **XXV** (1982), 290-308.
      Applies international law regarding external self-determination
      to recent political developments in Greenland. Explains that in
      1979 the Danish government had granted limited autonomy
      (home rule) to Greenland, including the Inuit. Categorizes the
      content and subject of self-determination into (1) external self-
      determination, referring to international status; (2) internal
      self-determination, pertaining to the preferred form of govern-
      ment; (3) territorial integrity; (4) minority rights in various as-
      pects of autonomy, possibly extending beyond state boundaries;
      and (5) right to cultural, social and economic development.
      Identifies only political decolonization and territorial integrity
      as binding rules in international law.   Maintains that
      Greenland's indigenous peoples could legally enjoy special
      rights supported by ILO Convention 107, the United Nations
      Working Group on Indigenous Populations, the 1978 World
      Conference to Combat Racism and Racial Discrimination, and
      the United Nations Study of the Problem of Discrimination
      against Indigenous Peoples. Traces the history of Denmark's
      relationship with Greenland, asserting that the three funda-
      mental criteria of colonial status (*i.e.*, foreign domination,
      separate geographic location, and distinct political unit) applied
      to Greenland.   Believes that Greenlanders were entitled to
      exercise their rights to external self-determination.

467. ALFREDSSON, Gudmundur. "International Law, Interna-
      tional Organizations, and Indigenous Peoples." *Journal of
      International Affairs*, XXXVI (1982), 113-24.
      Raises the question of remedies and redress vested in interna-
      tional law and organizations in view of consistent ignorance or
      institutionalized violations of indigenous peoples' rights. Cites
      only two concepts as being more or less legally binding: (1)
      political decolonization, or the external self-determination for
      colonial people; and (2) territorial integrity, thus excluding most
      indigenous peoples from the practical exercise of external self-
      determination. Finds substantive and procedural provisions of
      international human rights instruments wanting, and the imple-
      mentation of decisions rendered by international bodies on the
      basis of substantive international law insufficient. Advocates
      the more forceful application and extension of existing substan-
      tive and procedural rules of positive international law on behalf
      of indigenous peoples.

468. BENNETT, G. *Aboriginal Rights in International Law*.
      London: Survival International, 1978.
      Discusses various aspects of self-determination as it applied to
      indigenous peoples. Considers self-determination a legal right
      possessed by indigenous peoples, but subject to a possible
      governmental veto if "national interest genuinely requires it."

469. BERMAN, H. "Are Indigenous Peoples Entitled to Interna-
      tional Juridical Personality?" *Seventy-ninth Proceedings of
      the American Society of International Law*. Washington,
      DC: 1985.
      Argues that indigenous rights must be conceived as a restoration
      of preexisting rights which had been denied but not extin-
      guished. Points out that the U.N. recognized the international
      legal personality of indigenous peoples, so that they were enti-
      tled to exercise the right to self-determination, which might
      manifest itself in various forms.

470. Coalition Draft Declaration. "Draft declaration of principles
      proposed by the Indian Law Resource Center, Four Di-
      rections Council, National Aboriginal and Islander Legal
      Service, National Indian Youth Council, Inuit
      Circumpolar Conference, and the International Indian
      Treaty Council." U.N. E/CN.4/Sub.2/1985/22.

" 1.   Indigenous nations and peoples have, in common with all humanity, the right to life, and to freedom from oppression, discrimination, and aggression.

2.   All indigenous nations and peoples have the right to self-determination, by virtue of which they have the right to whatever degree of autonomy or self-government they chose.   This includes the right to freely determine their political status, freely pursue their own economic, social, religious and cultural development, and determine their own membership and/or citizenship, without external interference.

3.   No state shall assert any jurisdiction over an indigenous nation or people, or its territory, except in accordance with the freely expressed wishes of the nation or people concerned.

4.   Indigenous nations and peoples are entitled to the permanent control and enjoyment of their aboriginal ancestral-historical territories.   This includes surface and subsurface rights, inland and coastal waters, renewal and non-renewable resources, and the economies based on these resources.

5.   Rights to share and use land, subject to the underlying and inalienable title of the indigenous nation or people, may be granted by their free and informed consent, as evidenced in a valid treaty or agreement.

6.   Discovery, conquest, settlement on a theory of *terra nullius* and unilateral legislation are never legitimate bases for States to claim or retain the territories of indigenous nations or peoples.

7.   In cases where lands taken in violation of these principles have already been settled, the indigenous nation or people concerned is entitled to immediate restitution, including compensation for the loss of use, without extinction of original title. Indigenous peoples' desire to regain possession and control of sacred sites must always be respected.

8.   No State shall participate financially or militarily in the involuntary displacement of indigenous populations, or in the subsequent economic exploitation or military use of their territory.

9.   The laws and customs of indigenous nations and peoples must be recognized by States' legislative, administrative and judicial institutions and, in case of conflicts with State laws, shall take precedence.

10.   No State shall deny an indigenous nation, community, or people residing within its borders the right to participate in the life of the State in whatever manner and to whatever degree they may choose.   This includes the right to participate in other forms of collective action and expression.

11. Indigenous nations and peoples continue to own and control their material culture, including archeological, historical and sacred sites, artifacts, designs, knowledge, and works of art. They have the right to regain items of major cultural significance and, in all cases, to the return of the human remains of their ancestors for burial in accordance with their traditions.

12. Indigenous nations and peoples have the right to be educated and conduct business with States in their own languages, and to establish their own educational institutions.

13. No technical, scientific or social investigations, including archeological excavations, shall take place in relation to indigenous nations or peoples, or their lands, without their prior authorization, and their continuing ownership and control.

14. The religious practices of indigenous nations and peoples shall be fully respected and protected by the laws of States and by international law. Indigenous nations and peoples shall always enjoy unrestricted access to, and enjoyment of sacred sites in accordance with their own laws and customs, including the right of privacy.

15. Indigenous nations and peoples are subjects of international law.

16. Treaties and other agreements freely made with indigenous nations or peoples shall be recognized and applied in the same manner and according to the same international laws and principles as treaties and agreements entered into with other States.

17. Disputes regarding the jurisdiction, territories and institutions of an indigenous nation or people are a proper concern of international law, and must be resolved by mutual agreement or valid treaty.

18. Indigenous nations and peoples may engage in self-defence against State actions in conflict with their right to self-determination.

19. Indigenous nations and peoples have the right freely to travel, and to maintain economic, social, cultural and religious relations with each other across State borders.

20. In addition to these rights, indigenous nations and peoples are entitled to the enjoyment of all the human rights and fundamental freedoms enumerated in the International Bill of Human Rights and other United Nations instruments. In no circumstances shall they be subject to adverse discrimination."

471. CULTURAL SURVIVAL QUARTERLY (Cultural Survival, 11 Divinity Avenue, Cambridge, MA).

Quarterly publication since 1976, addresses immediate and long-term issues of concern to indigenous peoples.

472. DAVIES, Maureen. "Aspects of Aboriginal Rights in International Law." *Aboriginal Peoples and the Law: Indian, Metis and Inuit Rights in Canada.* Ed. Bradford W. Morse. Ottawa: Carleton University Press, 1985, pp. 16-47.
Traces the foundation of the rights of indigenous peoples in international law to the time of colonization. Through a discussion of international law sources explains how the opinions of legal scholars provided a substantive framework also applicable to domestic law. Explores Vitoria's advocacy of aboriginal rights echoed by Grotius and Pufendorf. Investigates the status of indigenous peoples under international law in terms of the principle of sovereignty, including the power to enter into treaties, and the concept of guardianship illustrated by views offered in judicial decisions. Considers doctrines of territorial acquisition used to legitimate colonization: discovery in itself was not a valid claim, whether it referred to inhabited or uninhabited lands. Discovery coupled with occupation required the lands in question to be *terra nullius*, that is, vacant, by which definition only aboriginal peoples could hold legal title. Similarly, conquest was not a suitable justification. Finally, legal cession implied voluntary action which had been questionable in many cases involving indigenous peoples. Concludes that, even though international law was created by Europeans, the principles, if interpreted correctly, would protect the rights of indigenous peoples.

473. DAVIES, Maureen. "Working Group on Indigenous Populations, Urgent and Effective Measures Called For." *Bulletin, World Federation of United Nations Associations,* No. 27 (September, 1983), 6-7.
Reports on the third annual session of the United Nations Working Group on Indigenous Populations, held in Geneva from 30 July to 2 August and on 6 August 1984. Explains that in keeping with the plan of action adopted at its second session, the Working Group focused primarily on issues relating to rights to land and natural resources, and the right to life, physical integrity and security of the indigenous populations. Underlines the unique spiritual relationship connecting indigenous peoples and the land. Maintains that the desperate situation many indigenous peoples face had resulted from the deprivation of their land base. Insists that indigenous peoples

were entitled to recognition as "peoples" and, therefore, had the right to self-determination. Urges effective international measures to end the internal colonization of enclave indigenous populations.

474. INTERNATIONAL WORK GROUP FOR INDIGENOUS AFFAIRS. *IWGIA Newletter* (Copenhagen: IWGIA, Fiolstraede 10, DK 1171 Copenhagen, Denmark).
Publication appearing three times annually deals with issues facing indigenous peoples in many states, and includes discussion of claims to self-determination.

475. JOJOLA, Theodore. "The Conflicting Role of National Governments in the Tribal Development Process: Two Case Studies." *Antipode*, XVI, 2 (1984), 19-26.
Examines the role of the tribal community in the regional development process by illustrating the conflicts that emerged between two countries and their tribal wards involved in two large-scale water projects: the Kinzua reservoir, located in the northeastern United States, and the proposed Chico River hydrodams in the Philippines. Alleges that in both cases, the dominant national society had attempted to prevent the tribes from participating in, and determining, their own regional development. The Seneca and Iroquois communities involved in the Kinzua case had been plagued with internal conflicts and the unfavorable political climate in the 1950s' United States. The Igorots might benefit from a high degree of community solidarity and the evolution of a positive international stance toward indigenous rights.

476. KNIGHT, David B. "'Minorities' and Self-Determination."
Our Geographic Mosaic: Research Essays in Honour of G. C. Merrill. Ed. David B. Knight. Ottawa: Carleton University Press, 1985, pp. 139-47.
Reviews recently published explanations of self-determination according to international law. Considers minorities to be linked with "people" and "nation." Questions the appropriateness of the U.N. term "populations" with respect to indigenous peoples. Expects internal self-determination to become increasingly pronounced to permit significant minorities (*i.e.*, sub-state group politico-territorial identities) to express their sense of "self" legitimately within their respective states.

477. LYONS, Oren. "Spirituality, Equality, and Natural Law."
      Pathways to Self-Determination - Canadian Indians and the
      Canadian State. Eds. Leroy Little Bear, Menno Boldt and
      J. Anthony Long. Toronto: University of Toronto Press,
      1984, pp. 5-13.
      Maintains that if an Indian government was to have any mean-
      ing, the Indian people alone must determine who they were.
      Suggests that Indian governments differed fundamentally from
      non-Indian ones in their recognition and respect for the prin-
      ciples of spiritual law, natural law, and equality of mankind.
      The fact that not all nations shared in these beliefs had caused
      a crisis for indigenous peoples, as they had become subjected to
      the attempted removal of their identity. Considers Indian
      claims to their land and everything under it the central issues.

478. LYONS, Oren. "Traditional Native Philosophies Relating to
      Aboriginal Rights." *The Quest for Justice: Aboriginal Peo-*
      ples and Aboriginal Rights. Eds. Menno Boldt and J.
      Anthony Long. Toronto: University of Toronto Press,
      1985, pp. 19-23.
      Asserts that the Creator had bestowed aboriginal rights on
      aboriginal peoples, and aboriginal rights thus were outside their
      jurisdiction. Indicates that aboriginal peoples' responsibility
      was to preserve the land for their children. As the land did not
      belong to them, they had no right to sell it, give it up, or make
      a settlement. Considers aboriginal rights part of natural law.

479. RABY, Stewart. "Aboriginal Territorial Aspirations in Political
      Geography." *Proceedings of the International Geographical*
      Union Regional Conference and Eighth New Zealand Geog-
      raphy Conference. Palmerston North: New Zealand Geo-
      graphical Society, 1974, 169-74.
      Self-consciousness, linked to a variety of cultural elements, uni-
      fied through common historical experiences, and aided by
      modern communications, had become a basis for tribal and
      intertribal cohesion within states and recently for tentative at-
      tempts at international identification. Isolates three varieties
      of native territorial situations, in legal and political terms: (1)
      areas of initiation, where there had been no legally defined and
      protected land base and where aboriginal land claims were or
      had been the subject of recent litigation and negotiations; (2)
      areas of enhancement, where the contemporary outcome of land
      claims had led to native demands for the entrenchment, exten-
      sion or reestablishment of their rights over the land base ori-

ginally given them; and (3) areas of omission, where the aboriginal peoples occupied a protected land base, although, from the native viewpoint, these tracts had not been part of a system for settling their land claims. Older forms of territorial consciousness, such as older forms of self-identification, were being radically reinterpreted over broader areal bases and through new forms of occupancy. Outlines the cases of aboriginal peoples in Alaska, Canada's north, and Australia.

480. STEA, David and Ben WISNER. "Introduction." *Antipode*, XVI, 2 (1984), 3-12.
Note a growing awareness among encapsulated native societies against shared oppression and destiny, and of the need to mount radical political responses to onslaughts upon their land, resources and cultures. Argue that a definition of Fourth World people must include their cultural-ecological attachment to land and their relation to the continuing process of its expropriation. Review various forms of resistance and resurgence in the face of attacks on Fourth World land, labor and culture. Discuss the analytical foundations utilized by the contributors to the volume.

481. World Council of Indigenous Peoples. Declaration of Principles Adopted at the Fourth General Assembly of the World Council of Indigenous Peoples in Panama, September 1984. New York: United Nations, E/CN.4/Sub.2/1985/22, Annex III.

"**Principle 1**. All indigenous peoples have the right of self-determination. By virtue of this right they may freely determine their political status and freely pursue their economic, social, religious and cultural development.
Principle 2. All States within which an indigenous people live shall recognize the population, territory and institutions of the indigenous people.
Principle 3. The cultures of the indigenous peoples are part of the cultural heritage of mankind.
Principle 4. The traditions and customs of indigenous people must be respected by the States, and recognized as a fundamental source of law.
Principle 5. All indigenous peoples have the right to determine the person or group of persons who are included within its population.

Principle 6. Each indigenous people has the right to determine the form, structure and authority of its institutions.

Principle 7. The institutions of indigenous peoples and their decision, like those of States, must be in conformity with internationally accepted human rights both collective and individual.

Principle 8. Indigenous peoples and their members are entitled to participate in the political life of a State.

Principle 9. Indigenous people shall have exclusive rights to their traditional lands and its resources, where the lands and resources of the indigenous peoples have been taken away without their free and informed consent such lands and resources shall be returned.

Principle 10. The land rights of an indigenous people include surface and subsurface rights, full rights to interior and coastal waters and rights to adequate and exclusive coastal economic zones within the limits of international law.

Principle 11. All indigenous peoples may, for their own needs, freely use their natural wealth and resources in accordance with Principles 9 and 10.

Principle 12. No action or course of conduct may be undertaken which, directly or indirectly, may result in the destruction of land, air, water, sea ice, wildlife, habitat or natural resources without the free and informed consent of the indigenous peoples affected.

Principle 13. The original rights to their material culture, including archeological sites, artifacts, designs, technology and works of art, lie with the indigenous people.

Principle 14. The indigenous peoples have the right to receive education in their own language or to establish their own educational institutions. The languages of the indigenous peoples are to be respected by the States in all dealings between the indigenous people and the State on the basis of equality and non-discrimination.

Principle 15. Indigenous peoples have the right, in accordance with their traditions, to move and conduct traditional activities and maintain friendship relations across international boundaries.

Principle 16. The indigenous peoples and their authorities have the right to be previously consulted and to authorize the realization of all technological and scientific investigations to be conducted within their territories and to have full access to the results of the investigation.

Principle 17. Treaties between indigenous nations or peoples and respresentatives of States freely entered into, shall be given full effect under national law and international law.

These principles constitute the minimum standards which States shall respect and implement."

482.   World Council of Indigenous Peoples. International Covenant on the Rights of Indigenous Peoples. Draft, Fugitive, 28 April 1981.

The preamble states that colonialism and its effects had been neglected or ignored with regard to Indigenous Peoples, despite United Nations General Assembly Resolution 1514 (XV), 1960, which urged the end of colonialism in all its manifestations; despite Convention 107 and Recommendation 104 of the International Labor Organization, 1957, which acknowledged the applicability of international standards to Indigenous Peoples, and despite the International Convention on the Elimination of All Forms of Racial Discrimination, 1965, which recognized the interrelationship of racial equality and decolonization. Part I, Article I, asserts that "All peoples have the right to self-determination. By virtue of that right Indigenous Peoples may freely determine their political status and freely pursue their economic and cultural development." Defines "indigenous people" and offers examples of applications of self-determination. Describes internal self-determination in terms of civil and political rights, including the determination of membership, economic rights, and social and cultural rights. Considers states and indigenous peoples as equal subjects of international law, and proposes scrutiny of domestic standards with regard to indigenous peoples. Concludes with conditions for ratification and implementation, including the establishment of a Commission of Indigenous Rights and a Tribunal of Indigenous Rights.

Indigenous Peoples: North America

483.   BERMAN, H. "The Concept of Aboriginal Rights in the Early
       Legal History of the United States." *Buffalo Law Review*,
       XXVII (1978), 637-66.
       Analyzes the conceptual development of recognition of distinct
       political rights for American Indian nations within the United
       States legal system during its formative period.

484.   BOLDT, Menno. "Philosophy, Politics, and Extralegal Action:
       Native Indian Leaders in Canada." *Ethnic and Racial
       Studies*, IV (1981), 205-21.
       Through interviews with Native Indian leaders in Canada, the
       author investigates the relationship of Enlightenment and
       Romanticist philosophical traditions on native attitudes toward
       extralegal action. Argues that the scale-increasing values of the
       Enlightenment and Romanticism were positively associated
       with attitudes approving of extralegal action to attain the "good
       society," and further, that a desire for increased self-
       determination was also positively associated with approval of
       extralegal action. Because Indians were not part of the political
       power structure and they were not influential in the political
       process, nationalist and autonomist leaders perceived little
       chance of achieving their political objectives through legal and
       official channels. On the other hand, the integrationists and
       adapted departmentalists did not view the law as an obstacle to
       their aspirations.

485.   BOLDT, Menno. "Social Correlates of Nationalism: A Study
       of Native Indian Leaders in a Canadian Internal Colony."
       Comparative Political Studies, XIV (1981), 205-31.
       Identifies four basic types of preferred political status among
       Canadian Native Indian leaders: (1) political independence
       within a sovereign territory; (2) autonomy, with the estab-
       lishment of Indian control over a socio-political-economic space
       without the specifications of a geographical space; (3) adapted
       departmentalism with the replacement of White by indigenous
       administrators; and (4) complete integration of Indians into
       Canadian society and the elimination of any special status for
       Indians. Postulates two influential social variables in orienting
       Indian leaders toward increased self-determination: (1) the
       leaders' experience of discrimination or exclusion at the hands
       of the dominant society; and (2) the leaders' proximity to the

indigenous cultural community. Contends that most Indian leaders were staking their future not on demands for better conditions and equality within the larger society, but on a movement to achieve increased self-determination and separation from the larger society.

486. BOLDT, Menno and J. Anthony LONG, eds. *The Quest for Justice: Aboriginal Peoples and Aboriginal Rights.* Toronto: University of Toronto Press, 1985.
Collection of twenty-three papers from mainly Canadian representatives of aboriginal peoples' organizations, of governments, and a variety of academic disciplines, along with introductions and an epilogue by the editors. Discuss aboriginal rights and what these rights meant in terms of land and sovereignty. Assert claims for self-government, with some authors demanding sovereign self-government, an idea that the Canadian federal and provincial governments were unwilling to entertain.

487. CANADA, Government of. *Indian Self-Government in Canada: Report of the Special Committee.* Ottawa: Queen's Printer for the House of Commons (First Session of the Thirty-Second Parliament, Issue no. 40), 1983.
Parliamentary Task Force on Indian Self-Government, composed of representatives from the three major political parties, reviews legal and related institutional factors affecting the status, development and responsibilities of Band Governments on Indian Reserves and offers recommendations. Its mandate was limited to the Indian peoples and therefore did not deal with the Inuit and Metis peoples. Treaties, which had allowed settlements in certain areas, reaffirmed Indian sovereignty and rights; however, non-Indians tended to view these treaties as the extinguishment of all rights and acceptance of external control. Determines that Indian peoples had moved from free, self-sustaining First Nations to a state of dependency, and suffered social disintegration and deprivation due to non-Indian domination. The Indian Act established a complicated relationship between Indian band councils, whose powers were restricted, and the Department of Indian Affairs and Northern Development (DIAND). Identifies three areas of critical concern: education, child welfare and health. Considers Indian jurisdiction over these areas essential in order to ensure cultural survival. Maintains the need for a new relationship between the federal government and the Indian First Nations, respecting their right to political self-determination, which ultimately

would benefit Canadian national unity. Proposes and recommends the entrenchment of Indian self-government in the Constitution of Canada, which would transform Indian First Nations into a distinct order of government; the enactment of an Indian First Nations Recognition Act, which would confirm the government's willingness to recognize the maximum amount of self-government now possible under the Constitution. Eventually, this would lead to full legislative and policy-making powers on matters affecting Indian people, and full control over the territory and resources within the boundaries of Indian lands; the creation of a Ministry of State for Indian First Nations Relations linked to the Privy Council Office in order to manage relations between the federal government and Indian governments and to promote the rights of the latter; the respect for the right of each band to determine its own membership; the promotion of Indian economic development through the speedy and just settlement of claims, and direct payment to Indian governments of federal funding and revenue trust funds. Recommends that, as Indian self-government became reality, DIAND programs relating to Indians be phased out over a period of five years. Believes that the best way to promote Indian rights for the time being was through Indian self-government and not by special representation in Parliament.

488. CLINEBELL, J. and J. THOMSON. "Sovereignty and Self-Determination: The Rights of Native Americans Under International Law." *Buffalo Law Review.*, XXVII (1978), 669-81.
Using the Montevideo Convention, examine criteria for recognition of indigenous nations in the United States. Argue that indigenous peoples had the necessary criteria for nationhood according to international standards, *i.e.*, permanent population, defined territory, capacity for government, and capability to carry on foreign relations.

489. CREERY, Ian. *The Inuit (Eskimo) of Canada.* London: Minority Rights Group, Report no. 60, 1983.
Investigates the history of the colonization of the Arctic and Inuit efforts to decolonize themselves, focusing on the Inuit of Canada. Traces Inuit origins and culture, the colonization period and the development of governmental interest and involvement in the area. Examines the growth of political consciousness highlighting the question of James Bay and the Mackenzie Valley Pipeline. Outlines the road to the division of

the Northwest territories as well as the education, communication and language aspects of the "quiet revolution." Compares the impact of these developments among the Inuit of the
Northwest Territories, Quebec, Labrador and the Western
Arctic. Links the historical and recent economic developments
to these political aspects. Economic goals mirrored the political
ones, reflecting the desire for self-sufficiency systematically
supported by the Canadian government. Discusses the potential future of the Inuit of Canada, and relates it to the evolution
of the Inuit circumpolar movement internationally.

490.   DAVIES, Maureen. "'Protection' of the Identity of Aboriginal
       Peoples with Particular Reference to Canada." *Nordisk
       Tidsskrift For International Ret*, LIV (1985), 23-8.
       Discusses the problems facing the fourth world. Focuses on the
       problem of assimilation and persistence of negative stereotyp-
       ing. Suggests that the only meaningful protection of indigenous
       identity lay in recognition of the right to self-determination.
       Distinguishes between "minority" or "ethnic" groups and
       indigenous peoples.

491.   DELISLE, Andrew. "How We Gained Control over Our Lives
       and Territories: The Kahnawake Story." *Pathways to Self-
       Determination - Canadian Indians and the Canadian State*.
       Eds. Leroy Little Bear, Menno Boldt and J. Anthony Long.
       Toronto: University of Toronto Press, 1984, pp. 141-47.
       Urges Indians to reestablish self-government and sovereignty,
       to gain control over their own lives and destiny within the
       traditional structure of Indian government rather than through
       negotiations with the federal government. Uses the example of
       the Kahnawake reserve, which had assumed control over its
       own health and police services, and had established its own
       schools. Stresses the need for mutual cooperation among native
       people for trade purposes as well as for a support network.
       Advocates the abolition of the Indian Affairs Department and
       replacement with an Indian-managed bureaucratic structure.

492.   DORRIS, Michael. "Twentieth-Century Indians: The Return
       of the Natives." *Ethnic Autonomy - Comparative
       Dynamics*. Ed. R. L. Hall. New York: Pergamon Press,
       1979, pp. 66-85.
       Explains that with increasing persistence over the past 400
       years, Native North American societies had been forced to de-
       fine themselves relative to an invading foreign population.

Since the inception, the European view of native people had been grounded in two hypotheses: (1) all inhabitants of the New World constitute a single ethnic community; and (2) human culture was universally and teleologically evolutionary, with Western civilization forever holding "most advanced" status. Asserts that native peoples had never considered themselves a part of the American cultural matrix.

493. EBONE, Andrew. "Federal Government Policies and Indian Goals in Self-Government." *Pathways to Self-Determination - Canadians and Indians and the Canadian State.* Eds. Leroy Little Bear, Menno Boldt and J. Anthony Long. Toronto: University of Toronto Press, 1984, pp. 90-6.

Explains that the Canadian federal government's long history of paternalism, and the lack of the Indian tribes' management and planning expertise had engendered serious economic development problems for the Indian people. Blames the dominance of Canadian federal bureaucrats in the decision-making process. Reports changing Indian attitudes, as tribes shattered the barriers that had kept them isolated on the reservations. Cites the return of young Indians to their reservations, utilization of natural resources on reservations, the creation of numerous Indian self-help organizations, and the development of special relationships with provincial governments, as signs of Indian progress.

494. Falk, Richard. "Brief on Behalf of the Dene." Thomas R. Berger. *The Report of the Mackenzie Valley Pipeline Inquiry.*, 6 UNCIO Doc. 396.

Discusses the principle of self-determination in light of the Dene nation's objection to a proposed pipeline that would encroach upon Dene soil, thus rendering Dene survival questionable. Refers to an international consensus citing self-determination as a fundamental legal right, initially applied to externally dominated territories that were potential states. Argues that self-determination also had an internal role that applied in various contexts to dependent nations lacking a state. Points out the need for autonomy in such cases in order to safeguard a dependent people's cultural integrity. Blames the reluctance to acknowledge the internal application of the doctrine of self-determination on the fear of secessionist movements. Cites the Vienna Convention of the Law of Treaties and the tradition of protecting minority rights expressed in several international documents which had attained the status of customary international law as additional vehicles for the protection of aboriginal rights. In situations of doubt, urges interpreters to favor dependent people. Maintains that international law compelled the Canadian government to respect the Dene people's right to self-determination, and required the authorities not to proceed with the proposed pipeline.

495. GIANNINOTO, James H. "Sovereignty under Reservation: American Indian Tribal Sovereignty in Law and Practice." *New York Law School Journal of International and Comparative Law*, IV (1983), 589-612.
Asserts that American Indian tribes had once formed sovereign entities exerting power domestically as well as internationally; their supremacy was curtailed only by the sovereignty of other, similar units. Contends that after the emergence of the United States as an independent state, Indian nations, although relinquishing external sovereignty, had retained the right to limited control over their own affairs. Believes that the American Indian peoples' claims to internal self-determination and the related policies of the United States government were proper subjects of international law and scrutiny. Argues that, notwithstanding congressional and constitutional limitations, national policies essentially recognized Indian self-government. Explains semi-sovereignty to be most notable in some criminal jurisdictions, adoption procedures and certain civil matters (while involving tribal members) on reservations. In light of recent native claims regarding unlawfully ceded lands, discusses the control over tribal property pertinent to the future development of natural resources. While conceding that the scope of Indian sovereignty depended on the will of Congress, concludes that the concept would survive because it was shaped by continuing pressures from native governments.

496. KICKINGBIRD, Kirke. "Indian Sovereignty: The American Experience." *Pathways to Self-Determination - Canadian Indians and the Canadian State.* Eds. Leroy Little Bear, Menno Boldt and J. Anthony Long. Toronto: University of Toronto Press, 1984, pp. 46-53.
Argues that Indian nations currently were more than merely social organizations or artificial creations of the United States government. Rather, they were sovereign nations, viable, functioning political units that exercised inherent sovereign powers. Maintains that the United States and other nations had recog-

nized this sovereignty. The fact that the United States and Europeans had entered into treaties with the Indian nations demonstrated that they had acknowledged such sovereignty. The United States Supreme Court had supported this position. United States law clearly stated that Indian nations possessed all the inherent power of sovereign government except those qualified or limited by treaties, agreements, or specified acts of Congress. Many Indian sovereign powers had not been fully exercised due to suppression by non-Indians and a reluctance by Indian governments to exercise such powers. Nevertheless, Indian sovereignty was a farreaching, vigorous reality today.

497. LITTLE BEAR, Leroy, Menno BOLDT and J. Anthony LONG. "Indian Government and the Constitution." *Pathways to Self-Determination - Canadian Indians and the Canadian State*. Eds. Leroy Little Bear, Menno Boldt and J. Anthony Long. Toronto: University of Toronto Press, 1984, pp. 174-80.
The authors outline the attitude of the indigenous Assembly of First Nations to the question of Indian government within the context of the Canadian constitutional process. Argue that the AFN supported a constitutionally-based Indian government as proof against parliamentary and political interference. Indian leaders had proposed the entrenchment of broad principles to enable an Indian government to enjoy the same jurisdictional authority in its relationship with the federal government as the provinces. Report that the federal government had unequivocally rejected Indian political sovereignty and assim- ilation, but that it favored a limited legislative role for Indians. Expect future negotiations over the meaning of aboriginal rights and self-government to be further complicated by the aboriginal groups' historical, legal and political distinctiveness. Believes that these differences would produce differing policy goals for these culturally and politically diverse peoples.

498. LONG, J. Anthony, Leroy LITTLE BEAR and Menno BOLDT. "Federal Indian Policy and Indian Self- Government in Canada." *Pathways to Self-Determination - Canadian Indians and the Canadian State*. Eds. Leroy Little Bear, Menno Boldt and J. Anthony Long. Toronto: University of Toronto Press, 1984, pp. 69-84.
The authors examine the most recent proposal submitted to Canada's aboriginal peoples by the Department of Indian Af- fairs and Northern Development for Indian Self-Government.

Discuss federal government strategy to achieve increased self-government for Canadian Indians. The government had planned limited self-government to replace the Indian Act, but had been uncertain over the meaning of aboriginal rights under the amended Constitution. Explain that in fact the government had already possessed authority under 91(24) of the Constitution Act to proceed, but had feared the opposition of various Indian groups. Identify five central tenets motivating the government's proposal: (1) the transfer of substantial administrative authority currently exercised by the Minister to Indian bands; (2) the delegation of legislative authority over land management, financial affairs, health, education and social services to individual bands; (3) band constitutions to determine the nature of internal government organization and procedures for accountability; and (4) authority to be vested in Indian bands regarding the authority to determine band membership and relations with all levels of governments, business firms, and other non-Indians. Criticize the federal government's intention merely to *delegate* parliamentary authority to Indian bands, but not to *substitute* Indian authority for parliamentary supremacy. Moreover, the federal government would still have to propitiate other peoples of aboriginal ancestry regarding Indian self-government, which would become viable only if Indians enjoyed a firm economic base.   `

499. MARULE, Smallface Marie. "Traditional Indian Government: Of the People, by the People, for the People." *Pathways to Self-Determination - Canadian Indians and the Canadian State.* Eds. Leroy Little Bear, Menno Boldt and J. Anthony Long. Toronto: University of Toronto Press, 1984, pp. 36-45.
Believes that the revitalization of Indian institutions, and a return to traditional Indian structures, systems and processes would best ensure combating the Canadian government's systematic policy of "detribalization," or subverting the Indian consensual political, kinship, and communal ownership and collective economic systems. Suspects the termination of Indian status and complete Indian assimilation to be the Canadian government's ultimate policy goals. The constitutional process had served only to divide Indians and divert their attention from this objective. Government control over funding had coerced Indian bands into surrendering their authority and responsibility, and had staved off Indian independence by encouraging reliance on government welfare. Proposes a four-pronged sol-

ution to Indian autonomy: (1) the Indian people's authority had to be reasserted; (2) an alternative government model with authority vested in the smallest political unit had to be devised; (3) tribal confederacies had to be reactivated to act as authoritative units in matters of shared tribal concerns; and (4) an Indian political unity had to be created to negotiate with the Canadian government.

500. NICHOLSON, David. "Indian Government in Federal Policy: An Insider's View." *Pathways to Self-Determination - Canadian Indians and the Canadian State.* Eds. Leroy Little Bear, Menno Boldt and J. Anthony Long. Toronto: University of Toronto Press, 1984, pp. 59-64.

Analyzes the Canadian federal government's policy development regarding Indian autonomy. Reviews historical developments in the relationship between the federal government and the Indians. Argues that a formal joint decision-making process had never been established, and that this, coupled with the serious communication gaps had caused many of the current difficulties in Indian-federal government relations. Developing an Indian policy had foundered on three structural and contextual variables: (1) stringent government restraints on all federal funding; (2) the "envelope system" of funding, which had forced the Department of Indian Affairs to compete with thirteen other departments for the limited resources within the Social and Native Affairs portfolio; and (3) the Department of Indian Affairs' practice of developing policy objectives without consulting the Indian people.

501. OLD PERSON, Chief Earl. "Problems, Prospects and Aspirations of the 'Real People' in America." *Pathways to Self-Determination - Canadian Indians and the Canadian State.* Eds. Leroy Little Bear, Menno Boldt and J. Anthony Long. Toronto: University of Toronto Press, 1984, pp. 148-51.

Urges Canada's Indian tribes to be realistic in facing their future and to cease pretending that grave dangers did not exist for the Indian people and culture. Recommends that the people evaluate their current situation and decide about the future. Reviews Canadian attempts to eliminate the Indian culture. Stresses the strength of the Indians, the "real people," in moving forward and preserving and maintaining the Indian way of life. Believes that the time had come for the Indian people to take a stand and to depend on Indian leadership and cooperation to protect the land and culture from ever-encroaching adversaries.

502.   OPEKOKEW, Delia. *The First Nations: Indian Government in the Community of Men.* Regina: Federation of Saskatchewan Indian Nations, 1982.
Provides a framework for the application of international human rights principles to Aboriginal and Treaty rights, especially with regard to Canada, and the Indian nations of Saskatchewan, specifically. Identifies the common goal of Indigenous Peoples as self-determination, in conformity with international law, especially since new classifications of colonial situations had been advanced. Explains that the Indian Nations had never surrendered their sovereignty, therefore they were entitled to international recognition and protection. Clarifies that the Indian Nations had recognized each others' sovereignty, and that the colonial powers had recognized the sovereignty of the Indian Nations by entering into treaties with them. Points out that if the Indian nations had sovereign status, then treaty rights could not be abrogated without the full and free consent of the Indians. Notes that the treaties had provided the Indian nations with a land base, known as reserves, over which they had retained sovereignty. Underlines the growing international concern with Aboriginal Rights expressed in several conventions and declaration, and the subsequent developments culminating in the United Nations Working Group on Indigenous Populations. Argues that until Canada recognized the Indian peoples' inherent right to self-determination, it was violating international law, in particular the International Bill of Rights.

503.   PONTING, J. Rick and Roger GIBBINS. "Thorns in the Bed of Roses: A Socio-Political View of the Problems of Indian Government." *Pathways to Self-Determination - Canadian Indians and the Canadian State.* Eds. Leroy Little Bear, Menno Boldt and J. Anthony Long. Toronto: University of Toronto Press, 1984, pp. 122-35.
The authors focus on internal Indian community problems and Indian-non-Indian relationships. Consider Indian government as an institutional innovation that might reduce although not eliminate racism, paternalism, external control of the Indian and Inuit Affairs Program (IIAP) and the Department of Indian Affairs and Northern Development (DIAND), and social disorganization and alienation. Argue that Indian self-government might also create internal problems: unrealistic expectations, intensified social tensions and cleavages, tribal rivalries, intertribal economic competition, tensions between

reserve and off-reserve Indians, Indian-non-Indian economic difficulties, abolition or emasculation of DIAND-IIAP, new problems in intergovernmental relations, and the adjustment of Indians into the national political community, or the status of Indians as Canadian and provincial citizens.

504. PORTER, Tom. "Traditions of the Constitution of the Six Nations." *Pathways to Self-Determination - Canadian Indians and the Canadian State.* Eds. Leroy Little Bear, Menno Boldt and J. Anthony Long. Toronto: University of Toronto Press, 1984, pp. 14-21.

Asserts that the Iroquois perception of the principles and concepts implicit in the term "Indian government" bore no relationship to the Western European perception. Notions of constitutions, parliamentary procedure, majority rule, prime ministers and presidents had no place or meaning in Indian government, which emphasized good leadership by a strong council of chiefs chosen for their personal qualities by clan mothers who also wielded the impeachment authority. Decision-making was thus achieved by consensus, not by majority rule.

505. POWDERFACE, Sykes. "Self-Governing Means Biting the Hand that Feeds Us." *Pathways to Self-Determination - Canadian Indians and the Canadian State.* Eds. Leroy Little Bear, Menno Boldt and J. Anthony Long. Toronto: University of Toronto Press, 1984, pp. 164-7.

Claims that if the Indian people were ever to develop independent Indian government, they must first declare their financial independence. As long as they were financially dependent on the federal government, Indians would not be able to "chart their own paths" or "set their own goals." Indian people must therefore be willing to accept responsibility for the development and financial support of political organizations, regardless of the form they took, which were necessary to achieve political independence. The Indian Association of Alberta clearly illustrated the significance of fiscal independence. Indian people must ask themselves whether they were willing to be accountable to the Department of Indian Affairs at the expense of meeting the needs and expectations of the people. The Indians had never relinquished their inherent right to self-determination, but in order to be able to claim this right, they must have control of the necessary resources.

506. RILEY, Del. "What Canadian Indians Want and the Diffi-
      culties of Getting It." *Pathways to Self-Determination -
      Canadian Indians and the Canadian State.* Eds. Leroy Lit-
      tle Bear, Menno Boldt and J. Anthony Long. Toronto:
      University of Toronto Press, 1984, pp. 159-63.
      Insists that the Indian people sought self-determination and ba-
      sic human rights, including the right to control the institutions
      that regulated Indian lives. To achieve this goal, the National
      Indian Brotherhood had acted through political channels, such
      as participation in the constitutional process and the application
      of political pressure through intense lobbying in domestic and
      foreign political arenas.   Asserts that although the consti-
      tutional negotiations had achieved some success, the battle was
      far from won. If the Indian people desired self-determination,
      they would have to institute it on their own authority. In order
      to achieve the types of results the Indians demanded, they would
      have to have strong leadership. This compelled the national
      Indian movement to overcome its vulnerability to the "divide
      and conquer" approach and its dependency on the federal
      government.

507. ROBINSON, Eric and Henry Bird QUINNEY. *The Infested
      Blanket: Canada's Constitution - Genocide of Indian Na-
      tions.* Winnipeg (Manitoba): Queenston House Publishing
      Co. Ltd., 1985.
      The authors analogize between the "gifts" the colonizers had
      sent the Indian nation centuries ago in the form of blankets in-
      fested with contagious diseases ensuring mass death, and the
      present attitude of the Canadian government expressed in the
      1982 Constitution Act, which in essence entailed assimilation
      and the end of Indian sovereignty, or cultural genocide. Main-
      tain that the Indian nations had never been conquered, yet
      treaties had not been upheld by the Canadian government. Ex-
      plain that the Assembly of First Nations, which prior to 1983
      had represented all Treaty and Status Indians, was divided, and
      the Coalition of First Nations was formed as a result. Consider
      this organization dedicated to the realization of self-
      determination for Indian Nations. Contend that International
      Human Rights Covenants had given binding legal status to this
      right and that the Helsinki Final Act had contributed a detailed
      definition through the doctrine of authoritative interpretation.
      Explain that self-determination included the right to define
      membership, and refute the concept of self-government devel-
      oped in the Penner Report as substantively false. Provides a

historical overview of the struggle between the Indian Nations and the federal government to indicate why this organization could not participate in the constitutional process.

508. RYAN, Joe. "Compared to Other Nations." *American Indian Journal of the Institute for the Development of Indian Law*, III, 8 (1977), 2-13.
Defines colonialism as unilateral political control, economic exploitation and cultural suppression. Suggests that the Indian relationship to the United States government resembled colonialism, and hence it constituted a proper subject of inquiry and action for the United Nations Decolonization Committee, particularly since Indian sovereignty had never been terminated. Illustrates the historical motives for colonialism, including economic exploitation, political control (neo-colonialism), land acquisition, and conversion of "barbaric and inferior" native peoples to Christianity. Declares that the United States hegemony over Indian nations must be viewed in light of new international law, which prohibited territorial acquisition by conquest or coerced cession.

509. RYSER, Rudolph C. "Nation-States, Indigenous Nations and the Great Lie." *Pathways to Self-Determination - Canadian Indians and the Canadian State*. Eds. Leroy Little Bear, Menno Boldt and J. Anthony Long. Toronto: University of Toronto Press, 1984, pp. 27-35.
Charges that nation-states, in conquering indigenous nations and establishing colonial regimes designed to confiscate indigenous lands and natural resources, had used the "great lie," *i.e.*, the fallacious argument that indigenous nations would not survive unless they rejected their own history, intellectual development, language and culture, and unless they replaced these indigenous attributes with Western values and ideals. Compares the application and relative "success" of the "great lie" in the United States, Canada, Nicaragua and Chile, noting the essential similarity in their patterns of oppression. Urges indigenous nations to assert their own values in government and nationhood as the only means of avoiding extinction.

510. SANDERS, Douglas E. "Some Current Issues Affecting Indian Government." *Pathways to Self-Determination - Canadian Indians and the Canadian State*. Eds. Leroy Little Bear, Menno Boldt and J. Anthony Long. Toronto: University of Toronto Press, 1984, pp. 113-21.

Argues that, although certain aspects of Canada's Indian Act
required amendment, legislative changes were unlikely to be
forthcoming immediately. Consequently, amendments would
have to await action by the courts, government agencies or the
Indian governments. The courts appeared divided on the question of band by-laws, which augured more litigation on the issue. Thus far, three Supreme Court of Canada decisions on the
application of provincial legislation to reserves had upheld
provincial laws. Records a long history involving band innovation and assumption of control in certain jurisdictions, but
deplores the general unwillingness of bands to assume more
power. Explains that this abdication of responsibility had left
the initiative for change largely in the hands of the Department
of Indian Affairs and Parliament. Asserts that such passivity
must end if the Indian government was to become a reality.

511. SANDERSON, Sol. "Preparations for Indian Government in
Saskatchewan." *Pathways to Self-Determination - Canadian Indians and the Canadian State*. Eds. Leroy Little
Bear, Menno Boldt and J. Anthony Long. Toronto:
University of Toronto Press, 1984, pp. 152-8.
Outlines the Federation of Saskatchewan Indians' approach in
pursuing self-determination to counteract the Canadian federal
government's detribalization policies and assimilation attempts.
Explains the Federation's development of indigenous political
institutions, especially those promoting the band chief's office
into the highest authority of Indian government. Identifies four
major functions to be served by the new political institutions:
educational, economic, social-cultural and political development. The Saskatchewan Indian Educational Commission
would monitor the development and administration of quality
Indian education; the Saskatchewan Indian Resource Council
would formulate economic policy; a technical group would
consider how to implement Indian law in the province, including how to establish an Indian judicial system; and a
Protectorate Office would arbitrate Canadian-Indian disputes,
and protect Indians under the principles of international law
against arbitrary Canadian government action. A Treaty
Enactment Office would scrutinize treaties involving Indian nations as well as those dealing with Crown-Indian relations.
Finally, an Indian government constitution would encompass
the broadest possible objectives and protect individual band
autonomy.

512. SHEPARDSON, M. "The Navajo Nonstate Nation." *Nonstate Nations in International Politics: Comparative System Analysis.* Ed. J. S. Bertelsen. New York: Praeger, 1979, pp. 223-44.

Describes the historical background, and argues that the Navajo constituted a thriving nation. Discusses the impact of the Marshall decisions on the status of the nation. Points out that ultimately European self-interest had triumphed over indigenous legal and moral rights. Asserts that the Navajo operated as a "domestic dependent nation" whose goals were to gain as much sovereignty as possible, and to exercise their right to self-determination within the legal framework of the United States.

513. STILLWAGGON, Eileen M. "Anti-Indian Agitation and Economic Interests." *Antipode*, XVI, 2 (1984), 13-8.

Denies that the recent upsurge of anti-Indian activity in the United States had signified a reaction to the aggressive Indian claims of the 1970s and the militancy of the American Indian Movement. Identifies the basic reasons for this activity in long-term issues and interests highlighted in the 1970s by the poor performance of the American economy and the national panic over energy resources. Presents evidence of corporate involvement in the activities of the anti-Indian Interstate Congress for Equal Rights and Responsibilities and its state affiliates during the struggle over Indian rights in the late 1970s. Reports that the Indian counteroffensive actions had faltered because they were legalistic, defensive and lacked economic analysis. Believes that the Indian trust status would not solve the problems of the present economic system, but might be used as a weapon in the larger struggle to strengthen Indians and progressive causes in general.

514. SUTTON, Imre. "Sovereign States and the Changing Definition of the Indian Reservation." *Geographical Review,* LXVI (1976), 281-95.

Discusses issues related to territories in the United States that had been designated as Indian reservations. Points out that most reservations lay within the bounds of a single state, sometimes within single counties, but that some reservations had been gerrymandered by states and local governments. Indian reservations had not fitted the Euro-American penchant for nicely segmented territorial units. Suggests that however variably comprehended among the states, the Indian reservation remained a semi-autonomous enclave, mostly immune to state jurisdiction except where the federal government had granted powers to the states. Indicates that tribal governments were legally distinct within their borders and had consummate powers to regulate and to manage their own resources.

515. THEISSEN, H. W. "Indian Self-Government: A Provincial Perspective." *Pathways to Self-Determination - Canadian Indians and the Canadian State.* Eds. Leroy Little Bear, Menno Boldt and J. Anthony Long. Toronto: University of Toronto Press, 1984, pp. 85-90.
Explains that Native leaders had identified four matters of fundamental importance: (1) the strong desire of the aboriginal people to protect their distinct culture and identity; (2) the need for clear assurances that rights already acquired by virtue of the aboriginal people's original occupancy would be honored; (3) the need for assurances that the native people would be afforded opportunities to participate as equals in the economic life of the larger society; and (4) the desire for the opportunity to exercise greater control over their own lives and destiny as a people. The Constitutional Act of 1982 and the Constitutional Accord on Aboriginal Rights had begun to address these fundamental aspirations, particularly the question of self-determination, principally by providing the aboriginal people with an opportunity to participate in the constitutional process. The province of Alberta recognized and supported the importance of Indian self-government, but this support did not extend to the concept of sovereign Indian nations. Although the basic question rested with the federal government and the Indian representatives, it would be necessary to involve the provinces in discussions of "jurisdictional interface." Urges the federal government to consider the need for consultation with Indians and the possibility that legislation might impinge on already-existing treaty and aboriginal rights. The federal government must consider, perhaps with close provincial liaison, the financial implications of Indian self-administration for Indian bands in order to avoid passing inadequate financial capability in the guise of local autonomy. The Alberta government, however, believed that provincial involvement should be initiated only upon request of the chief and band council.

516. WATKINS, Mel, ed. *Dene Nation: The Colony Within.* Toronto: University of Toronto Press, 1977.

A collection of papers selected from presentations made to Canada's Berger Inquiry on behalf of the Dene people and regarding the construction of the Mackenzie Valley pipeline. Express the following essential positions on behalf of the Dene people: (1) the aboriginal Dene right to self-determination was a universal human right. Canadians must therefore accommodate these demands within Confederation; (2) no pipeline project could be permitted before a land settlement was reached with the native people; the extraction of non-renewable resources before a settlement would deny the Dene right to self-determination; and (3) the Dene were expressing their vision of an alternative society with an economy based on renewable resources. The Dene nation would strive for decolonization in matters of economics, politics, education, law and culture.

517. WEAVER, Sally M. "Indian Government: A Concept in Need of a Definition." *Pathways to Self-Determination - Canadian Indians and the Canadian State.* Eds. Leroy Little Bear, Menno Boldt and J. Anthony Long. Toronto: University of Toronto Press, 1984, pp. 65-8.
Asserts that the Canadian government had difficulty accepting the formalized conception of Indian government as exemplified by a political science model. Believes that a band level government, supported by provincial and Indian organizations, would offer the most sensible and viable model of Indian government. Urges Indians to develop and define their own concept in order to eliminate the imposition of White bureaucratic values and world views on their people, and also to differentiate between the Indian concept of self-government and Quebec's demands for "sovereignty association." The latter would allegedly have negative consequences for Indians. Maintains that ultimately Indian autonomy would be achieved through band governments asserting their right to govern at the reserve level.

518. WEEKS, Nancy. "Autonomy of Indigenous Peoples in Canada." *Nordisk Tidsskrift For International Ret,* LIV (1985), 17-23.
Points out that the degree of indigenous people's autonomy indicated the probability of their survival. Suggests the need for four criteria in order to assess autonomy for indigenous groups in Canada: (1) If the indigenous group comprised a minority, did the state acknowledge its existence?; (2) Did the group have the capacity to determine its own membership?; (3) Did the group have some measure of self-government as a group?; (4)

Did the group have access to and control of its lands and resources? Points out that indigenous peoples in Canada were recognized constitutionally. Describes legal relations between indigenous peoples and Canada. Suggests that the prognosis for indigenous autonomy in Canada was good, but points to the fundamental problem of a collision of values which must be resolved.

519. WHYTE, John D. "Indian Self-Government: A Legal Analysis." *Pathways to Self-Determination - Canadian Indians and the Canadian State.* Eds. Leroy Little Bear, Menno Boldt and J. Anthony Long. Toronto: University of Toronto Press, 1984, pp. 101-12.

Reviews the legal claims advanced to support the arguments for Indian political autonomy in Saskatchewan. Explains that even if the rights to self-government were not aboriginal rights, common law courts in all former English colonies had recognized Indian possessory and hunting rights. In contrast, the Canadian government had characterized aboriginal rights merely as the right of enjoyment, but not of possession of property, whereas the United States Supreme Court had suggested the existence of superior Indian rights dealing with Indian customs that determined occupation rights predating state intervention. Suggests that the interpretation of the new Canadian Charter could influence the future of aboriginal rights in Canada, but suspects that judges would avoid the issue simply by denying the existence of any such rights.

520. WILSON, J. *The Original Americans: U.S. Indians.* London: Minority Rights Group, Report No. 31, 1976.

Examines the system of domination of the indigenous people in the United States. Considers how the present situation had developed in terms of administrative institutions and control of natural resources and water rights. Discusses the origin of the administrative system through overviews of the indigenous societies in pre-Columbian America, the flood of White immigration, the "new puritanism" of the 1820s to 1840s which saw the clearing of native peoples from major areas of the South and West, and the Civil War. Emphasizes the role of the myth of the natives as inferior in these processes of oppression. Describes the attempts to ameliorate the position of the Indians in the Dawes Act of 1887 and the Meriam Report of 1928, and comments on their relative successes and failures. Reviews renewed efforts to resolve the "Indian problem" spurred by the politicization of the Indian communities in the 1960s. Asserts that the Indians desired self-determination to be carried out mainly in terms of self-sufficiency, which must be based on long-term economic development. Concludes that self-determination would be achieved only if the majority population accepted this right.

Indigenous Peoples: Elsewhere

521. AWATERE, Donna. *Maori Sovereignty.* Auckland: Broadsheet, 1984.
Reconceptualizes colonial experience from a Maori point of view, and stresses the cultural base of different forms of oppression. Argues that the Maori people had no choice but to reject New Zealand's "biculturalism" and to seek sovereignty. The practice of separate development and its partner, White hatred, had resulted in the loss of the Maori social and economic base and the perpetuation of White privilege. Maori hegemony required the formation of alliances. However, the Pacific Islanders, feminists, trade unionists, and the Left were all captives of White culture. Exposes some elements underlying White culture as obstacles to Maori sovereignty; they could, however, be overcome through decolonization and the radicalization of Maori youth. The objective of the movement in the 1980s was to overcome the White/Maori split consciousness.

522. BALLARD, Patricia L. "Toward Indigenous Liberation: The Sandinistas and the Miskito of Northeastern Nicaragua." *Antipode*, XVI, 2 (1984), 54-64.
Considers the populist/indigenist position adopted by some American progressives toward the Miskito question in Nicaragua as being ahistorical and failing to address the crucial problems posed by development theory. Locates the roots of Miskito separatist demands in the practice of British indirect rule and the failure of subsequent weak Hispanic and Mestizo states to establish territorial hegemony. Identifies the historical divergence between the Pacific and Atlantic regions as the source of Miskito hostility and mistrust toward western Nicaraguans, aggravated by counterrevolutionary forces exploiting this mistrust by utilizing historic caciquismo political

structures to manipulate the Miskito against the Sandinistas. Credits the Sandinista program with enriching indigenous cultural consciousness, while facilitating national integration and socialist transformation, despite enduring tensions regarding the ownership and control of the northeastern region's resources. Recommends the unification of Nicaragua's progressives to ensure the resolution of conflicts, and the exclusion of imperialist forces.

523.   BOLLINGER, William and Daniel Manny LUND. "Minority Oppression: Towards Analyses that Clarify and Strategists that Liberate." *Latin American Perspectives*, IX, 2 (1982) (special issue on "Minorities in the Americas"), 2-28.
The political essence of minority questions included: who was mobilized, and around what analysis of the oppression and with what strategy for resolving the oppression? Who could be won to support the minority struggle, and whose interest did the continued relations of oppression serve? How did the struggle intersect with the class struggle, and what was the content of this intersection? Assert that the exploitation and oppression of minority groups in the United States and Latin America could not be properly analyzed without first distinguishing between racial and national oppression; that the oppression of indigenous peoples could not be understood solely within the categories of racial and national oppression but rather must be taken up as a distinct form of oppression; that distinct forms of minority oppression might in fact be combined in a given concrete situation and intersect with class contradictions as well. Although resistance had often taken nationalist or even separatist form, many indigenous peoples as well as socially defined "racial" groups were not nationalities. Distinguish between oppression of a national social formation, which required a struggle for self-determination, oppression of a national immigrant minority, which required a struggle for democratic rights, and class oppression, which called for class struggle and social revolution. Just as Marxism must come to terms with the persistence of national and indigenous struggles, so *indigenismo* movements had to reckon with historical dialectics and the complex positive and negative heritage of the conquest. Link the reproduction of indigenous peoples as minority groups within Latin America to the perpetuation of precapitalist relations which had not permitted minority groups to evolve into viable nationalities capable of a separate national existence.

524. CASTRO-CLAREN, Sara. "Huaman Poma and the Space of Purity." *Ethnic Autonomy - Comparative Dynamics.* Ed. Raymond L. Hall. New York: Pergamon Press, 1979, pp. 345-69.
Examines 16th-century Indian writer Huaman Poma de Ayala and his plan to expel the Spaniards from what is now Peru and bring about an ethnically homogeneous state. Points out that separatism appears to be absent from Latin America because by the mid-16th century, Indians had succumbed to the power of the colonial invaders and the forces of integration they had put into play. Cites the 1848 Yucatan war of the castes as the last large-scale historical event that expressed a desire for a separate ethnic rule. The depth of this ideology of Indian supremacy was expressed by Huaman Poma, whose influence was still felt among segments of the Peruvian Indian population. Poma's blueprint would establish a separate state in two stages: the Spaniards and their black slaves would occupy the cities and towns, and the Indians would return to their villages and pre-Inca lifestyles. Indian government would be based on the old Indian culture, on an idealized yet concrete experience as a model for the future. Poma believed that the two greatest threats to Indian future were depopulation and the loss of indigenous control over the reproductive and kinship system of Indian society. Contends that Poma's dream was rooted in reality, and could have come about if these problems had not galloped ahead of his expectations.

525. O'SHAUGHNESSY, H. *What Future for the Amerindians of South America?* London: Minority Rights Group, Report No. 15, 1973.
Summarizes the conditions of the various Amerindian peoples of South America, the policies of the governments of the various republics toward them, and suggests ways in which their lot might be improved. Focuses on the jungle and plain dwellers of the Amazon basin and the adjacent lowlands. Outlines the basic dimensions of the problems in terms of demography, geography, and living standards. Reviews the role of the Roman Catholic Church and the armies in the survival of the indigenous cultures. Examines governmental attitudes toward the indigenous communities in three groups: (1) those without an effective policy (Bolivia, Ecuador, Paraguay and Venezuela); (2) those whose policy was in the course of formation or major change (Colombia and Peru); and (3) those with a firmly established policy (Brazil). Suggests for the future: (1) concerted

action by international organizations and individual experts forming a new international body which would formulate and execute a rescue plan; (2) help coordinate national policies; and (3) facilitate processes of persuasion and diplomacy with the states of the region. The body would have the mandate of aiding all indigenous peoples of the world.

526. STEPHEN, David and Phillip WEARNE. *Central America's Indians.* London: Minority Rights Group, Report No. 62, 1984.
The authors survey the indigenous rights movement in Central America, the colonization process, and the evolution of the new Indian consciousness in this region. Highlight the 1980 Congress of Indian Movements in Peru, seeing it as a watershed in ethnic politics in Latin America. Examine the 1977 Declaration of Barbados, which described the Indian peoples as suffering economic and cultural discrimination, and demand the liberation of native peoples. The problem of identity rested on the lack of a single definite criterion, so that the Indian position in society must be understood in terms of adaptation and survival. Describe the Indians' place in Guatemalan society and outline the forms of discrimination and the government's cultural absorption policies. Trace the growing sense of self-awareness among the indigenous population since 1944, and emphasize the role of religion and a socio-economic consciousness.

527. VALKEAPÄÄ, Nils-Aslak. *Greetings from Lapland: The Sami - Europe's Forgotten People.* London: Zed Press, 1983.
Discusses the Sami people, whose cultural existence and traditional way of life were seriously threatened. Links the political, economic, and cultural encroachment of dominant societies in Nordic countries into Sami territory with the plight of indigenous peoples all over the world. Claims that the Samis had the right to preserve their own culture, and issues a call of action in support of this cause.

PART VI

FUTURE DIRECTIONS

Future Directions

528. BRUNN, Stanley D. "Future of the Nation-State System." *Political Geography: Recent Advances and Future Directions.* Eds. Peter Taylor and John House. London: Croom Helm; New York: Barnes and Noble, 1984, pp. 149-67.
Addresses the future of the nation-state in the emerging postindustrial world. Identifies a number of salient features of the postindustrial economies and the features of the emerging postindustrial state system and delineates some basic differences with the industrial state society and economy. Includes matters of loyalties, boundaries, territorial conflicts, the creation of superstates and the emergence of regionalism and secession.

529. BRUNN, Stanley D. "Geopolitics in a Shrinking World: A Political Geography of the Twenty-First Century." *Political Studies from Spatial Perspectives.* Eds. A. D. Burnett and P. J. Taylor. Chichester: John Wiley and Sons, Ltd., 1981, pp. 131-56.
Explores a framework for studying the political geography of the future. Reviews pertinent literature that focuses on geopolitical futures. Develops a number of geopolitical scenarios likely to be characteristic of the late 20th and early 21st centuries, including (1) the influences of emerging regional powers; (2) the demands of a new international political order; (3) the destinies of ministates in a macropower world; (4) the exploration and sovereignty of outer space; (5) the reorganization of political spaces; (6) the renaissance of regionalism; (7) transnational states as the new corporate states or neo-imperialists; (8)

adjusting to the realities of a four-dimensional world; (9) government and governments redefined; and (10) apocalypse: Gardens of Eden or Armageddons.

530. BURGHARDT, Andrew F. "Nation, State and Territorial Unity: A Trans-Outaouis View." *Cahiers de géographie du Québec*, XXIV (1980), 123-34.
The concept of "nation" could be applied on more than one level. Whereas many Québécois maintained that a nation should be a state, world experience showed many nations forming constituent parts of larger-scaled nations. Asserts that sovereignty must have priority over "association." Québec secession would split Canada into at least three portions, and would cause a reorientation of the remnant pieces away from the center. Several potential boundary problems would exist. The recent development of Canadian nationalism should not be overlooked.

531. KEEGAN, John and Andrew WHEATCROFT. *Zones of Conflict: An Atlas of Future Wars.* London: Jonathan Cape, 1986.
The authors describe twenty-eight possible conflicts, with accompanying maps. The cases include reminders that demands for self-determination might involve violent conflict, *e.g.*, Ethiopian minorities, the Palestinians, the Kurds, the Baluchis, and more.

532. KNIGHT, David B. "Maps as Constraints or Springboards to Imaginative Thought." *Bulletin of the Association of Canadian Map Libraries*, XVIII (1975), 1-9; *idem*, "Future Maps of Canada as a Pedagogical Device." *The Monograph*, XXX, 2 (1979), 3-5.
Finds students having difficulty in accepting that a state's political boundaries need not remain as they were. Considers future territorial changes to Canada. Takes as a basic premise that Québec would secede from Canada. The fanciful mapped suggestions plus written rationales were intended to stimulate thought.

533. Old, Colin. *Quebec's Relations with Francophonie: A Political Geographic Perspective.* Ottawa: Carleton University, Department of Geography, Discussion Paper No. 1, 1984.
Examines the means by which Québec had been able to develop international linkages even while remaining part of the Cana-

dian state. Canadian provinces were allowed some flexibility in their foreign relations in areas assigned to their jurisdiction by the Canadian Constitution (*e.g.*, culture and education), but Québec had taken the issue of international activity furthest. Antagonisms existed between the Federal and the Québec governments, yet the Canadian government had permitted Québec to have international representation in fora that normally involved only sovereign states. The Canadian experiment with such linkages suggested new forms of international relationships for substate nations lacking full sovereignty.

534. PARKER, Geoffrey. *The Logic of Unity: A Geography of the European Economic Community.* Third edition. London: Longman, 1981.
Examines the Community as a unit, covering population, industry, agriculture, energy resources, transport, international trade, and regional development to set the patterns of geographic activity of each member state within the overall EEC context. Explores the political and economic implications of the Community, and proposes what the Community might be like in structural terms in the years beyond 2000 A.D. If disintegration did not occur, a federal structure might be based upon eight "provinces": Scandia, Celtica, Gallia, Iberia, Italia, Aegea, and, at the center, the territories of Germania and the Federal Province (Alpina).

535. SHAFER, Boyd C. *Nationalism and Internationalism: Belonging in Human Experience.* Malabar, FL: Robert E. Krieger, 1982.
This source book includes primary literature on nationalism. Discusses the development of nationalism emphasizing its possible move toward internationalism. Suggests that people had always sought one or more human groups to share the fulfilment of their emotional and material needs, and that the nation as an ideal had been especially able to gratify these identity, security and satisfaction requirements. Surveys the development of nationalism in the West since medieval times, and records its spread to Africa and Asia. Proposes that this nationalizing process had evolved as a learned sentiment through "conjuncture" of ideas, institutions and "happenings." With all its "blessings" and "curses," nationalism had changed, but had remained viable and was still growing. Believes that internationalism had a chance of developing into a sentiment someday.

AUTHOR INDEX